PERUVIAN REBEL

PERUVIAN REBEL

The World of Magda Portal, with a Selection of Her Poems

Kathleen Weaver

The Pennsylvania State University Press
University Park, Pennsylvania

Spanish texts of poems by Magda Portal are
© The Estate of Magda Portal. Translation and citation of texts by Magda
Portal by permission of Rocío Pareja Revolledo and Graciela Pareja Moreno,
The Estate of Magda Portal. Translation of poems by permission of Magda
Portal. Excerpts translated from the interview "Yo soy Magda Portal," by Esther
Andradi and Ana María Portugal, by permission of Ana María Portugal.

Unless noted, all other photographs and graphics are held by the Estate of Magda Portal
(Documentos/archivos de Magda Portal, in the care of Rocío Revolledo Pareja)
and reprinted by permission.

Map of Peru, page xvi, taken from "Peru: A Portrait," in *Peru: A Short History,*
by David P. Werlich. © 1978 by Southern Illinois University Press. By permission.

LIBRARY OF CONGRESS CATALOGING-IN-PUBLICATION DATA

Weaver, Kathleen, 1945–
Peruvian rebel : the world of Magda Portal, with a selection of her poems /
Kathleen Weaver.
p.   cm.
Summary: "Examines the life and poetry of Magda Portal, a major figure in
Latin American revolutionary politics. Includes a selection of her poems available for the
first time in English translation"—Provided by publisher.
Includes bibliographical references and index.
ISBN 978-0-271-03549-9 (cloth : alk. paper)
1. Portal, Magda, 1901–1989. 2. Poets, Peruvian—20th century—Biography.
3. Women poets, Peruvian—Biography. 4. Revolutionaries—Peru—Biography.
5. Peruvian poetry—20th century. 6. Peruvian poetry—Women authors. 7. Political poetry.
8. Partido Aprista Peruano—History. 9. Peru—Politics and government—1919–1968.
I. Portal, Magda, 1901–1989. Selections. English. 2009.
II. Title.

PQ8497.P75Z93 2009
861'.62—dc22
[B]
2009007392

WE HOLD THESE TRUTHS TO BE SELF-EVIDENT:
THAT ALL MEN AND WOMEN ARE CREATED EQUAL. . . .
—Elizabeth Cady Stanton,
Seneca Falls Declaration, 1848

AMPLÍAME O DIOS LOS HORIZONTES
—Magda Portal

CONTENTS

ILLUSTRATIONS

FIGURES

ACKNOWLEDGMENTS

Many people helped me complete this work, not all noted here, but all held in gratitude. Magda's closest relatives, her half-sister, Graciela Pareja Moreno, and her daughter, Rocío Revolledo Pareja, Magda's niece, offered not only friendship but also practical assistance of many kinds; without their generous support and confidence this project would hardly have been feasible. Magda herself provided materials and took pains to correct the long typescript of her San Francisco interview. Professor Daniel Reedy kindly shared some of his own research gathered in Peru during his seminal work on Portal and shared his thoughts on a number of points. Janet Rigg played a central role in the early phase of the work, helping to host Magda in San Francisco, participating in the interview, helping with translation. In Lima, Sara Beatriz Guardia provided her sense of Peru's women's movement, along with insights into Portal's interactions with younger women activists. Eduardo Galeano reoriented the project by insisting on Portal's importance as a political figure, and Claribel Alegría lent support to the translations at their inception. Donald Gibbs and archivists of the Nettie Lee Benson Latin American Collection provided assistance over many years. Horacio Tubio, Stephen Kessler, Bernardo Garcia Pandavenes, and Agnes Dimitriou made translation suggestions, while Willis Popenoe, Bernadette Szafranskia and Judy Wilkinson read early drafts of the manuscript.

A crucial debt is to Professor Mihai Grünfeld of Vassar College, for much needed and exceedingly generous support of the manuscript at a key moment in its development, as well as for providing many corrections and suggestions for improvements. Gloria Bowles also provided greatly valued support, furthering the work decisively, as did Jane Dickson with her editing suggestions. My first husband, the late film documentarian Allan Francovich, director of the three-hour film *On Company Business: A Documentary History of the c.i.a.,* strongly encouraged the entire effort. As the son of a U.S. mining engineer who worked at the Cerro de Pasco mines in the 1950s, he witnessed as a child the humiliating conditions in which miners lived in Peru's

highlands. In his draft translations of a number of Magda's poems I first
heard the voice of Magda Portal.

My profound appreciation goes out to Sandy Thatcher, distinguished
director of Penn State University Press. I also wish to acknowledge the work
of others at the Press, especially that of Romaine Perin, who did a great deal
of work on the manuscript. It was a pleasure to work with them all.

Grateful acknowledgment to Georgiana M. M. Coluile, and to the edi-
tors of the following reviews in whose pages a number of translations have
appeared: *Alcatraz, The Bitter Oleander, Exchanges, The Monserrat Review,
Tecalote,* and *Translation Review.*

Finally and beyond others I am indebted to Bob Baldock, my husband. His
forbearance as the project persisted; his difficult, shaping questions; his hands-
on editorial guidance and sacrifice to the effort—his work has amounted to
a collaboration.

KW, Berkeley, 2008

INTRODUCTION

On May 29, 1929, Magda Portal, a political deportee traveling with her five-year-old daughter, arrived in San Juan, Puerto Rico. The two had come from Cuba on the steamship *Guantánamo*. Five foot two, slender, her chestnut hair cut in a stylish bob, she waited on the dock. Also traveling on the steamship was a troupe of dancers, all of whom had disembarked and disappeared along with the other passengers. In her baggage, in addition to hats, dresses, shoes, and her daughter's clothing, were manuscripts—texts of four talks she wrote in Mexico City and would deliver many times in the course of a four-month-long speaking tour of the Caribbean. Eventually she made her way to the offices of a newspaper whose editors she had thought would be meeting her at the landing. There, as she later recounted, she introduced herself.

> "You? Magda Portal?" They seemed astonished. "We went to meet you," they said, "but we ended up leaving, we didn't recognize you, we thought you were one of the dancers."
>
> "What were you expecting," I asked, "somebody fat and middle-aged, with hands in her pockets and a bomb in each hand?"
>
> They burst out laughing and immediately we were friends, enjoying that spontaneous sympathy and affection that so quickly unites people of like-minded politics.

It was not so easy for Magda Portal to escape notice in her own country, Peru, especially in the 1930s and 1940s. Having chosen to live in the public eye, she was, as she said, a "public woman," humorously describing herself with a phrase denoting a woman of ill repute. Acclaimed as a poet early in the 1920s, she would later gain prominence as a social fighter. Finally she would be acknowledged as a foundational figure in women's struggles in Peru.

Her immersion in the revolutionary mood of Lima in the 1920s and her association with such brilliant compatriots as César Vallejo, José Carlos Mariátegui, and Víctor Raúl Haya de la Torre—all members of an outstanding generation of Peruvian activists—would awaken her to the social struggles that would dominate her life. As a member of this "vanguard generation," Portal counted herself part of a momentous battle to elevate the lives of the impoverished majority in Peru—mostly Indians, workers, and campesinos. As part of this battle she assaulted the social rules that constrained so many women of her time to remain at home, unable even to think of themselves as responsible individuals capable of uniting with others and effecting social change.

As the editor of the Buenos Aires review *Claridad* stated in 1935, their epoch was one of incessant material progress but a progress out of joint with genuine improvement in humanity—advance, that is, toward equitable distribution of the social wealth. But major redress seemed more than ever possible, if not inevitable. The editor concluded that great currents were now in motion that could no more be held back than "a surging sea could be contained by the narrow channel of a river."

Observing these powerful currents, Portal at first hesitated, but soon flung herself into action. Impelled by a rootless, modernist drive for freedom, she subdued her own libertarian spirit, accepting the discipline of a political party, the Alianza Popular Revolucionaria Americana (American Popular Revolutionary Alliance; APRA). In 1931 she cofounded the Aprista Party of Peru and for two decades was the principal women's leader of that party. She undertook strenuous forays into Peru's hinterlands, traveling high into the Andes and deep into the Amazonian jungle, exploring what it meant to be Peruvian—desirous of helping forge a more inclusive continental identity, one honoring the indigenous legacy. Once described as "a small engine indefatigably in motion," she worked with bold initiative to incorporate women, and men, into the first mass political party in Peru's history. In fact, the party she cofounded would contribute substantially to the tumultuous disorder and protracted violence in Peru during the 1930s. Her partisan choices would exact harsh personal costs.

A comrade of Portal's once referred to her as "the protagonist of a broken dream." Some aspects of this dream may now be seen as purely utopian and of a bygone era. But the basic problems faced by Portal's generation—above all, the glaring social inequities—have not been solved. So too the anti-imperialist Pan-American ethos so militantly promulgated by the APRA remains vital today, evident in the resurgence of left-wing nationalism to the south. The following narrative, then, is the story not just of a particular woman but also of a "vanguard generation" and a social vision that proved exceedingly influential in its time, with ramifications extending to the present.

Map of Peru

BEGINNINGS (1900–1919)

The sea, our sea, lies open again; perhaps there has never yet been such an "open sea."
—FRIEDRICH NIETZSCHE, *THE GAY SCIENCE*

As a young man, Pedro Pablo Portal Ortega traveled from Peru's Pacific coast across the Andean cordillera to seek work harvesting rubber in the Amazonian jungle basin, a highly dangerous occupation. Rubber workers often died in the jungle—of tropical diseases, snakebite, exhaustion—but Pedro Portal survived, eventually returning to the coast with amazing stories to tell his future children and plans to launch a construction business in the Lima area.

Nearly forty years old in 1895 and eager to start a family, he married Rosa Amelia Moreno del Risco, then sixteen. A devout Catholic whose convent schooling was just finished, she "preferred to marry rather than go on living in her stepfather's house." Her own father, Alejandro Moreno, died as a soldier in the War of the Pacific (1879–84), the bloody conflict between Peru and Chile that ended in defeat and devastation for Peru. Snatched from her cradle by marauding Chilean soldiers—so the family story goes—the infant Rosa Amelia was hastily retrieved by a watchful servant. Her family was comfortably, if not affluently, middle class. Rosa Amelia's mother, Juana de Risco Cáceres, had Spanish aristocratic antecedents, in Seville. An ancestor on her mother's side was a signatory to Peru's Declaration of Independence.

Pedro Portal settled his young family in Barranco, a wind-scoured resort town situated on a magnificent bluff overlooking the Pacific. The bracing salt air and vast ocean vistas attracted many of the wealthier residents of nearby

Lima, who made the journey to the seaside in horse and buggy, leaving behind the fetid air of the increasingly crowded and unsanitary capital city. On May 27, 1900, Julia Portal (christened María Magdalena, later shortened to Magda), second among four children of the Moreno-Portal union, was born on a tranquil block of adjoining single-story dwellings, possibly at number 122 or 124 Calle Colón, a brief walk from the ocean and a stone's throw from a gracefully spired local church, the Iglesia de San Francisco.

One of Magda's earliest and most vivid memories was of seeing the ocean. Carried in her mother's arms down to the shoreline and placed on the rocks, the small child was "astounded, completely dazzled by the marvel of the sea." The sea would become the cardinal metaphor in her poetry, a recurrent image of her own inveterate restlessness.

When his second daughter was nearly three, Pedro Portal, wanting to be nearer his construction sites, moved his family from seaside Barranco to nearby Callao, Peru's main port city, recently connected to landlocked Lima by rail. Through Callao moved a steady stream of agricultural and mining commodities to be shipped abroad. Portal's construction business flourished, profiting from the building boom then transforming the greater Lima-Callao area, whose population at the time was some two hundred thousand. A century later Lima and the outlying towns, including Barranco, would form a single urban complex with upward of 7 million inhabitants.

In Callao the Portal family settled into a huge, rambling house on the far edge of town, again near the ocean. Previously the house was a seminary and prior to that a barracks for the Chilean soldiers who occupied the port city in the aftermath of Peru's humiliating rout in the War of the Pacific. Her father, Magda surmised, "was no doubt attracted by the large meadow, the interior patios, and the orchard, as well as by the house's many rooms. He most certainly envisioned a larger family." There were three children by the time of this move, María Amelia, María Magdalena Julia, and Felix Alfonso; Juana de Dios would soon be born. Replete with legends and stories of local ghosts, the sprawling house with its many corridors was seen by many in the neighborhood as a place of mystery, especially at night. Phantoms loomed in the febrile imaginations of the children, who loved being frightened. Magda and her elder sister heard whispers and strange noises. They once experienced a vivid apparition of their father in shirtsleeves drawing water from the garden pump, though they soon learned from their mother—with an eerie thrill—that their father was still at work, not yet having returned home to enjoy lunch with his family.

By the time Magda was three, both she and her sister knew how to read, having been taught by their mother. A beautiful, dignified woman, Rosa Amelia greatly valued education and would take considerable pains to send all her children to school, which in Peru in those days meant Catholic school at private expense. In the peaceable routine of these years, in the morning while their mother did household chores, Magda and her sister Amelia dragged their miniature chairs to a nearby patio where young women in the neighborhood were operating a sort of preschool. Here the small girl memorized nursery rhymes and verses extolling the lives of the saints, happily reciting these to any audience she could find. On long afternoons, as her mother looked on, arms crossed, smiling indulgently, the fanciful child often walked the perimeter of the large interior patio, always with something to read tucked under her arm. She enjoyed these simple childhood pleasures, secure in the midst of a stable, prospering family. Although Rosa Moreno did not marry for love, as she later confided to her daughters, she found her taciturn husband to be a good man, hardworking, honest, and devoted to his family.

Pedro Portal regretted his own lack of a university education and hoped to provide better for his children, including the girls. He once laughingly remarked, referring to his contentious second daughter, "I'm going to have to send her to law school because she's always arguing with me, always disputing some point." He said to his wife, holding his daughter's upturned face in his hand, "This child will do something in life. You'll live to see it but I won't."

Magda had no doubt she was her father's favorite. Her principal memory of Barranco, besides her dazzling impression of the sea, was of precious time spent with her busy father. She recalled that he didn't mind her interruptions but gladly admitted her into the sanctum of his office. "'Papa, it's me, Julita,' I used to say, knocking softly on his door. That was the password. My father liked to call me Julita, and he would let me in and sit me on his desk and we would chat. He never allowed this with the other children, not even with my older sister."

This idyll abruptly ceased when one day Pedro Portal, sitting on a damp marble slab at one of his construction sites, experienced a sudden chill and went home feverish. Within the week he would succumb to a virulent strain of bronchial pneumonia. Magda retained a vivid memory of seeing her father's lifeless body.

This was my first experience of death, although I didn't grasp its significance. As the adults kept watch over my father, forbidding any child to come near, I waited my chance and slipped in when the others were somewhere else. I turned five in May, and my father died in July. I approached the bed and just stood there quietly. He was very still. Then I noticed that his feet were rigid. . . . I wasn't afraid but inside me something strange and extraordinary was happening. I don't know how long I stood there but finally I left, not wanting to be there when the others came back into the room.

Perhaps fortunately at this time, the Portal family owned a dog, León. The faithful pet followed their father's funeral procession to the cemetery then took off running as the coffin was being lowered into the ground. Eight days later the children found his limp body in the orchard weeds. With gentle solicitude they nursed him back to health, the beloved pet's condition distracting them from the harsh reality of their father's death. "I have to confess," Magda later reflected, "that our grief for our father was much less than the pain we felt when León disappeared."

She often withdrew, taking refuge in the orchard behind their house, spending hours alone. She did not, however, ignore the needs of her siblings when their mother had to be away meeting with lawyers and judges, attempting to sort out the tangled estate of mortgaged properties. According to Juana de Portal, Magda's sister and the last Portal child, Magda became responsible out of necessity, because the eldest girl, Amelia, lacked the temperament to take charge when their mother was not at home. It was Magda who put order in the household, taking care of the younger children like a grown-up. Magda's own childhood, Juana believed, effectively ended the day their father died.

While awaiting their mother's return, Magda recalled, the children would huddle together in the front doorway, singing melancholy songs while the dog lay nearby. "How many times on those lonely days when my mother traveled to Lima to see judges . . . did León wait with us, silent, attentive to the least noise, on those long afternoons when the only sound was the distant murmur of the sea."

The sudden death of Pedro Portal left his family in financial trouble. It was up to Rosa Amelia, just twenty-six and with four small children, the youngest only three months old, to salvage whatever assets she could. To raise urgently needed cash, she sold valuables and household items. Their main asset being the great house, she decided to rent it out, moving with the children into smaller accommodations. Unfortunately, the man to whom she rented the house did not pay his rent, even though he sublet apartments in the large building, thereby collecting rent himself from several families. He insisted he needed the money to make critical repairs to the property. Frustrated and bewildered, the young widow took her children and moved back into an empty wing in the house. Her tenant then insisted that *she* pay rent to *him.* Which she indignantly refused to do. At this point her tenant took her to court, charging her with trespassing. A judge responded with a patently unfair ruling: the family was evicted by court order from their own property. One day when Rosa Moreno was not at home, police authorities entered the house and put the children and household furnishings into the street. Magda recalled the scene.

> I was seven, my brother four, and the youngest, my father's last daugh-
> ter, was two and a half. My eldest sister, ten, wasn't with us at the time.
> The officials put a huge padlock on the door and we just stood there
> sobbing in the street. Everybody in the neighborhood knew the house
> was ours. "This is impossible," they said. "How can it be that these chil-
> dren can be evicted from their own house?" When the officials turned
> to go, I picked up a stone and threw it as hard as I could. Screaming and
> sobbing I picked up a huge rock and battered the padlock until it broke.
> Then I opened the door and with the neighbors' help started dragging
> the furniture back into the house. Nobody tried to stop us. The police
> and the officials just stood there and watched. But what a scene when
> my mother finally got back home!

This episode infuriated the young girl, as if a buried anger associated with the loss of her father was now erupting into consciousness, confounded with the present outrage. Her indignation at being put in the street, at seeing the shock and distress of her siblings, at experiencing the family's helplessness in the face of official power—all that, she believed, predisposed her from that day on to identify with society's ill-treated, unprotected, and unjustly dispossessed. The early loss of her father may also have predisposed her to attach herself to powerful men, to whom she could look as mentors in the battle for social reform.

Eventually the various properties her father was acquiring were auctioned to pay debts. The family moved from the port of Callao to adjacent Lima, where they lived in a series of cramped rental apartments. Her mother, "inept at earning money" yet needing to support herself and four children, solicited sewing from friends and found work stitching uniforms for the Peruvian army.

Magda would later decry what she saw as the propensity of those born into the middle class to be deeply ashamed if they became poor, trying to hide their penury while persisting in the belief that at any moment some miracle would occur to restore them to their former position. In their own case, the hoped-for miracle came in the form of a second husband for Rosa Moreno—Juan Crisóstomo Pareja, whose stable job paid a good salary. Financial cares were allayed, and in rapid succession the young mother would give birth to five additional children. Magda could now enjoy a fairly carefree girlhood. "I was very vain," she confided in a late interview given to *La Tortuga* magazine. "My mother used to say that we should install mirrors everywhere so I could look at myself from every possible angle." She also recalled liking to stay up late and look at the moon: "This worried my mother, who was afraid I'd be exhausted the next day in school."

By early adolescence Magda was writing prolifically, churning out stories, poems, even a sentimental novel (in the course of which her heroine became pregnant from having kissed her boyfriend). When she read this innocent passage to her adult relatives they burst out laughing. "In the too-austere atmosphere of our household," she disclosed to *La Tortuga,* "sex was never mentioned."

Members of her extended family may have been amused by her naive prose but they were not impressed by her incessant writing and studying and were frankly irritated by her tendency to point out errors in her elders' speech. Some of Magda's relatives—aunts, uncles—referred to her sarcastically among themselves as "la princesa" (the princess) or "la letrada" (Miss Erudition). Rosa Moreno, however, encouraged her daughter's literary experiments. She scolded Magda for destroying her manuscripts, a typical occurrence as the neophyte author's critical sense often told her the writing was worthless.

Magda also suspected that her relatives were reading her manuscripts when she was out of the house. "I always felt harassed," she later confessed, "intruded upon, persecuted by the curiosity of those around me." This sense that her writings were being violated produced in her a kind of disgust. "An almost physical need to write," she also recalled, coincided "oddly" with her tendency to destroy her work. "It seemed to me that my writing was so naked, so vulnerable, so newly born, even embryonic, that if someone should come across it, it wouldn't have the strength to remain alive. Any violation would require its death. But at the same time its destruction, my self-destruction, was a painful thing, like something I didn't do of my own accord, like something forced upon me. Like a suicide."

Being protective of her writing did not, however, deter her, when she was older, from submitting it for publication. She wanted to see her work in print. She once noted that what set her apart from many women writers was her willingness to put forward her efforts. This tension between wanting to reveal and at the same time wanting to destroy her writing may never have been fully resolved.

Even as her adolescent writing continued, she embarked upon a course of practical studies. For four years she took courses in typing, dictation, bookkeeping, and related subjects at the Colegio para Señoritas Decentes (Academy for Respectable Young Ladies). By the age of twelve she was exasperated with being schooled by nuns and yearned to acquire the marketable skills that would enable her to become self-supporting and to help her mother. "I was never frivolous," she said. "My most urgent desire was to prepare myself to become independent."

Only recently established in Lima, the Colegio para Señoritas Decentes had as its mission the imparting of secretarial skills to young women (whites only, no Indians or mestizas) who were eager to find employment in the newly opened commercial offices in the bustling capital city, then in the throes of economic expansion.

At age sixteen, having completed her program, Magda was ready to seek work. Her mother accompanied her to job interviews. When one of her very first employers took the inexperienced wage earner out of the office for an afternoon drive to the sea, her mother forbade her to return to that job. Eventually she found a position in the lithography studio of a courtly German immigrant. There she worked for two years, pleased that her mother no longer needed to purchase her clothing or provide her with spending money. She felt herself on a new plateau. "I adjusted to this new way of life, repellent in some aspects yet providing the satisfaction that comes of knowing oneself to be useful."

At the time when Magda first began earning wages, it was widely thought improper for women to work outside their homes—women, that is, of Peru's tiny middle and upper classes. Published in 1918, a novel by Angélica Palma explored the shame felt by its protagonist, a young lady of social standing, when financial need compelled her to go to work. But social mores were undergoing intense pressure to adapt to changing conditions. By the early 1920s Peruvian women, at least some of them, were taking liberties never before dared. They exposed their bodies in short-sleeved flapper-style dresses or in form-fitting bathing suits; they drove about town in sputtering motorcars;

they wore cosmetics, smoked cigarettes; they even opened their own shops. Not only were "respectable" women beginning to earn their own livelihoods, they were very much in demand to serve as secretaries, receptionists, bank tellers, and telephone switchboard operators in Lima's rapidly modernizing commercial economy.

Throughout her life Magda worked for pay, most typically as a journalist or in some aspect of publishing, though it's not always clear how she managed to stay afloat. Her income, often precarious and frequently interrupted, allowed her to provide her mother with a small sum each month—"the blessed remittance from Magda"—that her youngest sister recalled as often arriving from outside the country.

On August 24, 1917, when Magda was seventeen, her mother's second husband unexpectedly died, leaving neither life insurance nor personal savings. Three months pregnant with her ninth and last child, Magda's mother, again impoverished, began taking in sewing, and the tiny salaries of Magda and her elder sister, Amelia, became the principal support of the large household.

ENTERING THE VANGUARD (1920–1927)

A NEW SPIRIT

We shared an idea, an inarticulate vision, of a world organized in such a way that all the happiness would not belong to just a few.
—*Magda Portal*

Magda Portal came of age at a moment of exceptional social ferment and intellectual vibrancy in Peru's capital. After centuries of insularity the country was open to international influences. The Mexican Revolution, the Soviet Revolution—cataclysmic events were in the air, and dissident young people in Lima were exhilarated by dreams of a radically transformed social order. José Carlos Mariátegui, Peru's great labor leader and Marxian social theorist, called this pervasive yearning for change a "new spirit." Magda soon identified with this generational attitude, which she first encountered in the bohemian world of Lima's students, writers, and artists, a world she entered through the portals of the University of San Marcos.

Although the inquisitive young woman would have liked to study law, medicine, history, or perhaps philosophy, attaining a university degree "was out of the question" because she needed to work. Unable to enroll as a matriculating student, she was all the more fascinated by San Marcos.

> Every day as I walked home from the office where I worked I passed its imposing entry and glanced in at the interior gardens and patios. One

day on impulse I crossed the threshold and entered the university grounds. I made my way into a classroom where a lecture, I think on philosophy, was in progress. I took a seat in the back row. No one said anything and I sat there quietly listening for several long minutes. That was how I began attending a number of classes. I made friends, who never asked about my enrollment status, and I felt part of the most elevated center of learning in Peru, though I was there just by accident.

She would audit classes sporadically as her work schedule permitted, gradually becoming aware of the great questions of her day.

Chartered in 1551—arguably the first university in the New World—and a bastion of Peru's landholding elite, San Marcos only recently had opened its doors to women and nonwhite candidates. But student reformers were now calling for more sweeping changes, demands given fiery impetus by the university reform movement, which erupted in 1918 in Córdoba, Argentina, its radical ideas quickly spreading to other countries on the continent.

Student activists were calling for the dismissal of professors they regarded as fossils, relics of an outmoded feudal era, incompetent guides for their reform-minded generation. They regarded the traditional curriculum—law, literature, theology, philosophy—as far too narrow, if not totally irrelevant, in light of the needs of their sorely backward country. Students called for co-governance and the introduction of courses in such disciplines as sociology, anthropology, and civil engineering. The university, they insisted, should be a force for modernization, a vital resource in the task of building a modern secular state.

In the local squares, in coffeehouses, and in little bars near the university, students passionately debated local and international issues. Many cut classes to attend rallies and demonstrations. In 1919 they took to the streets to support textile workers on strike for the eight-hour day. Protest against the staid structure of the university rapidly became part of a larger, more ambitious movement challenging all entrenched privilege and calling for social revolution.

BOHEMIAN CIRCLES

It is not clear exactly when Magda began auditing classes at San Marcos and making friends among artists and political dissidents, but by 1922 she was attending gatherings of several bohemian groups. At the photography studio of the Goyzueta brothers, Federico and Diego, she met writer María Wiesse and her husband, painter and woodblock artist José Sabogal, whose recent exposure to Diego Rivera's groundbreaking mural art in Mexico City stimulated his own exploration of indigenous themes in Peru. Magda also associated and felt most at ease with a group of writers who came to Lima from the north coast city of Trujillo. In that group she met Peru's great poet César Vallejo, composer Alfonso de Silva, poet-journalist Alcides Spelucín, and philosopher-journalist Antenor Orrego.

At gatherings of this group, Magda recalled, drugs were much in evidence—cocaine, ether, opium. But she held back, she said, looking on while her friends indulged, except for once sniffing a handkerchief doused with ether—to no effect. In fact she was wary of drugs, afraid she might become dependent and above all not wanting to upset her mother by coming home under the influence of a narcotic; she continued to live at home with her mother and siblings. Intrigued, however, by tales of incredible opium dreams, she once ventured into the narrow alleyways of Lima's Chinatown to rendezvous with friends at an opium den. Arriving before the others at the appointed meeting place, she lost her nerve and "furtively withdrew," later confessing her cowardice to her friends.

Her connection with César Vallejo began in 1922 when Magda was twenty-two and the older poet about thirty. "We were close," she said, "like brother and sister. We went to the sea together with our group of friends. We sang songs, sad songs, *yaravíes*. . . . We were sad because life told us that happiness was impossible." Vallejo was back in Lima after a disastrous trip the previous year to Santiago de Chuco, his native village in the northern Andes, a remote mining community four days on horseback from the nearest train station. This village is described by H. R. Hays, one of Vallejo's translators. "The inhabitants of the town retain much of the Indian's closeness to the soil; houses are primitive adobe shells, without sanitary conveniences and sparsely furnished; chickens and guinea pigs swarm in the kitchen and patio. . . . Whole clans live together, uncles, aunts, cousins, grandparents, swarms of children, in patriarchal unity."

Vallejo's ties to his native region and to his family were strong. The last of eleven children, he grew up in an atmosphere of maternal solicitude and devout Catholicism. Both his grandfathers were Spanish priests and both grandmothers Chimú Indian. His bronze skin, high cheekbones, and thick black hair bore ample witness to his indigenous blood. His father enjoyed social standing in the impoverished town but could not afford to pay for his sons' higher education. Vallejo therefore left home very early to work as a tutor and at other jobs, saving almost all his earnings to make possible his university studies in Trujillo and later in Lima.

His fateful return trip to his natal town resulted in his being unjustly imprisoned, a nightmarish episode that changed the course of his life. Vallejo arrived in Santiago de Chuco during the annual festival honoring the town's patron saint, a celebration that devolved into a drunken riot in the course of which a town official was slain and a local store burned down. Although he did not participate in the violence, even tried to subdue it, he was nevertheless charged by local officials with complicity in the crimes. To escape detention the poet fled to the coast, living in hiding until eventually being arrested and jailed in Trujillo. For three profoundly demoralizing months he remained jailed while his friends worked frantically to secure his release. Finally he was let go, but the charges against him remained standing.

During this incarceration Vallejo drafted a number of the poems that would appear under the title *Trilce* in October 1922, when Magda was part of his circle. José Carlos Mariátegui viewed Vallejo as a great poet and the first in Peru to express an authentically indigenous American sensibility, one imbued with the fatalism, piety, and suffering of the Indian people. Describing Vallejo's first book, *Los heraldos negros* (*The Black Heralds*), 1919, as marking "the dawn of a new poetry in Peru," Mariátegui saw in Vallejo's writing an incipient yearning for societal change and believed Vallejo to be "the precursor of the new spirit and new conscience."

Although Vallejo's friends enthusiastically praised his unusual talent, the new book, *Trilce*—with its nonsensical title, cryptic passages, and peculiar idiom—met with general incomprehension. One critic called him "a poet without poems." The negative reviews hurt and discouraged the poet, who, as Magda recounted, "told his friends that he felt ashamed, as if he were guilty of a contemptible crime." As part of this group Magda recalled that she preferred to listen while the others talked. She must have seemed to her more sophisticated and somewhat older friends, mostly men, to be very limited in her education and knowledge of the world. Already an accomplished poet, Vallejo, for example, held an advanced degree in Spanish literature. He had witnessed the humiliating treatment endured by workers in the high-sierran mines and on the great coastal plantations. Antenor Orrego and Alcides Spelucín—later to become leaders along with Magda in the Partido Aprista Peruano—were already veteran writers and social agitators, active in the labor movement in Trujillo. Orrego was editor in chief of the daily newspaper *La*

Reforma, then of *La Libertad,* which authorities shut down in order to silence its repeated calls for better treatment of farmworkers in the fertile Chicama Valley to Trujillo's north, the Chicama being one of several river valley oases on Peru's otherwise desert coast. By early 1923 Orrego and Spelucín were publishing yet another militant paper in Trujillo, *El Norte,* in which they resumed their battle to improve the lot of the farm laborers. César Vallejo served as correspondent for *El Norte* in Lima. Magda had yet to acquire firsthand experience of the harsh facts of Peruvian life that gave rise to these journalistic protests.

Vallejo and his friends from the provinces perceived themselves as outsiders in the former seat of the Spanish viceroys. Lima exemplified for these activist-intellectuals the worst of colonialist presumption and parasitism. Still comparatively unformed in 1922, and quick to be engaged by what concerned her friends, Magda internalized their anti-Lima attitudes to such an extent that she felt flattered when someone told her that she did not seem like a *limeña.*

Vallejo felt out of his element in Peru's capital. He disliked the attitudes of assumed superiority he experienced there, especially the condescending smiles of those *limeños,* who, Magda recalled his saying, "seemed always to be giving you patronizing pats on the back." Vallejo also suffered from Lima's dreary climate, with its endless overcast days. He missed the sierran landscape of his childhood and above all he missed his mother, whose death was recent. He longed for the warmth of the familial circle he had left behind and that in fact no longer existed. Vallejo is said to have so yearned for the sierra that he regularly left a water faucet running in his rooms in Lima so as to be reminded of the mountain rains.

It may have been through this early connection with César Vallejo that Magda first became aware of the tragic gist of Peru's postconquest history. To have enjoyed the companionship of such a formidably gifted poet and intellectual—considered by Thomas Merton to be the greatest universal poet since Dante—to have observed his preoccupations and to some extent absorbed them, was crucially formative for the young poet and future political leader. Many times Magda acknowledged her debt to Vallejo, but it's unlikely that she remained in touch with him following his departure from Peru. Fearing he might again be arrested and jailed on the old charges, Vallejo left for Europe on June 17, 1923. In Paris he lived in extreme poverty, writing prolifically and becoming even more ardently involved in left-wing politics, including Peruvian politics in exile. He never returned to Peru.

LEGACY OF CONQUEST

Perou: in Renaissance Europe a synonym for inestimable riches.

Hostility toward Lima on the part of these young dissidents formed part of an ongoing debate over what in fact constituted Peru. What was Peru? Hardly a nation, but much the same cobbled-together aggregate of distinct geographies and disparate peoples it had been as an outpost of sixteenth-century Spain. Even following its independence from Spain, Peru failed to cohere as a nation, a social construct enshrined in myths and unifying symbols. By the early twentieth century, the problem of national identity was approaching a state of crisis. Some reformers believed that the only true Peru was indigenous Peru. A few went so far as to envision the destruction of the Spanish influence—rather perversely imagining a cathartic fire sweeping down out of the Andes to burn away all traces of the Hispanic culture that was dominant in Lima and along the Pacific coast. Still others wanted to create an entirely new Peru, integrating Hispanic and native elements into a socially equitable and fully modern nation-state.

This fervent questioning of Peru's identity cannot be understood without reference to the country's extreme inequities in land ownership and in social power, a legacy of the Spanish Conquest. At the time of Magda's birth in 1900, the vast majority of Peruvians, perhaps as many as four-fifths, were indigenous and rural. Isolated from the Europeanized cities on the coast, they lived in the Andean foothills, in largely inaccessible highland villages, and in high-altitude urban centers such as Cuzco or in the vast expanses of the Amazonian jungle basin. Social relations continued very much as in colonial days. An enormous cultural chasm separated Hispanic Peru from deep Peru—*el Perú profundo*—the semiarchaic world of the native peoples. Neolithic folkways persisted in the hinterlands; in various Andean regions the knowledge endured of how Incan priests made human bones into turquoise amulets; ritual combat might well end with human sacrifice to the Mountain; and local people venerated the Virgin Mary as Pacha Mama, mother earth.

This simplified vision of Peru as two highly polarized and self-contained realities prevailed in the 1920s among progressives concerned with the plight of the indigenous people. The fact of *mestizaje*—race and cultural mixture—and the problems of Black and Asian Peruvians did not much figure in the conversation. Although many Africans were brought as slaves to work on the great plantations, and Asians in considerable numbers came later as farm laborers, the primary concern of the new generation of Peruvian activists was the misery of the indigenous majority.

In great numbers Indian campesinos were living in semifeudal conditions on enormous haciendas, great landed estates. Often managed by overseers while the landowners lived abroad in Paris, Madrid, or Barcelona, some of these estates covered as many as a quarter of a million acres. Herds of llama and alpacas grazed in mountain pastures on landholdings that might extend from the Andean highlands to the Pacific-coastal valleys. Some Indians worked as *yanaconas*, tenant farmers, on these vast estates, while others toiled as *colonos*, or serfs, legally bound to the land and required to pay their feudal masters, the *gamonales*, in labor, livestock, shearings, or farm produce—for which they were given the right to till a plot of ground so small it barely afforded subsistence. Indians on high-sierran holdings were sometimes paid a token wage of four cents a day. Obliged to do domestic service in the home of the landowner or his manager, Indian women and girls were routinely subjected to the sexual exploitation denounced by Clorinda Matto de Turner in her excoriating 1889 novel of social criticism, *Aves sin nido* (*Torn from the Nest*). Badly nourished, often sick, sometimes living in windowless shacks whose walls were plastered with evil-smelling dung, the sierran Indians were known for their collective resignation; they did not want to be separated from their native lands, which they revered as Pacha Mama, mother earth.

Although the indigenous economic unit and land collective, the *ayllu*, still flourished in many localities, communally held lands continued to be lost—sometimes sold or even given away. But more frequently such lands were occupied by force, murderous force, as armed settlers, even the Catholic Church, took over territories that were then incorporated into privately owned haciendas. Dispossessed Indian campesinos were thus rendered easy prey for *enganchadores*, labor recruiters who made seductive promises of a better life working for wages in the mines or on coastal plantations. Some of these great farms employed as many as four thousand workers, disdainfully called *peones* by their employers.

Sugarcane, the "white gold" imported to the Americas from the Canary Islands by Columbus, provided enormous wealth for the influential families that owned the massive agribusiness operations in the Chicama Valley, but the workers on these lands suffered fearful exploitation. In his job as assistant to the paymaster at Hacienda Roma—the site in 1910 of a violently suppressed campesino uprising—César Vallejo witnessed the bleak ritual of indigenous and mestizo workers gathering at dawn in the great courtyard to march out for a long day's toil in the fields. They earned for their labor the equivalent of pennies a day. Obtaining alcohol and meager necessities on credit at the company store, these workers soon found themselves in irreversible debt peonage.

While many of Peru's indigenous resigned themselves to such conditions, many did not. From the first days of the Spanish Conquest native people rebelled, with women in the forefront of major revolts. As Sara Beatriz Guardia's research indicates, in an eighteenth-century uprising led by Túpac Amaru II, indigenous women led troops against Spanish forces; they defended rivers, laid siege to towns, and died grisly deaths when captured. Túpac Amaru II's wife, the legendary Micaela Bastidas—who commanded a rebel army—died by hanging after gruesome tortures. Parts of her dismembered body were exhibited in Cuzco, Arequipa, and Tungasuca. Another female leader in this revolt, Bartolina Sisa, was crowned with feathers, tied to a horse, and dragged through the streets with a town crier trumpeting her crimes. Her severed head and hands were displayed in her native village, a grim caution to would-be rebels. By the early twentieth century, native rebellion on a massive scale had been more or less quelled. But exploitation continued, accompanied by mass unrest and sporadic uprisings.

A CRUCIAL YEAR: 1923

O God widen my horizons.
—*Magda Portal, "Anhelo"*

On a May morning in 1923 Magda Portal stood on a street corner in Lima. Intently, she watched as a raucous street demonstration drew nearer, a mass action that would extend over several days and culminate in deadly violence. University students and factory workers came together to protest reigning autocrat Augusto B. Leguía's recently announced plan to consecrate Peru to the Sacred Heart of Jesus. The volatile anti-Leguía movement viewed this plan as a shamelessly anachronistic attempt by Peru's strongman to ingratiate himself with high officials of the Catholic Church while simultaneously distracting the uneducated masses with colorful religious pageantry. Protesters saw this plan as all too emblematic of the centuries-old symbiotic relationship between church and state in Peru, a relationship that proponents of the new spirit—a secular spirit—refused to tolerate. The protesters despised Leguía with a youthful fury. They saw in him both a tyrant and a traitor. He was, they believed, eagerly surrendering the country's wealth to a new breed of conquistador—the foreign capitalists who were extracting exorbitant profits from Peru.

By the time of Augusto Leguía's ascension to power, Peru's economy was undergoing a boom; a phase of astonishing dynamism was under way, an expansion that had begun some decades earlier, following Peru's catastrophic war with Chile. Just when it seemed that the roving eye of international finance capital might possibly have overlooked Peru, that desolating war opened the way for an influx of foreign capital to rebuild the country. The task of reconstructing Peru's shattered rail system, for example, was entirely given over to a British company, which assumed Peru's huge debt to that concern. To offset the huge risks of investing in such a devastated and geographically daunting country, the firm received extraordinary incentives from the state—exemption from taxes, a million-acre land grant in the Amazonian jungle, and cash payments in pounds sterling to be made annually over several decades. Similar incentives were offered mining concerns. By the 1920s this influx of capital was a flood, stimulated by the opening of the Panama Canal in 1914 and by the heightened demand for Peru's raw materials occasioned by the Great War in Europe.

Impeccably groomed, mustachioed, invariably described as "dapper," the entrepreneurial Leguía—already immensely wealthy, enriched by his many and far-flung business ventures—was duly elected to Peru's presidency in January 1919. Eager to accelerate Peru's great leap into modernity, and aiming to remove all obstacles to developing the country at breakneck speed, Leguía soon declared himself above the law: he suspended Peru's constitution on July 4, 1919, a date thereafter celebrated as Peruvian-U.S. Friendship Day.

Leguía greatly admired the prosperity and streamlined business practices of the United States, then well on its way to becoming the "boardroom state" predicted with dismay by U.S. President Woodrow Wilson. "Foreign capital," Leguía grandly declared, "will be given facilities and opportunities for the development of Peruvian resources which have never heretofore been accorded and which may never be accorded again." He then set about arranging deals with Wall Street bankers, who consolidated Peru's debt and restored the country's ruined credit. Business confidence soared—along with deficit spending—as the Yankee dollar edged out the formerly dominant British pound. Peru's national debt during Leguía's eleven-year rule rocketed from $10 million to $100 million, mostly owed to New York banks. While investment capital poured in from abroad—only the tiniest merchant class existed in the country—Peru's great landholding elite retained its traditional power, even increasing it by investing in the new economy.

To compete with other international centers of commerce, Lima, some concluded, could no longer remain "a dirty, miserable little hamlet . . . without water, without light, without pavement, a sad leftover of what was colonial grandeur." Electric streetcars replaced horse-drawn trams, and tall buildings dramatically altered the skyline, but modernization of the city was only just beginning. Leguía worked indefatigably to advance this process, setting in motion ambitious sanitation and electrification projects, arranging as well for the construction of a major network of asphalted thoroughfares with names such as Avenida Leguía or Avenida Progreso—wide boulevards connecting central Lima with the outlying coastal towns of Callao, Barranco, and Miraflores. The capital city's population exploded as thousands poured in from the hinterlands to seek work in construction or in textile factories or simply to escape conscription into Leguía's road-building crews, almost entirely Indian, whose dreaded unpaid labor built rugged, unpaved roads that cut through Peru's mountainous interior.

The quick fortunes then being made in Peru's commodities, and in the newer industries of finance, transportation, and communications, were conspicuously displayed in lavishly built homes in exclusive new suburbs of Lima. At Talara, on Peru's north coast, International Petroleum, a subsidiary of Standard Oil of New Jersey, pumped prodigious quantities of oil. Coal extraction was stepped up to power the trains hauling ores from Andean mines down to the sea. Ports were expanded; refining plants were under construction; and agribusiness flourished, dominated by three giant concerns on the north coastal plains. Leguía's promise of prosperity was largely being delivered, and not just to the elites. This economic boom created jobs and aroused great expectations. But it also provoked strikes and labor riots as anarchosyndicalist ideas began penetrating the small urban proletariat. Indigenous communities were also undergoing turmoil. Violent rebellions were taking place in the sierran cities of Cuzco and Puno. Through it all, however, the collective unit—the *ayllu*—survived, offering a native precedent for the communitarian ideals that appealed so strongly to the self-declared vanguard generation with which Magda Portal increasingly identified.

That day in May as Magda stood watching the approaching demonstration, her interest was tempered with hesitancy. Not yet caught up in the quasi-revolutionary mood of marching students and workers, she stood on the sidelines, hanging back, "put off by the turmoil and threat of arrest." She later viewed the year 1923 as crucial in her personal development, for during that year she became conscious of Peru's social problems. In the aftermath of this violently suppressed protest, Magda first met the charismatic Víctor Raúl Haya de la Torre, who would figure so decisively in Peru's history and in her own career.

HAYA DE LA TORRE

Haya de la Torre came to Lima from the northern coastal city of Trujillo. There he participated in a brilliant circle of aspiring writers and social reformers—the "Trujillo bohemians," a group that included César Vallejo and Antenor Orrego. Haya was born into the local manorial class and descended from colonial aristocracy; his family was no longer wealthy but nevertheless managed to live very comfortably in a spacious Persian-carpeted home, routinely enjoying seaside vacations and employing maids for each child. But when it came time for Víctor Raúl to attend university, there was no money to support his studies away from home. He had no choice but to make his own way, which he did with the help of various benefactors.

Although his family took pride in having a bloodline that was traceable over many generations back to Spain, the young Haya repudiated this attitude, which amounted to a white supremacist presumption. He greatly admired the indigenous culture. On a moonlit excursion to the indigenous ruins of Chan Chan, center of the once flourishing Chimú civilization, Haya as a very young man underwent a life-altering mystical experience that bound him, as he announced at the time, to promote in all his future endeavors the indigenous heritage of Peru. In fact he felt honored to recognize his own distinctive features in the faces sculpted at Chan Chan, a resemblance said to be truly uncanny. As historian Fredrick Pike observed in his preeminent study, *The Politics of the Miraculous in Peru: Haya de la Torre and the Spiritualist Tradition,* Haya's affinity for the indigenous was highly unusual—"To be white of skin and relatively free from racial prejudice was a stunning attribute for this time in Peru."

Víctor Raúl threw himself into student politics at San Marcos. Year after year he remained a first-year student, contemptuous of the very idea of attaining a degree. In 1919, Haya, then twenty-four, led university students in a major political action. They put their bodies on the line between embattled textile workers on strike for the eight-hour day and armed police who were threatening to open fire on the strikers. This heroic gamble paid off. The police backed down and Haya's prestige soared as he went on to negotiate terms for the creation of a textile workers' union, secure in his leadership of the newly forged worker-student alliance. He went on to found, in 1921, what soon became a major radical institution—the popular university movement, inspired by the thought of nineteenth-century social theorist and poet Manuel González Prada, who called for the privileged youth of society to share their knowledge and skills with manual workers. Traveling by horse-drawn buggy over nearly impassable mountain terrain, the audacious leader helped inaugurate popular universities not just in Lima but also in other Peruvian cities—Arequipa, Trujillo, Cuzco, Chiclayo, Piura, Huaraz, and Puno. Many labor leaders studied at these radical schools, which often met at night in union halls. Providing instruction from an anticolonialist perspective, popular universities quickly developed into a potent movement. The famous saying of González Prada—"The old to the tomb, the young to work!"—succinctly expressed the impatient spirit of a militant new generation.

Haya de la Torre's prestige was further heightened when once again he led a protest that united students and workers. It was during this famous protest in May 1923, that Magda for the first time saw the dynamic leader.

> A young man—whose name I would only later learn—walked fearlessly at the front of the march, his arms linked with two student friends. This scene made a powerful impression. A few days later a friend took me to meet him. He was in a boardinghouse, in bed with a fever and congested lungs. On the second day of the mass demonstrations, at the burial of the two victims, a student and worker killed by the police, there was another clash with the police and Haya de la Torre escaped arrest by jumping into the Rímac River. That exposure led to his illness.

The two deaths in this demonstration were said to have sealed in blood the worker-student alliance from which would emerge the Frente Único de Trabajadores Manuales y Intelectuales (United Front of Manual and Intellectual Workers), which became identified with Haya's most influential formulation, the Alianza Popular Revolucionaria Americana (APRA). At the funeral of the slain demonstrators, the eloquent leader gave an electrifying speech, profoundly moving his followers and possibly alarming Augusto Leguía—for no more was heard of the autocrat's plan to consecrate Peru to the Sacred Heart of Jesus.

After an intensive months-long search by the authorities, the fugitive Haya was arrested and jailed on the bleak prison island of San Lorenzo. Leguía offered his young antagonist a government stipend to study abroad, which Haya refused on principle, whereupon he was promptly deported. Almost four years would pass before he and Magda would meet again, in Mexico City, by which time Magda herself was in exile, expelled from Peru as a political "subversive."

Gaunt from his incarceration, Haya de la Torre disembarked from the steamship *Negada* in Havana. There he received a rousing hero's welcome. It was November 1923. Julio Antonio Mella, the militant Irish Afro-Cuban student leader, hosted Haya on a whirlwind tour of speeches to student and labor groups throughout the island. Haya's presence in Cuba greatly contributed to the revolutionary ferment already under way in the country. Modeled on its Peruvian counterpart, the José Martí popular university movement was established during Haya's visit, and in a short while a Cuban Aprista Party would be founded, tributaries of which, three decades later, would feed into Fidel Castro's 26th of July Movement, which inaugurated the Cuban Revolution. Mella described Haya's charisma on that tour. "He subjugated his listeners so powerfully they seemed like purring lions dominated by their tamer. He made us laugh, cry, think, fear. With magisterial finesse he ran the full gamut of feelings. . . . He is the archetype of Latin American youth, a dream of Rodó made flesh; he is Ariel."

For some time Haya had been corresponding with Mexico's revolutionary minister of education, José Vasconcelos, an extraordinary figure, as described by U.S. writer and Communist Party activist Bertram D. Wolfe, Vasconcelos's contemporary: "He surrounded himself with poets, painters, and visionary counselors of all descriptions, [and he] rode forth with this motley train on burro and horseback to all the corners of the land, warring on the illiteracy and rudeness of the times, laying foundations for schools, urging the preparation of the people for entrance into democratic political life."

Vasconcelos now invited the exiled Peruvian to come to Mexico. In Mexico City, working as Vasconcelos's personal secretary, Haya became aware of the magnificent mural art then being commissioned by his employer. By 1923 Diego Rivera was the undisputed leader of what Wolfe described as the most significant revival of fresco painting since the late Italian Renaissance. When working in Paris, Rivera was encouraged by Vasconcelos to develop a more civic conception of art by touring Italy. In Rome, Venice, Ravenna, and other

' Mexican painter made hundreds of sketches inspired by such
'o, Michelangelo, and Mantegna. In his subsequent mural
_ ......ings he would manage an uncanny integration of the disparate styles,
perspectives, and palettes he had observed in both Italy and France. When
Rivera returned to Mexico, Vasconcelos urged him to become more familiar
with his own country's indigenous heritage, personally escorting the painter
to the indigenous sites of Chichén Itzá and Uxmal in Yucatán.

Working preternaturally long hours, applying pigments with ferocious
speed to wet plaster, Rivera was already embarked, by the time Haya arrived
in Mexico City, on his most famous mural project. His monumental murals
in the new edifice housing Mexico's Ministry of Education illustrated Vas-
concelos's own seminal concept of the Indo-American—a creative fusion of
European and indigenous elements. Haya was so impressed with this concept
and with the term *Indo-American* that he immediately incorporated it into the
phraseology of his fledgling APRA movement. A five-pointed star represented
the movement's broad points of unity: (1) anti-imperialism, (2) Pan-American
unity, (3) internationalization of the Panama Canal, (4) nationalization of
lands and industries, and (5) concern for Indo-America's indigenous heritage
and solidarity with all oppressed peoples. When Haya officially inaugurated
this movement in Mexico City on May 7, 1924, he displayed the distinctive
APRA banner, whose design Diego Rivera helped create. The colorful banner
featured Central and South America in gold outline on a scarlet ground, the
gold Aprista star ascendant.

In the late spring of 1924, Haya traveled with Vasconcelos to Texas. From
there APRA's architect, as a member of a delegation led by the young Com-
munist Bertram Wolfe, proceeded to New York City to embark on a trip to
the new Russia. Such an excursion was made possible for Haya by Anna
Melissa Graves, whose personal wealth helped support numerous peace and
social justice efforts. In fact, Graves's generosity would enable Haya to study
in England and to devote himself full time to building his APRA movement.
During his years in exile abroad Haya energetically traveled, studied, lec-
tured, and wrote, all the while sending back greetings and news of his activi-
ties to his many friends and comrades in Peru.

TOURNAMENT OF FLOWERS

In August 1923, just weeks prior to Haya de la Torre's arrest and deportation,
Magda Portal won first prize in Peru's most prestigious literary competition:
the Juegos Florales (Tournament of Flowers), a contest sponsored by the

University of San Marcos. Submitted under the evocative pen name Lorelei, Magda's winning entry consisted of three poems collectively titled "Nocturnos." In the pages of the Lima newspaper *El Tiempo*, the contest judges pronounced her worthy of standing "alongside Juana de Ibarbourou and Gabriela Mistral in a radiant trinity of women poets."

That Magda's early poetry elicited such generous appreciation must be understood in the Peruvian context—educated women, women who wrote, were a tiny minority in Peru, and women poets of distinctive accomplishment were few. In 450 years of Peru's postconquest history, only one purportedly female poet—writing under the pseudonym Amarilis—achieved substantial recognition. In fact, it's not certain that a woman actually wrote Amarilis's verses, originally sent to Spanish playwright and poet Lope de Vega, who published them along with his own work in 1621. Another pseudonymous poet of that era wrote under the pen name Clarinda, but that poet too may have been male—at least one critic has concluded that the female pen name "was a device used to conceal a masculine identity." In Peru as in other Latin American countries, women with intellectual gifts often sought refuge in convents. A good deal of writing went on in such cloisters, as documented in *Untold Sisters: Hispanic Nuns in Their Own Words*, by Electa Arenal and Stacey Schlau. Peru's most famous saint, Rosa of Lima, for example, wrote a number of conventional verses. But it appears that no poetry of strong interest emerged from Peru's convents, certainly no work comparable to that of seventeenth-century Mexican nun Sor Juana Inés de la Cruz, whose poetry and other writings exhibit genius.

Although a number of women poets were part of the illustrious group of Peruvian literary women known collectively as the Generation of 1870, those women were dismissed without mention by José Carlos Mariátegui, who credited Magda Portal in his influential essay on Peru's literature as being "Peru's first poetess as distinguished from mere women of letters." He went on to say that he believed Magda to be "important in Peru's literature" because she represented the emergence of a poetry "spiritually emancipated and differentiated from men's" and by means of which women were expressing their entire beings. Other Latin American women who embodied this tendency, he said, were Delmira Augustini, Juana de Ibarbourou, Gabriela Mistral, and Blanca Luz Brum. "Poetry, grown old in man," Mariátegui declared, "is born again, rejuvenated in woman."

Magda was twenty when she first began seeing her poems (and prose writings) in print in Lima's *Mundial*, a general-interest weekly magazine in which poems by Federico Bolaños also appeared. Magda met this temperamental poet and critic (four years her elder) either through *Mundial* or through mutual friends at the university. Bolaños came from the Andean city of Huancayo. Their subsequent love affair, as Daniel R. Reedy recounts in his major study, *Magda Portal: La pasionaria peruana; Biografía intelectual,* led to a painful estrangement between Magda and her mother, a practicing Catholic whose religious beliefs and sense of propriety were offended by her daughter's unconventional behavior. In a sequence of untitled poems, "18 cantos emocionados de 'Vidrios de amor,'" Magda examined the emotions she experienced as a result of this estrangement and during the pregnancy that resulted from her affair with Bolaños, with whom she openly lived and traveled. Dated as having been finished in 1924 but not published until 1929, these poems express feelings that range from exquisite tenderness for her unborn child to a sense of the oddity of being pregnant and a resistance to embracing the natural process under way in her womb. Above all in these writings she articulates her unhappiness at being estranged from her beloved mother, confiding an anguish at her own willfulness and seeming inability to live other than strictly on her own terms. While yearning to be forgiven and soothed, she cannot alter her own stubborn resistance to ending the silence and distance between them. In the first poem in this series she addresses her mother directly and asks her pardon.

> forgive me smile on me
> from the plenitude of your silence
> vast field inhabited by your dead
> you whose eyes are lost
> I too stand on that field
> because I am among your dead
> FORGIVE ME

When Magda won first prize in the Juegos Florales competition in 1923, a critic writing in *Mundial* observed that "Magda Portal's soul is a landscape of clouds, mist, and sorrow. . . . Her poems are full of pain, genuinely disconsolate." The sadness noted by this early critic Magda herself believed to be intrinsic to her poetic voice. In fact her poems manifest a range of moods and tonalities, among which sadness or something akin to it may well be predominant.

Her triumph in this contest brought her early recognition as a poet, this prize having never before been awarded to a woman. Steeped in medieval pageantry, the awards ceremony, a major date on Lima's social calendar, required the winner of first prize to serenade the queen of this annual event, a tradition that presented a new problem: obviously a woman could not serenade another woman. The contest's director visited Magda at her home to explain the situation and suggest a solution. "I don't believe I understood much of what he said," Magda recalled, "except that first prize couldn't go to a woman." She agreed to accept a special prize, ostensibly one equal in prestige, so that first prize could be awarded to a man and the traditional serenade be performed as usual.

At the awards ceremony, however, Magda refused at the last moment to go on stage and accept this special prize. But she did this for a reason unrelated to the serenade difficulty, which, she recalled, she didn't regard as of much importance at the time. A contemporary observer recalled the incident, which turned on autocrat Augusto Leguía's unexpected arrival in the auditorium.

> The auditorium of Lima's Municipal Theater was jam-packed when Leguía came in. A few scattered police informants broke into feeble applause. The audience hissed. . . . Frowning, Leguía took a seat. Magda stood backstage, lovely in her evening dress and radiant with anticipation. When the curtain rose and she was summoned to go on stage . . . I saw her delicate young face flush and become set with decision. "No," she told the master of ceremonies. "I don't want to greet Leguía, not even out of courtesy. I renounce the prize." The audience burst into applause, immediately understanding her protest.

Magda's own account of the incident suggests a reluctance to remove herself entirely from the proceedings. "I asked the master of ceremonies, poet [José] Gálvez to excuse me from going onstage and asked him to read my poems in my place. . . . He gave an excellent reading . . . and the audience applauded." News of her defiant gesture spread, bringing her substantial notoriety. Still fresh in the minds of Leguía's adversaries was the fact that only months earlier the autocrat's police had shot dead a student and a worker, participants in the massive May protest led by Víctor Raúl Haya de la Torre. At the time of the awards ceremony, Haya remained in hiding, a fugitive in Peru.

In later years Leguía would be judged a good deal more leniently as his police brutalities were seen in the light of atrocities committed by later strongmen in Peru and elsewhere in Latin America. For the moment, however, the autocrat was viewed, at least by many of his young opponents, as a homicidal despot and venal servant of foreign capital. Magda experienced no official reprisals for her sensational insult to Leguía, who apparently did not see her as any threat to his regime.

What appears to have gone unmentioned in public comment on Magda's protest was the fact of her being substantially pregnant at the time, and unmarried, quite possibly an additional motive for her refusal to go on stage. The extremely unconventional nature of her personal life seemed not to detract from the praise accorded her as a poet in a number of established print forums. Given the predominantly conservative mores of the time, this toleration, or discretion, suggests that at least in some circles women were permitted certain liberties. Magda's first and only child, Gloria, fathered by Federico Bolaños, was born November 11, 1923. Magda and Federico were married July 31, 1924.

ARROWS

Later that year in Lima, the couple were co-editing and publishing the literary review *Flechas* (Arrows), a journal that emerged under the broad aegis of Italian artist F. T. Marinetti's *Futurist Manifesto*, first published in 1909 in France. That enormously influential statement exalted "the new" and celebrated speed, dynamism, youth, and risk, not to mention exhaust-belching motor cars and even war itself—hailed as the epitome of extreme experience. In a hyperadrenalated tone, Marinetti declared that the past should be obliterated and that museums and libraries as repositories of its dusty artifacts should be destroyed.

The natural affinities between a futurist spirit in the arts and that same spirit in social reform were manifest in a shared desire to remove from the scene—at once—the outworn, the antiquated, the traditional, whether the outmoded thing be a vault of antiquities or even, ominously, in the social arena, an entire class of persons deemed by its critics to be standing in the way of progress. The futurist tendency to exacerbate conflict to the point of violence would soon be a major tendency in radical politics in Peru. The review *Flechas* is credited with being the first in that country to articulate the futurist-vanguard spirit in the literary arts.

A fertile mix of constructive and destructive impulses characterized this handsome journal, which appeared in only four issues (in six numbers, from October to December 1924). In the inaugural issue's "Prologue-Manifesto," writing in a feverish style and addressing themselves "to a few pure and lucid spirits," the editors announced the journal's grandiose mission: "We want spiritual renovation. . . . And more. We want to destroy, to decimate all false values, values like cadavers that would float forever on waves of the multitude . . . if bold, revitalizing youth did not demolish them." In the pages of *Flechas,* the editors proclaimed, Peru's young people would reject the cultural isolation of "the senile and hermetically sealed generations of the past" and instead embrace all kindred spirits, their contemporaries from all over the continent.

Dedicated to Simón Bolívar, the final issue presented writers from Venezuela, Colombia, Bolivia, Ecuador, and Peru. Women poets were also featured, including Chile's future Nobel Prize–winner Gabriela Mistral, Uruguay's Juana de Ibarbourou, and the Argentinean Alfonsina Storni. Magda provided brief appreciations of both Mistral and Storni. Praising Storni's "tormented lyricism," she acknowledged that reading Storni's work was her first experience of poetry by a woman writer, except for a few verses by Saint Theresa.

Generally appreciative when commenting on specific contemporaries, Magda's byline contributions contrasted sharply with Federico's reviews, which lurched from hyperbolic acclaim for writers he admired to vitriolic denunciation of those he did not. A section of the review, "Flechazos" (Arrow Wounds), was reserved for his barbed remarks, invariably delivered in a scathingly superior tone. Luis Alberto Sánchez described Federico as "inwardly disturbed and outwardly arrogant, . . . a writer who disappeared from the scene after publishing one promising book."

Federico's denunciatory zeal reflected a depth of rage and scorn that Magda may have shared but did not articulate when writing solely in her own voice. Their bylined contributions to *Flechas* suggest a potentially explosive combination of personalities. As co-editors of the journal, however, the two were united in nonambivalent advocacy of the new spirit, and they self-righteously and belligerently attacked in print anything or anyone who offended their sensibilities.

If certain accounts are to be believed, Federico did not confine his animosities to book reviews. According to Graciela Pareja Moreno, Magda's half-sister, Federico subjected Magda to abusive treatment and failed to contribute financially to the household, instead confiscating the salary his wife earned working in a print shop. Magda herself characterized Federico as controlling and abusive. Whatever in fact transpired in the relationship, keeping in mind that we lack Federico's view of the matter, the marriage failed, and it did so in an especially scandalous way. Deserting her husband, Magda began living with his younger brother, Reynaldo Bolaños, known by his pen name Serafín Delmar. On the *Flechas* masthead Serafín is listed as secretary, indicating his collaboration on the review and suggesting the context in which he came to know his sister-in-law.

Magda and Serafín were in their mid-twenties when they became a couple, Serafín a year younger than Magda. Both were instinctive rebels and dedicated poets. In March 1925, in the Lima review *Variedades*, Magda commented enthusiastically on Serafín's first book of poetry, *Los espejos envenenados* (Poisoned Mirrors). Praising Serafín as "the most conscious" of Peru's young poets, she exuberantly remarked that his poetry resembled "a train hurtling toward the Future along rails of Thought." Serafín's words were penetrating, she said, but they were also "a triumph of impenetrability." Some readers, she concluded, might dislike the effort involved in attempting to make sense of difficult modern poetry, but she defended such work as providing a needed spur to "the dormant steeds of thought."

The love affair between Magda and Serafín could only have hurt and deeply angered Federico, who must have felt badly betrayed by his wife and brother. The situation might have culminated in violence. As her half-sister Graciela reported, after Magda had abandoned Federico for Serafín, Federico kidnapped their daughter, Gloria, and gave her to a family in Huancayo in the high sierra. It was Graciela's understanding that the family believed the child was an orphan. "Federico did this," Graciela speculated, "to get revenge." As Magda recalled the episode, "I had a revolver and was ready to use it. I was ready to kill to get my daughter back." With the assistance of a local prefect, Magda succeeded in retrieving her daughter, then recovering from a case of scarlet fever. Shortly thereafter Federico disappeared from their lives.

BOLIVIA

Late in 1925, Magda and Serafín, with Gloria, left Peru for Bolivia, ostensibly to escape the oppressive political climate in Lima but perhaps also, as has been speculated, to escape the scandal occasioned by Magda's liaison with her husband's brother. Many assumed that Gloria Delmar was Serafín's biological child. By all accounts, however, she was his niece. As Graciela reported, Serafín treated Gloria as a daughter and "with great affection."

Traveling south and inland, into the Andes, ascending beyond Cuzco, the great urban center of the Incan civilization, the small family arrived in the high-sierran city of Puno. There they lingered in the company of Alejandro Peralta and his brother, Arturo (also known by his pen name Gamaliel Churata)—poets of native blood and leaders in the pro-Indian (*indigenista*) movement. Magda's friendship with these writer-activists strengthened her sense of being part of a Peru that was not solely Hispanic but extended beyond the cultural confines of the coast to embrace the vast indigenous interior. "From the very moment I took Gamaliel's hand in mine," she said, "I ceased being a *limeña* and became entirely Peruvian." Across from Puno on the other side of the vast Lake Titicaca lay Bolivia, their destination. As they ascended into ever-thinner air, the Hispanic influence dissipated and the indigenous world of the high mountains appeared unveiled, like the stars that in Lima were so often obscured by mist. In Bolivia's capital, La Paz, nestled in a natural basin in the high Andes, Magda for the first time came into contact with native speakers of Quechua and Aymara. Their severe poverty, seeing it directly, was a new experience.

Serafín, however, knew this deprivation well, having grown up in Huancayo, a high-sierra town that served as the central market for Indian villages throughout the region. Studded with Quechua words, Serafín's stories of Andean life, *Los campesinos y otros condenados* (Campesinos and Other Condemned Men), 1941, revealed his knowledge of indigenous life and landscape. In his early youth he had explored the sierran countryside in three years of wandering "among hills and condors until his mother found him and brought him home," a boyhood episode he alluded to but did not detail in the preface to his Andean stories. Critic and historian Luis Alberto Sánchez characterized Serafín as "an inveterate romantic, . . . an authentic poet and dissident, a chronicler of history and a storyteller whose militant politics and personal suffering compromised the high level his fiction might have attained." Sánchez believed that Serafín's work, though flawed, merited much greater recognition; his achievement in fiction, Sánchez said, should be considered along with that of Serafín's more famous contemporaries—also novelists of indigenous life—José María Arguedas and Ciro Alegría. While dedicated to his Andean heritage, Serafín was drawn to Russian anarchism, political and literary vanguardism, and the Soviet poet Vladimir Mayakovsky. His cosmopolitan interests helped draw Magda into a broader intellectual sphere, one oriented toward social revolution.

Tall and slender, with green eyes and dark hair, a shock of premature white falling over his forehead, Serafín cut a strikingly handsome figure. Of a milder temperament than his brother Federico, more circumspect, less domineering, he did not rush to speak his mind. "Magda and Serafín loved each other very much. They were very happy together," said Graciela, Magda's half-sister, who as a child shared a household with the young couple when they lived with her mother in Lima in 1931 and 1932. Carlos Manuel Cox, later their friend and comrade in the Aprista movement, described the two as creatively enhancing each other's work. Their energies in combination, he said, were "geometrically raised to new powers"—they became "more productive," their writings "of finer quality."

Although a strongman ruled Bolivia in those years, the voluntary expatriates were left to their own devices, free to study, write, and participate in the agitations of the revolutionary student movement in La Paz. They distributed fliers; they marched in the street; they helped bring out the incendiary student newspaper *Bandera Roja* (Red Banner). During this interlude the two poets jointly authored (and privately published in a limited edition) the provocatively titled book *El derecho de matar* (The Right to Kill). With a copyright by "agitación" and a dedication to French socialist Henri Barbusse, this book with a red cover bore a warning label: "Dangerous to the bourgeois of literature."

The prose poems in *El derecho de matar* reveal the influence of futurism, criminal anarchism, and Dadaism, this last tendency absorbed perhaps through the writings of Gamaliel Churata, who is described by Magda as the Tristan Tzara of the *indigenista* movement. In this collection there are many allusions to Christian story and symbol, often conflated with enthusiasm for Lenin and the Russian Revolution, as in Magda's "El viento" (Wind): "Christ at the last supper, no Judas at the table, shared out bread to the workers of Progress, bread of Freedom, wine of jubilation. . . . Christ's tomb is in Leningrad. Wind skips over its ledges, hearing calls for liberty." One of her bleaker visions is revealed in "Círculos violeta" (Violet Circles), in which she depicts the listless wanderings of a young mother who flings her infant child into a river and walks away, feeling nothing. "El poema de la cárcel" (Prison Poem) is a lyrical evocation of a sunless prison—a site of utter abandonment, ignored by those who are free.

José Carlos Mariátegui described *El derecho de matar* as exhibiting "the rebellious spirit and revolutionary messianism that in these times are indisputable evidence of an artist's historical awareness." He did not, however, think that this collection—whose very title, he said, "rings of anarchy and nihilism"—truly represented Magda's compassion and "exalted tenderness." This slim volume, and the couple's *Bandera Roja* connection, may have attracted the official attention that led to their deportation. After nearly a year in La Paz they were abruptly expelled from the country. Police escorted them, along with Gloria, across the Bolivia-Peru border; they were released well inside Peru.

TRAMPOLINE

By the last months of 1926, Magda and Serafín were back in Lima, editing and publishing a review of "supercosmopolitan art." Each collectively produced issue—a single large sheet of twice-folded colored paper—had a new title: *Trampolín* (Trampoline), *Hangar* (Hangar), *Rascacielos* (Skyscrapers), and *Timonel* (Helm). The first number appeared in October 1926, the last in March 1927. The little review provided a showcase for their own poems and those of their friends, including Blanca Luz Brum, Gamaliel Churata, Alejandro Peralta, and Julián Petrovick (aka Oscar Bolaños, Serafín's second brother). Poems by the young Chileans Pablo Neruda and Vicente Huidobro were also presented.

Just back in Latin America, coming from France, Huidobro had been in the thick of the avant-garde artistic ferment in Paris, first in collaboration with French poets Guillaume Apollinaire and Pierre Reverdy, then in the Dada movement. Huidobro's affinity for literary manifestos and his own exuberant poetic production were enormously influential in shaping the generational style of the vanguardist movement in Latin American poetry. This international Dada-surrealist style captivated Magda; in it she would write some of her most successful poems. As editor of *Timonel*, Magda emphasized in her editorial the rebellious internationalist spirit of their small group: "We despise as inhuman the very idea of the NATION." She also offered a personal credo encapsulating the basic themes she would develop over the coming decades:

    —I believe in love, which unites us and effaces borders
    —I believe in education, which illumines hitherto unknown roads
       toward joy
    —I believe in work, which gives us dignity
    —I believe in revolution, which will be our salvation.

Colorful and impertinent, the little magazine created a splash, but neither it nor any of the various and usually short-lived reviews—*Boletín Titicaca, Guerrilla, Poliedro,* and many more—were remotely comparable in intellectual scope and substance to the monumentally ambitious *Amauta,* widely regarded as the most influential journal of its time in Latin America.

AMAUTA

In 1926 Magda entered into one of her most crucial associations. She became the friend and collaborator of José Carlos Mariátegui. Only a few years earlier, in 1923, José Carlos, twenty-nine, was back in Lima following a four-year exile in Europe. There he allied himself with Víctor Raúl Haya de La Torre, then working hard to strengthen the popular university movement, mainstay of the worker-student alliance. Invited by Haya to lecture to popular university audiences, Mariátegui at first was poorly received; his thin voice did not carry well when he spoke to large groups. But Haya insisted that his colleague be heard out with respect, and in a short while Mariátegui's talks became hugely popular. Popular university lectures began attracting immense audiences, "as many as one thousand workers, men and women, would gather in the Palacio de la Exposición . . . to hear Haya de la Torre expound on social justice or José Carlos Mariátegui lecture on the new Russia." Following Haya's arrest and deportation after the demonstrations in May of that year, Mariátegui assumed leadership of the popular university movement. The following year, however, when Augusto Leguía cracked down on the free schools by jailing a number of students and instructors, Mariátegui found himself in no position to organize a protest.

In childhood, a kind of bone cancer had left Mariátegui with a debilitated leg. In 1924 this disease recurred, now attacking the other leg. His condition became grave. His close friend María Wiesse reported that he lay in a delirium, apparently near death, at which point his wife, Ana (over the objection of his mother, who thought him better off dead), instructed doctors to proceed with amputation. When he awoke to the realization that his leg was gone, he began screaming in uncontrollable anguish. Once the shock had subsided and he felt steadied by the presence of his wife, Mariátegui stoically refused to mention his condition and discouraged his friends from making inquiries about his health. Confined from then on to a wheelchair, he resumed his activities, including his prolific writing. He wrote with astonishing efficiency; the many articles he composed on his battered Underwood typewriter were sent to the printer in their initial drafts.

In September 1926, Mariátegui sent to press the first issue of *Amauta,* his seminal review of art, literature, and social theory. Magda's association with the group of writers, artists, and labor leaders who came together around this journal marked her entry into Peru's most brilliant and dynamic intellectual circle. *Amauta*'s first issue announced the socialist, broadly Marxist perspective of the journal, as well as an editorial intent to resist dogmatism and remain open to all progressive, regenerative points of view.

Always a militant journalist on the side of labor, active during the textile workers' strike in 1919, Mariátegui at that time was given a peculiar ultimatum by Leguía: either be jailed in Peru or travel to Europe on a government stipend. Not surprisingly, he chose travel over jail, and a four-year exile began.

It seems oddly fitting that the capitalist Leguía, an inveterate developer and entrepreneur, should have provided the means for the European sojourn of the young Peruvian who would become a major interpreter of Marxist sociology and one of Latin America's most prominent socialists. Travel in Europe, the Grand Tour, the standard finish to a privileged education, would not otherwise have been possible for José Carlos, who quit school at age fourteen to work, adding to his mestiza mother's earnings as a seamstress his meager wages as a printer's assistant. His father had abandoned the family.

In Europe Mariátegui immersed himself in the ideas then animating conversations in cafés, music halls, and labor locals. The riches of European art opened to him, and he studied not only art but also contemporary social movements, observing in Italy how a left-wing movement could very quickly degenerate into fascism. Reading voraciously, he absorbed the thought of Friedrich Nietzsche, Georges Sorel, Benedetto Croce, Henri Bergson, and Pierre Gobetti. He deepened his knowledge of Marxist texts, encountering as well an extraordinary array of personalities, including Russian novelist Maxim Gorky and Henri Barbusse, founder of the French Communist Party. In Italy the Peruvian observer became a participant, embroiling himself in left-wing factional struggles, as Italian workers mounted massive labor actions. Also in Italy, in Florence, he met the beautiful Ana Chiappe, who became his wife. The couple settled briefly in Frascati before traveling together to Paris, Munich, Vienna, and Berlin. Because of the difficulties of traveling with a small child—their first son, Sandro (named for Botticelli), having been born—they decided against making the strenuous journey to Russia.

Throughout his travels in France, Italy, Germany, Austria, and Hungary, as he observed the vicissitudes of the social movements then vying for power, Mariátegui gained insights that he would later apply to the Peruvian case, with its distinctive mix of feudal, capitalist, and indigenist elements. To revitalize Peru, Mariátegui believed, it would be necessary to "Peruvianize Peru," which meant incorporating the indigenous majority into an alliance capable of transforming the country. But before this transformation could be accomplished the Indian would have to be liberated from serfdom, as he explained in his foundational study, *Siete ensayos de interpretación de la realidad peruana* (Seven Interpretive Essays on Peruvian Reality; 1928). Initially published in *Amauta,* these essays were described by Magda as "X-rays revealing the body of Peru in its most vulnerable aspects."

Far more than a methodology, Marxism for Mariátegui was a faith and an ethical pursuit. Even if socialism was never instituted as a social order, he wrote, "its formidable work of education and elevation of humanity would be sufficient to justify its place in history." Mariátegui did not believe that history favored the proletariat, or that victory for socialist forces would inevitably come about. "The messianic millennium," he wrote, "will never come." He granted that it might be good for the masses to believe that their struggle was the final struggle—indeed, he remarked, for those in the midst of it, it was the final struggle. Mariátegui, however, viewed history as a process in which myths arose, shaped cultures, and then declined as other myths arose in their place. "The masses" he insisted, " . . . can't do without myth, can't do without faith."

The editor of *Amauta* rejected a narrow-minded Marxist preoccupation with economics and other material concerns, believing that the religious impulse should not be derided. The theories of Georges Sorel, Miguel de Unamuno, Friedrich Nietzsche, and Henri Bergson helped form Mariátegui's conviction that will, faith, and myth were key forces in shaping social life. As he observed, following Sorel, "Revolutionary and social myths can occupy man's deepest consciousness just as entirely as the religious myths of the past."

Mariátegui also believed that even the most humane ends could not justify unprincipled means. The creator of *Amauta* repudiated the practice—so prevalent in Peru—of attempting to seize state power by insurrectionary or conspiratorial means. He favored a gradualist approach to achieving socialism, one of steadily organizing workers, heightening class consciousness, and studiously clarifying the principles of Peru's vanguard movement. The *Amauta* journal would provide a forum for this indispensable clarification. Painter José Sabogal suggested the name for the journal—*Amauta* is a Quechua word meaning "sage" or "priest"—and created its distinctive logo of the Incan sower. Sabogal also edited a regular art section in the journal, in which pre-Columbian artifacts were presented along with handsome reproductions of contemporary works, including woodblock prints by painter Julia Codesido and powerful bronzes by sculptor Carmen Saco, two artists whose works merit far wider recognition.

Even as multinational corporations were extracting wealth from Peru, *Amauta* provided a countervailing transfusion of thought from abroad. Among the international figures whose writings appeared in the journal were George Bernard Shaw, André Breton, Louis Aragon, José Ortega y Gasset, Diego Rivera, Rabindranath Tagore, Vladimir Lenin, Sigmund Freud, Leon Trotsky, and F. T. Marinetti.

As efforts to make sense of the world fragmented into a kaleidoscopic round of disciplines—ethnography, history, psychology, political economy, and so on—*Amauta* reflected that expanding range of inquiry, its concerns extending beyond Europe and America to China, Japan, and India. *Amauta* also presented poems, stories, book reviews, letters to the editor, and editorial comment, all interspersed with graphics, including a few ads for Ford motor cars.

Magda was a regular contributor, mostly of poems, along with Serafín and many other intellectuals who were later to become militants in the Partido Aprista Peruano. Sent from abroad, articles by Haya de la Torre also appeared; *Amauta* editorially embraced the APRA's five points of unity.

With the stated aim of broadcasting "the voice of a generation," *Amauta* nonetheless bore the unmistakable stamp of one man's genius. Mariátegui not only articulated the ethos of the journal, he solicited manuscripts; wrote editorial and feature articles; and personally undertook to assemble and publish and then package and mail the journal to a far-flung network of friends, associates, and organizations. During its four years of publication, 1926 to 1930, the periodical proved to be a prodigious disseminator of ideas, influential in leftist circles in Latin America and far beyond.

Mariátegui's struggle with serious illness no doubt intensified the dedication he brought to his tasks. The ideas of Spanish philosopher Miguel de Unamuno, author of *Del sentimiento trágico de la vida* (The Tragic Sense of Life) and *La agonía del cristianismo* (The Agony of Christianity), confirmed Mariátegui's sense of existence as fundamentally an arena for conflict and exertion; the agonic man, or woman—who lucidly accepted such terms of existence—was the pure type, he believed, of the social revolutionary. His quiet heroism inspired many who visited his home at 146 Jirón Washington, widely known as "the red corner."

It seemed to Magda at this time that Mariátegui existed in a far loftier sphere than her own. He was, she said, "out of my league because of his great knowledge. I thought of myself as just barely a poet." When a friend invited her to visit the red corner, she gladly went along and soon became a regular visitor. "Mariátegui was the teacher and guide for the young people of my generation," she said. "At the gatherings in his home, he always spoke, giving lectures or lessons on the social and political concerns he encountered in Europe in the years when Nazism and fascism were on the rise." Refusing to dismiss Europe as having nothing more to offer them than a vile legacy of conquest and plunder, Mariátegui insisted that the European in many respects was a civilization superior to their own, one that, even in its decadence, bore within it strong powers of social renewal. Historian Jorge Basadre described Mariátegui as he knew him in those days.

> His black eyes, gleaming in his wasted, pale brown face, commanded attention. His features were sharp and his thick, black hair was always carefully groomed, but with a bohemian lock sometimes falling onto his forehead. He dressed in a plain, spotlessly clean suit and he invariably wore a black bow tie. His conversation was free of vanity and expansive autobiography, rhetoric, and vague banalities. On the contrary, he was objective in his judgment and always ready to listen and ask questions, reluctant to discuss himself, and immune to commonplaces. . . . Mariátegui's wife occasionally appeared on her return from shopping or the post office. . . . No attempt was made to proselytize. Current events were commented on, especially those relating to books, paintings, or music. There was no sign of the heavy atmosphere, charged with gossip and backbiting, of political cliques.

Frequenting *Amauta's* informal salon were writers, artists, students, labor leaders, archaeologists, historians, and sociologists. Foreign radicals were sometimes present, and delegations of factory workers or miners often stopped by to confer with Mariátegui on specific labor issues. Here Magda encountered many notable individuals: "Julia Codesido and activist Ángela Ramos, my friend Carmen Saco, the great sculptor, and Martín Adán, José María Eguren, [and] Ricardo Martínez de la Torre, a close political associate and defender of Mariátegui. There was also the young historian Jorge Basadre, and the American radical author Carleton Beals." Having recently been part of photographer Tina Modotti's circle in Mexico, Beals was then writing his classic sociocultural study and travel narrative, *Fire on the Andes*. Also at one of these gatherings Magda met the Bolivian poet Tristán Marof, as well as Uruguayan poet Blanca Luz Brum, widow at age twenty of the recently deceased Peruvian poet Juan Parra del Riego. While many of Mariátegui's visitors were accomplished in their fields, others were young and politically unsophisticated—"hardly more," Magda observed, probably thinking of herself, "than sorcerers' apprentices in social protest."

Adhering to a rigorous schedule, Mariátegui typically reserved certain hours for his own writing. He composed articles in the same room that later in the day would accommodate visitors, who began arriving around five o'clock. The appealing room was furnished with an overstuffed armchair and a divan draped with a red carpet. On the walls hung prints and oil paintings; recent books and periodicals from abroad were stacked on all the tables and overflowed the bookshelves.

When Magda appeared at the door, Mariátegui acknowledged her presence with a slight motion of his hand. As the room was usually very crowded, she frequently sat on the floor near their host's wooden wheelchair. Her friend Blanca Luz Brum also sat on the floor near Mariátegui, "not wanting," Magda recalled, "to miss a single one of his words." The feeling in the room, she said, was often intense. "Mariátegui radiated a simple, fluent wisdom. All his friends and disciples listened with great emotion as he talked. Though weakened by his illness he was still young and full of light, energy, and confidence in the future. Mariátegui never believed he would die so soon, not with so much left to be said and to be done."

By 1927 the popular universities, again free to operate, were going strong. Nearly every week Magda accompanied Mariátegui, along with Blanca Luz Brum, Ángela Ramos, and others—"intellectuals," she insisted, "not just women," to the workers' city of Vitarte, ten miles inland from Lima and the site of a textile factory owned by one of Peru's wealthiest families. "When the workers finished their shifts," she explained, "we did a sort of proselytizing from a cultural perspective. We discussed ideas. We talked about rights and responsibilities." Many of the factory workers were Spanish-speaking mestizos. Historian Jeffrey Klaiber described photos of popular university teachers posing with their students on picnics in the nearby woods. Haya and other instructors (university students) were dressed in dark suits and ties. The darker-skinned workers wore white shirts and trousers, while their wives wore colorful highland dress, their babies wrapped in mantas on their backs. Many Quechua-speaking hacienda workers rode in on horseback to attend lectures in the local cinema that housed the popular university programs, including courses in history, math, Spanish grammar, hygiene, and first aid, as well as morality plays on the evils of alcohol and dramatic sketches honoring the Inca heritage. A highlight of the popular university year was the Tree Planting Festival, which included poetry readings; Magda, Serafín, and Blanca Luz Brum were among those who recited their poems to the textile workers assembled in the football stadium at Vitarte.

At the same time in the central highlands, distressed miners were again up in arms. They were calling for safer conditions, demanding that the smokestacks at the Cerro de Pasco and La Oroya smelters be made higher so as to vent toxic emissions into the upper air. A notorious polluter from the start of its operation, Cerro de Pasco Mining was incorporated in 1902 in New York City, counting among its principal investors J. Pierpont Morgan, Cornelius Vanderbilt, and Phoebe Apperson Hearst. Quickly establishing itself in Peru's central highlands, the corporation installed industrial smelters that spewed arsenic and other poisons throughout the formerly bucolic region. Magda described some of what happened when the U.S. mining company moved in.

> Cerro de Pasco, despite its climate and altitude, was a green pasture where cattle grazed, producing meat and milk. When the corporation came, it built no mechanism to vent the smoke from the smelters and refineries, and the pasturage and cattle couldn't survive, leaving the campesinos no choice but to seek work in the mines. . . . Children suffered the most from the poisonous fumes. Their hair quit growing, and their teeth blackened. The same thing happened to the old people who lived in the zones contaminated by La Oroya mines.

Smaller mines were subsumed as Cerro de Pasco came to symbolize the most ruthless incursion of foreign capital into Peru. The corporation amassed so much power that its U.S. manager, rumor had it, gave orders to the American ambassador in Lima.

As a journalist and leading labor leader, Mariátegui involved himself closely in the miners' fight for better working conditions. As protests mounted and unrest intensified, Augusto Leguía ordered his police agents to arrest key individuals in the labor movement and in other dissident organizations. Several days before this sweep of arrests, the archaeologist and indigenist Luis Valcárcel, author of *Tempestad en los Andes* (Tempest in the Andes) and a frequent contributor to *Amauta*, gave a public lecture introduced by future Aprista leader Carlos Manuel Cox. Contrary to established procedures, the indigenous delegates at this gathering were accorded equal standing with the whites. In Leguía's sudden crackdown, Valcárcel was arrested and summarily jailed on San Lorenzo prison island, and Carlos Manuel Cox was deported to Mexico. Some forty "subversives" were imprisoned on San Lorenzo. The pretext for these arrests—meant to debilitate the increasingly militant labor and indigenous movements—was a purported plot to overthrow strongman Leguía.

On June 10, 1927, the Lima daily *El Comercio* announced the government's discovery of a "communist plot" and the arrest of "a group of communists" in the building that housed the *Amauta* press. Magda learned of these arrests as she read the paper; reading beyond the huge headlines, she was even more stunned: "Two women implicated in plot"—Blanca Luz Brum and herself. Both women were ordered to present themselves at police headquarters, which they obediently did. Several days later police agents informed them they were being deported, immediately, Blanca Luz to her native Uruguay, Magda to Cuba.

Only when at sea, aboard a ship steaming for Havana, were the seven or eight deportees in Magda's group, which included Serafín Delmar, issued passports and shown news clippings detailing Mariátegui's arrest and imprisonment in the military hospital of San Bartolomé. International protests helped secure the release of the wheelchair-bound leader, who was held for more than a week. Mariátegui later reported that the *Amauta* arrests were triggered by the June issue, "in which article after article drew attention to *yanqui* penetration of our country and other countries of America." According to his sources, Mariátegui continued, "the U.S. Embassy exerted pressure on Leguía to shut down *Amauta* and silence its editors and contributors." By the time *Amauta* was permitted to resume publication several months later, a good number of its most active contributors were in exile.

In Havana, U.S.-backed dictator Gerardo Machado was struggling to contain a surging resistance to his regime. When the Peruvian deportees arrived at Cuban customs they were greeted with overt hostility. A number of books in their "ambulatory library" were impounded, notably any with red covers or whose authors were Russian, including books by Karl Marx, Lenin, Maxim Gorky, Leonid Andreyev, and Anton Chekhov. All the men in the group were jailed. Magda, however, enjoyed privileged treatment. Placed under house arrest, all the while with her daughter, she stayed in the Havana home of her friend Cuban poet Mariblanca Sabas Alomá. Daily she visited the prison, where she met a number of incarcerated Cuban dissidents, including novelist Alejo Carpentier, critic Juan Marinello, and writer and future diplomat Raúl Roa.

Serafín and Magda brought with them a letter of introduction from Mariátegui to Havana intellectual Emilio Roig de Leuchsenring. "I hold poets Serafín Delmar and Magda Portal in the highest personal and artistic esteem," Mariátegui wrote. "They are living emblems of our message. Please welcome them as authentic representatives of the Peruvian vanguard, now experiencing its darkest moment." In the blazing heat of midsummer Havana, the men in her group were held for forty-five days and then released under strict orders to leave the island immediately.

FIRST EXILE (1927–1930)

MEXICO: A GREAT SCHOOL

We are 100 million.
—*Serafín Delmar,* El hombre de estos años

Rise with me, American love.
—*Pablo Neruda,* Las alturas de Machu Picchu

Some of the Peruvian deportees in Cuba went on to Europe, while Magda, Serafín, and several others preferred to stay in the Americas, eager to study Mexico's agrarian reform. "Triumphant Mexico," they believed, not "decadent Europe," might serve as a model for their own backward Peru. Traveling in miserable conditions third class aboard a United Fruit banana boat, the small group arrived at the Gulf port of Veracruz, with barely enough money to be allowed entry into the country.

In Mexico, the Peruvian travelers were not entirely foreigners. The dominant language was their own. Mexico, like Peru, had arisen in the midst of indigenous civilizations. Looking out the window on the long train ride from Veracruz to Mexico City, Magda noted the indigenous cast in the faces she saw in passing. In Mexico, she observed, the Spaniard seemed less enthroned as conquistador, less frequently elevated in equestrian monuments than in Peru. She would also note in Mexico a different, more militant mood among the people; she would contrast the plaintive, sorrowful tone of Peru's high-sierran songs with the joyfully combative spirit of the Mexican *corridos*, the folk ballads that emerged in the revolutionary fighting. In a working-class district in Mexico City on May Day, 1928, Magda experienced firsthand the martial spirit of Mexico's 1910 revolution. She watched intently as a militant parade of campesinos filed past her, all shouting the Zapatista cry—*¡Tierra y Libertad!* (Land and Liberty!). "An overwhelming impression of power—the campesinos in pristinely white trousers, colorful serapes draped over rifles and cartridge belts—I'd never seen anything like it. The emotional impact was tremendous. In Mexico I think I finally understood, or began to, the indigenous Peruvian, the indigenous American, that creature held in the utmost contempt, comparable only to the Russian peasant before the October Revolution." She'd seen abject poverty, the "harsh, tragic" poverty of the Andean Indian, but never before had she witnessed the mass militancy of an oppressed people. Italian American photographer and Communist militant Tina Modotti, then active in Mexico City, captured this combative tone in her photographs of the period. In one of these, the entire frame is filled by men wearing broad-brimmed sombreros, crowded together and peering over an issue of the Communist newspaper *El Machete*. In another photo a straight-backed Indian woman strides forward, the staff of an enormous banner balanced on her shoulder. In a March 1928 issue of *Repertorio Americano,* Magda praised Modotti as "a great and forceful photographer" whose "precisely beautiful" compositions—with their motifs of corn, cartridge belt, sickle, and guitar—symbolized the Mexican *corrido* and its militant mood. In Mexico the young poet, mother, and social rebel would be transformed into a dedicated political activist. On that train ride from Veracruz, entranced by the onrush of novel, intensely colorful images of the Mexican landscape and its people, she could not have imagined just how extensively and how quickly she would be, as she said, "fundamentally changed" by this country. In Mexico she became imbued with what seemed to her "a new concept of a Latin American people, one no longer disinherited or exploited." That the Mexican Revolution remained unfinished did not trouble her. "It didn't matter," she reflected, "that the many goals the revolution proposed for itself were not attained because revolutionary feeling still permeated the country, suffusing the atmosphere and the awareness of all Mexicans."

From all over the world, artists, writers, and political activists were converging on Mexico's capital. They came seeking refuge or simply wanting to participate in the ferment of "the triumphant revolution." In Mexico City the Peruvian deportees formed a closely knit group that included Magda, Serafín (and Gloria), Manuel Vásquez Díaz, Carlos Manuel Cox, Oscar Herrera, and Esteban Pavletich; Pavletich's letters to Mariátegui from Panama were implicated in the so-called communist plot in Peru, the pretext for the arrests and deportations. The displaced Peruvians immediately sought out their counterparts in the Mexican capital. "We became associated," Magda recalled, "with left-wing elements and with the intellectuals and visual artists who were vitally active in aesthetic and revolutionary causes, . . . painters of the international stature of Diego Rivera, José Clemente Orozco, Rufino Tamayo, [David] Alfaro Siqueiros, Fernando Leal, Frida Kahlo."

When Magda and her group arrived in Mexico's capital, Diego Rivera was enjoying remarkable prominence as a mural artist and as a militant in Mexico's Communist Party. Following a bad fall from a scaffold earlier that year, Rivera was back at work on his great mural project at the newly constructed Ministry of Education building—an epic work eventually to be composed of 117 panels. That year he would finish the provocative *Wall Street Banquet* panel, featuring caricatures of capitalist titans John D. Rockefeller, J. P. Morgan, and Henry Ford. Minister of education José Vasconcelos conceived of this new edifice as not just a building but "a moral organization." The belief that architectural and other art forms could be weapons in the battle for social reform was current during these years, when revolutionary artists were urgently debating and not necessarily agreeing upon what role art should play in social struggle. Some viewed the more avant-garde painters as self-indulgent elitists whose efforts were incomprehensible to campesinos and factory workers, and therefore contemptible. At the same time those who favored a social realist approach came under attack as reducing art to no more than a vehicle for propaganda. Diego Rivera, along with other notable Mexican painters, called for a public art—a monumental art—declaring in the vibrantly opinionated manifesto of their artists' union that public art belonged to everyone, unlike easel painting, which they reviled as a decadent form whose practitioners catered solely to a tiny class of wealthy patrons.

Although revolutionary fervor remained intense, especially in Mexico City, the counterrevolution was rapidly gaining power. By 1927 the mood in the country had turned ominous. Under grueling political pressure, José Vasconcelos resigned his post as minister of education and went into exile. The Soviet ambassador to Mexico, Aleksandra Kollantai—a libertarian feminist and the only woman in Lenin's cabinet in the new Russia—also resigned her position and then abandoned the country. Deeply fatigued, her heart condition aggravated by Mexico City's high altitude as well as by the strain of repeatedly being attacked in the Mexican press, Kollantai boarded a ship for Europe in June, just weeks before the Peruvian exiles arrived in Veracruz. She embarked with a painting by Diego Rivera under her arm and with photos by Tina Modotti and Edward Weston in her baggage. Her association with such radical artists and intellectuals, her support for the worker-campesino movement—the very fact of her being a Russian revolutionary—made her presence in Mexico anathema to conservative forces. Her departure was no doubt applauded by U.S. secretary of state Frank Kellogg, who made it his personal mission to drive "the Bolshevik" Kollantai out of the hemisphere. Kollantai's pioneering feminism thoroughly impressed Magda, who in her 1933 pamphlet *Toward the New Woman* paid tribute to the free-spirited Russian.

Shortly before the Peruvians arrived in Mexico City, a massive street demonstration had been held to protest the imminent executions in the United States of anarchists Nicola Sacco and Bartolomeo Vanzetti, convicted of robbery and double murder on suspect evidence in a highly politicized trial. Italian American Tina Modotti helped coordinate this protest, during which she first met the Cuban exile and Communist revolutionary Julio Antonio Mella. Some months after this mass protest their legendary love affair began.

Deported from Cuba for his Communist and anti-Machado agitations, Mella came to Mexico following travels in Europe and the Soviet Union. Earlier that year in Brussels he had attended the World Anti-imperialist Congress, which attracted not only Communists but representatives of many left-wing tendencies. Highly visible at that conference was Víctor Raúl Haya de la Torre, vocally representing the APRA. Although Mella very cordially had hosted Haya in Havana in 1923, he now opposed the APRA leader, who took issue with the Communist movement on a number of key points. A heated polemic between the two leaders began in Brussels and would continue in Mexico City, where revolutionary energies were increasingly in bitter conflict, not just with one another but with counterrevolutionary forces, including elements of the immensely powerful Catholic Church.

During the Mexican Revolution's first wave of land expropriations, the great properties owned by the church were not spared. When armed campesinos stormed haciendas and burned deeds to the land, local priests sought refuge in the fortress-manors of wealthy protectors. Rural churches were shut down or converted to public libraries, health clinics, or shelters. By 1926, however, ecclesiastical forces were on the offensive—proponents of the fierce "Christ the King" movement set about terrorizing rural districts. With a number of Catholic bishops abetting the violence, armed gangs burst into schools, gunned down literacy teachers, and left the mutilated bodies shrouded in "Cristero" banners.

During better days in the literacy campaign, Chilean poet Gabriela Mistral, invited to Mexico by José Vasconcelos, put together a collection of readings for newly literate rural women. When Magda reviewed a similar collection in *Amauta,* she praised Mexico's ambitious literacy campaign as a "formidable work of mass education" and "a giant step forward in the battle to break up the great colonial landholdings, whose continuing power is based on the campesinos' illiteracy." This important movement was now in retreat.

By 1927 a number of powerful interests—the Catholic Church, the local oligarchy, and U.S. corporate investors—were united in opposition to Mexico's revolutionary nationalist agenda, which included the literacy program as well as major land reform and other radical measures, all aimed at redistributing wealth. Responding to the alarm of Standard Oil executives, U.S. officials were pressuring the Mexican government to exempt U.S. companies from any taxes that might conceivably be levied on profits from Mexican oil, fees stipulated by the new Mexican Constitution—a document so menacing to moneyed interests that it remained unratified and a matter of extreme contention. Any individual who swore allegiance to this constitution faced excommunication by the Catholic Church.

William Randolph Hearst, with his wide array of business ventures in Mexico, also demanded protection. While Mexico's president, Elias Plutarco Calles, and U.S. secretary of state Dwight Morrow went about (in the words of Carleton Beals) "ripping the heart and soul out of the Mexican revolution," many feared that the colossus to the north would tire of its diplomatic exertions and simply invade Mexico and occupy the country.

HAYA ABROAD

In the autumn of 1927, after three years abroad, Haya de la Torre returned to Mexico by way of New York City, where Norman Thomas, head of the U.S. Socialist Party, arranged for him to lecture at Columbia University. The high-voltage fast-paced dynamism of Manhattan thrilled the Peruvian agitator. In New York he exchanged views with novelist Upton Sinclair at a luncheon given by the editors of the *New Republic*. In Boston he debated with students at Harvard. Haya admired many aspects of the United States and greatly enjoyed his associations with U.S. intellectuals, students, and political leaders, including influential figures in Washington, D.C.

Once back in Mexico City, he quickly drew into his orbit Magda and the other Peruvian exiles, who were eager to hear details of his years abroad. These were formative, productive years in which his exertions won for his APRA movement an international profile.

In the first year of his exile, 1924, Haya traveled to Russia as part of a delegation of young left-wing activists, including Communists. As reported in his account of that trip, *Impresiones de la Inglaterra imperialista y la Rusia soviética* (Impressions of Imperialist England and Soviet Russia), the group sailed from New York Harbor on a Baltic-American ship, formerly named the *Tzar* and rechristened the *Estonia*, which took the delegation as far as the Baltic coast, from where they traveled on for three days by rail—destination Moscow. As the train crossed the border into Russia, a great cheer went up in the car adjoining that of the American delegation. Finally they were entering the revolutionary homeland—the world's first socialist state!

A scant seven years had passed since the fall of the Romanoff dynasty, and only three since Lenin's founding of the first Communist International, or Comintern. Everything Haya saw as he entered Russia impressed him favorably: the huge banners blazoning in several languages the radical imperative—"Workers of the World Unite!"—the robust look of the peasants seen from the train window, the richly abundant fields of yellow grain. Haya did not observe (or at least made no mention of) signs of the hunger and deprivation the Russian people suffered during the civil war and throughout the terrible famine of 1922, from which the country had not recovered.

In Moscow the excited young delegates would attend the Fifth Congress of the Communist International, a grand convening of representatives from France, Germany, England, Ireland, the United States, Spain, Italy, Japan, India, and a number of other nations. From gavel to gavel the delegates were regaled with speeches in Russian, German, French, or English, with simultaneous translations into the various languages of those in attendance. Day after day Haya absorbed these speeches, including an inaugural address by Leon Trotsky and a four-hour talk by Clara Zetkin, "the grandmother of the revolution." He also heard addresses by the influential Bolshevik leaders Nikolai Bukharin and Grigory Zinoviev, both of whom would be executed in Stalin's purges.

Sessions were held in the sumptuous Alexander Palace, with the pressroom situated in equally imposing quarters. Haya reported that "people of all races milled around work tables, a thousand typewriters clicking away . . . [while] at day's end there lingered in the air the triumphal strains of the 'Internationale.'" Although a number of the speeches may have bogged down in minute discussion of contentious tactical points, the delegates shared an overriding concern with battling imperialism and colonialism and with lessening the enormous disparity between rich and poor nations. Haya might well have glimpsed in this extraordinary gathering an incipient world government, a progressive union of nations, a global council representing diverse geographies and cultures—an organization capable of transforming the world.

The Russian Revolution, however, remained in crisis. Severe shortages, widespread hunger, and systemic disorganization plagued the country. Stunned and stunted by years of war, famine, and civil unrest, the new Russia was not going to be structured as a confederation of workers' councils. That anarchist ideal quickly succumbed to Vladimir Ilich Lenin's vision of centralized power and top-down rule by a vanguard party of the proletariat. The founding father of Bolshevism and the principal leader of the October Revolution, Lenin died of a massive stroke in January the year of Haya's visit. But his Bolshevik party retained its hold on power. With more than a little awe Haya observed the cult growing around the recently deceased leader. "One understands after just a few weeks in Russia," he declared, "why the mere mention of the name Lenin provokes such widespread public admiration and why his tomb is constantly surrounded with groups of ecstatic people."

Haya's account of his experience in Russia is a self-portrait of a young man who is superbly confident but out of his element and eagerly absorbing impressions of a society in great upheaval. He carried with him a letter from the renowned French pacifist Romain Rolland, an introduction he presented to Anatoly Lunacharsky, commissar of arts and political education. Among Lenin's most trusted collaborators, a cultivated, genial man—in many respects the counterpart of José Vasconcelos in Mexico—the urbane Lunacharsky used his exceptional administrative and political skills to protect and advance the arts. He rejected the prevailing notion that art forms baffling to unsophisticated workers should be suppressed in favor of simpler modes. Instead he believed in educating the workers so as to enable them to appreciate the more difficult works of art. In the meantime he protected the Moscow Symphony, whose disbanding was being called for by some Bolshevik functionaries, ostensibly to cut costs in a time of severe scarcity.

Lunacharsky cordially received the Peruvian visitor, inviting him to spend a weekend at his dacha. At this special gathering in the countryside Haya exchanged views with some of the most powerful figures in the new Bolshevik state. Evidently at some point Lunacharsky invited Haya to establish a local branch of the Communist International in Peru, in other words, a Peruvian Communist party. But any such invitation was declined. By Haya's own account he had doubts even then about Communism as a solution for the ills of his native land—reservations, he said, that he discussed frankly with his Russian hosts. Although he granted that Communism was right for Russia, he would insist repeatedly in years to come that Communism was not suitable for Peru.

One of the things that Haya found most striking in Russia was, he wrote, "the new organization of the Party or its bolshevikization as Zinoviev called it." The selfless dedication and strict adherence to party discipline he observed among the Bolshevik cadre impressed him deeply and favorably. This strict discipline in fact enabled a small minority like the Bolsheviks to dominate a huge population. Or so American anarchist Emma Goldman concluded in *My Disillusionment with Russia,* 1925, an account of her experience in that country in the early years of revolutionary turmoil. The Bolshevik minority was able to wield such tremendous power, she believed, not only because the citizenry was exhausted, but also because the Bolsheviks suppressed all competing forces, including anarchists and social democrats. She argued that never before had the state proved so inherently reactionary—in fact, counterrevolutionary. What was happening in Russia, she charged, was the antithesis of genuine revolution.

Despite her criticisms of the Bolsheviks, Goldman greatly appreciated Anatoly Lunacharsky. She particularly liked his receptivity to becoming more familiar with John Dewey's new theories on education. She regretted that Lunacharsky's tolerant policies were being stymied by his having to contend with narrow-minded ideologues in his own Bolshevik party.

Meanwhile, constructivism was emerging as an international art movement, its practitioners setting aside their easels in favor of a virtual adoration of mechanization and utility. The Russian artist El Lissitzky pronounced the machine "simply a paintbrush . . . for shaping the canvas of our picture of the world." In fact the most avant-garde directions in painting, poetry, and cinema flourished in the new Russia, perhaps because (some say) the more conservative artists failed to come forward in support of the workers' state. The brilliantly experimental poet and dramatist Vladimir Mayakovsky became prominent as a ferociously high-spirited supporter of the new regime. Agitprop performances were held in factories and public squares. Painter

Wassily Kandinsky gave classes to workers in proletarian art studios established by Lunacharsky, while Dziga Vertov's brilliant Kino-Eye cinematography captured the dynamism of industrial workers, compounding their strength with that of titanic machines, machines whose power augured, many fervently believed, universal liberation from brutalizing toil. In less than a decade, however, the forced mechanization and collectivization of Russian agriculture would demonstrate that modernization did not necessarily liberate human potential. At the time of Haya's visit to Russia, Joseph Stalin was not yet in power, and the revolutionary government retained a certain liberality, especially in the spheres of art and education.

For all the heady innovation, disturbing rumors of Soviet abuses of state power nevertheless abounded among intellectuals outside Russia. Such rumors troubled Haya, who made inquiries about allegations that works by Tolstoy and by the anarchist philosopher Kropotkin were being suppressed. Quickly reassured, he concluded that such rumors were part of a smear campaign by the capitalist press, one meant to discredit the revolutionary process.

Apparently Haya remained unaware of repressive measures that were in fact already under way in Russia—the suppression of non-Bolshevik left-wing tendencies that Emma Goldman would decry and the persecution of some of the country's most talented poets. Soviet authorities were already refusing to allow the great Anna Akhmatova to be published in state-supported journals, Bolshevik critics denouncing her work as the product of a decadent aristocratic sensibility.

After a number of months in Russia, with the hard winter setting in and his lung congestion still unresolved, Haya refused the offer of his hosts to convalesce at a resort on the Black Sea, preferring to prolong his stay in Moscow. He wanted to see more of the social programs then in formation and also to attend the huge rallies whose crowd-moving effects would provide a model for later mass rallies in Peru.

In late autumn, 1924, Haya left Russia for Switzerland. There he entered a sanatorium. But he would not be able to rest—for almost immediately after his arrival Swiss police raided the premises, confiscated nearly all his papers, and took him into custody, allegedly at the behest of Peruvian authorities. Soon released, Haya traveled on to Italy, France, and England.

In England Haya would establish his base, studying unofficially at the London School of Economics and at Oxford University. As a member of the Oxford debating team, the charismatic orator dueled successfully with a team from Yale on the subject of the Monroe Doctrine. That doctrine articulated the intention of the United States to consider Latin America as a sphere of interest exclusively its own, a position unacceptable to the anti-imperialist Peruvian. Throughout his travels abroad, Haya sent back to Latin American newspapers journalistic reports on his observations abroad. In these dispatches, he bluntly criticized the foreign policy of England, his host country, denouncing it as colonialist and imperialist. He left Russia strongly in support of revolutionary action and convinced (as he wrote to a friend in Lima) that an uprising of workers and campesinos should be fomented immediately in Peru. He rejoiced at the professorial interest in Marxist analysis he observed at Oxford, referring to the noted professor G. D. H. Cole, whose study, *A Short History of the British Working Class,* he lauded as being imbued with insights paralleling those of Marx himself. The Oxford dons who recognized the import of Marxian sociology seemed to Haya rather more restrained in their appreciation of the master than the members of the Marxist club to which he himself belonged. Enthusiastically, he announced, "We aren't just a few . . . who go forward with firm resolve in the economic and philosophical path of the genial Marx."

Strongly sympathizing with the fledgling Soviet state, in those days Haya de la Torre favored socialism. But this attitude proved short-lived. The word *socialism* would soon be expunged from his revolutionary lexicon. In a short while he would be promoting only his own concept, "Aprismo." English Labor Party leader Harold Laski invited Haya to write up his much heralded but in fact little-known APRA agenda for the political review the *Labor Monthly.* Written in Haya's English and appearing in December 1926, this fundamental defining of the APRA program begins with the five points of unity already mentioned and concludes with a summary statement.

> The A.P.R.A. represents, therefore, a political organisation struggling against Imperialism and against the national governing classes that are its auxiliaries and its allies in Latin América. The A.P.R.A. is the united front of the toiling classes (workers, peasants, natives of the soil) united with students, intellectuals, revolutionaries, etc. The A.P.R.A. is an autonomous movement, completely Latin American, without foreign interventions or influences. It is the result of a spontaneous movement in defense of our countries in view [of] the experiences of México, Central América, Panama and the Antilles, and the present position of Perú, Bolivia, and Venezuela, where the policy of penetration by Imperialism is already [k]eenly felt. For this our watchword is to be the following:

"Against Yankee Imperialism, for the unity of the peoples of Latin
América, for the realisation of social justice" (Paris, October 1926).

Throughout his travels in exile, Haya worked indefatigably to promote his
Aprista vision and organization. In 1925 he explained the APRA agenda and
conveyed his still-fresh enthusiasm for the Soviet experiment to fellow Peru-
vian expatriates in Paris, including Luis Eduardo Enríquez, Eudocio Ravines,
and poet César Vallejo; they responded by organizing themselves into an
Aprista cell. Aprista groups then in formation in Latin America sent modest
donations to support Haya's activities. Along with the contributions of more
affluent benefactors, these donations enabled Haya to enjoy a not entirely
abstemious lifestyle. One of his followers recalled seeing the APRA leader in
a train station in Paris as he descended from the exclusive deluxe coach,
"surrounded by porters carrying shiny leather suitcases" and nattily dressed
in gloves, hat, and "a trench coat straight from Piccadilly." As Luis Eduardo
Enríquez recounted, Haya's followers in Paris ate Peruvian soup in their
modest rooms in the Hôtel Monge so as to pool their money to meet the costs
of their itinerant leader's residing in the comfortable Hôtel Saint-Michel
on the Left Bank. Their sacrifice, Enríquez recalled, "was nothing to them
compared to safeguarding the health of the man who incarnated the well-
being of Peru."

A COMMITMENT

Once situated in Mexico City, Haya continued to promulgate his anti-
imperialist views. In December, he lectured twice weekly at the Universidad
Nacional Autónoma de México; Magda and Serafín had helped to arrange
this series prior to the APRA leader's arrival. The lecture titles included
"Europe and the Two Americas," "A New Indo-American Nationalism," "The
Message of Mexico and of America," "Pan-American Unity," and "The North
American People and Us."

Haya encouraged the Peruvians, Magda recalled, to constitute themselves
as an APRA cell, which they did, in fact reviving a preexisting APRA cell
that had fallen dormant. Magda was appointed secretary-general of the new
cell, and this grand title, perhaps a euphemism for *typist*, suggests the scope
of Aprista ambitions at the time. A master plan was taking shape, overtly
Marxist and similar in scope to the Communists' expansive vision, yet differ-
ing from the Communist agenda in many respects. Aprista cells now existed

in Paris, Panama City, La Paz, Buenos Aires, and Havana. Aprista reviews were also appearing. In Mexico there was *Indoamérica,* edited by Magda and Serafín; in La Paz there was *Meridiano*; and in Cuba, *Atuei,* named for an aboriginal chief who died resisting the Spanish conquerors.

Haya's well-known personal warmth, his concern for the development of his associates, his talent as a teacher—all this, combined with the stimulus of revolutionary Mexico itself, moved Magda toward real political commitment. Although anti-imperialist and related ideas circulated in José Carlos Mariátegui's *Amauta* group, she had not quite registered their significance. As she later said, "I didn't understand yet what imperialism was." Haya's anti-imperialist emphasis now struck her with revelatory force. In those "months of Hayista influence" she acquired a new perspective, as she later explained. "Haya's arrival in Mexico and the lectures he gave at the Escuela Superior offered models of understanding distinct from Mariátegui's and having to do with Latin American nationalist ideas. We hadn't really noticed this new attitude in Haya's letters to *Amauta* or in his articles."

The Peruvian exiles, it seems, were being recruited by Haya into a sectarian campaign and gradually being estranged from their friend Mariátegui, whose socialist convictions (and Communist leanings) Haya denigrated, pronouncing them imitatively European and inappropriate for Peru. Haya also charged Mariátegui with lacking political sense and with devoting too much time to exploring intellectual or theoretical questions at the expense of urgently needed activism. Looking back, Magda attempted to account for her shift in allegiance at that time from her friend Mariátegui to Haya de la Torre. "With J. C. Mariátegui, at the get-togethers in his home, the conversations were always open-ended, freewheeling, always having to do with socialist thought but not geared toward ideological definition, political education, or proselytizing. Haya, however, put forward a specific goal. His intention was to lay the groundwork for a new sociopolitical movement in Latin America." Haya's insistence on organization building strongly appealed to the pragmatic aspect of Magda's sensibility. She recalled the special quality of their frequent discussions. "Night after night, Haya conversed with us, the newly born Apristas, in 1928, under a Mexican sky." In these gatherings, she said, "Haya … went straight to the point, illustrating, motivating, clearing up confusions, clarifying many things that until then had been obscure to most of us in the group, and to me in particular." She later noted that before coming to Mexico, she was "barely contaminated by political thought." Until then, she explained, her ideas "were vague, unformulated, barely more than impulses toward solidarity with workers and campesinos." Some observers thought at the time that Haya came to Mexico with the express aim of recruiting the Peruvian deportees into his APRA movement. "It was nearly inevitable," Magda herself later concluded, "that when Haya arrived from Europe we would be won over."

Haya, it seems, had the remarkable ability to simplify, to reduce all the flux and confusion of reality to easily understood formulas, while at the same time intriguing his followers with dialectical notions that seemed to embrace all the complexity in the world. Following Haya's lead, Magda could now discern a line for action. A distinct enemy now came into sharp focus: Uncle Sam, and corporate capital's formidable power throughout Latin America.

This focus on the United States as an imminent threat to local sovereignties came in response to the recent emergence of that country as a major power, one with particular designs on Latin America. Historian Howard Zinn, in his indispensable study, *A People's History of the United States,* catalogs U.S. incursions in that region and elsewhere, starting with the U.S. war against Mexico in the nineteenth century.

> [The United States] had instigated a war with Mexico and taken half of that country. It had pretended to help Cuba win freedom from Spain, and then planted itself in Cuba with a military base, investments and rights of intervention. It had seized Hawaii, Puerto Rico, Guam and fought a brutal war to subjugate the Filipinos. . . . It had engineered a revolution against Colombia and created the "independent" state of Panama in order to build and control the Canal. It sent five thousand marines to Nicaragua in 1926 to counter a revolution, and kept a force there for seven years. It intervened in the Dominican Republic for the fourth time in 1916 and for the second time in Haiti in 1915. . . . By 1924 the finances of half of the twenty Latin American states were being directed to some extent by the United States.

No doubt with such precedents in mind, Haya advised members of the Aprista cell to inform themselves and, more particularly, to study Marxism. He directed Magda, "half joking, half in earnest," to snap out of her absorption in poetry, which he considered an obstacle to her political development. She disagreed in principle, but—aware of deficiencies in her education—she would act on this advice, even as her first book of poetry had just been published in Lima.

Edited by Mariátegui from a sheaf of her poems, this slim volume, *Una esperanza y el mar* (A Hope and the Sea), and another in the same format by Serafín Delmar, *Radiogramas del Pacífico* (Radiograms from the Pacific), appeared in 1927 under the imprint of Mariátegui's Minerva Press. A number of Magda's poems in this collection echo in imagery and phrasing some of Serafín's in his; the two shared an affinity for the international "vanguardist" style then in vogue. In these works the two poets acknowledge their mutual love and their gratitude for the transformation each had wrought in the other's life. Serafín, for example, writes in a poem titled "to magda portal":

> GREAT FRIEND
> LIFE'S PRISM
> in which I learned to love you—
> flinging a childhood
> of bad memories at the first cross
> formed by your hands—
> . . . .
> with you came a panorama
> of landscapes and on your lips
> time's whirling propellers
> destined
> for my gypsy soul

Magda writes in a similar vein in a section dedicated to Serafín in *Una esperanza y el mar*.

> Midnight birds
> circled my heart's shipwreck
> —desolate sands
> BUT YOU CAME—
> You—my arms opened
> in a cross for you
> dream-spiders wove
> amnesia's infinite silk

Their books are indeed companion volumes. Mariátegui not only took pains to get these works into print, he also praised Magda's poetry, describing her sensibility (in his essay "Literature on Trial") as "essentially lyrical" and "compassionate in the same way Vallejo is compassionate." He went on: "This poetess [*poetisa*] of ours whom we should hail as one of the foremost poetesses of Indo-America, does not descend from Ibarbourou, or Augustini, or even Mistral, whom she nonetheless resembles more than anyone else because of a certain similarity of tone. She has an original and autonomous temperament." Her work merited, he said, far greater recognition. Mariátegui perceived in Magda's poetry, and in her sensibility, profound contradictions that her work could express but not resolve.

> The eternal and dark contrast between the life and death principles that govern the world is always present in the poetry of Magda. At the same time that she longs for oblivion, she is eager to create and live. Magda's soul is a soul in agony. And her art is a total translation of the two forces that lacerate and inspire her. . . . This dramatic conflict gives the poetry of Magda Portal a profound metaphysics, which her spirit easily reaches through her lyricism without the aid of any philosophy. It also gives her a psychological depth that enables her to record all the contradictory voices of her dialogue, her combat, her agony.

Mariátegui's appreciation, along with the appearance of a first book, helped raise Magda's profile as a poet and began establishing her reputation as a significant figure in Peruvian letters. By 1928, however, her concerns were broader than poetry. "If my poetry's an obstacle," she answered Haya, "fine, I'll give it up." She recalled her promise to Víctor Raúl that she "would not publish another book of poems until [she] understood the meaning of imperialism in Latin America." To seal that vow, one afternoon on a picnic in the country with members of their group in Mexico, she impulsively committed what she called "a homicidal act."

> I opened my handbag, took out my manuscript "Anima absorta" . . . and standing on a bridge over a little stream I ripped it up—to the astonishment of my good friend Esteban Pavletich—and tossed the pieces into the water, which carried it away. . . . I felt like I was giving up something precious but that it wouldn't be forever. If I thought it would be forever I would've burst into tears but it wasn't like that. We simply went on talking while my friend stared at me as if to say, "What is this? What in the world has come over you?" But that was my

way of responding to a new attitude, that of social struggle. I now had a commitment. During my two years in Mexico I studied the Mexican Revolution and learned everything I could about political economy, a rather tedious subject. . . . But it was necessary for me to broaden my understanding. I couldn't continue simply as a poet.

By Daniel Reedy's count, at least twenty poems from this unpublished manuscript survive; seventeen appeared in the Lima review *Mundial*. Magda described the "Anima absorta" collection as having been "saturated with a certain precocious fatalism, undoubtedly influenced by my first readings, especially the 'Nocturnos' of Colombian poet José Asunción Silva."

Decisively formative both politically and intellectually, Magda's two years in Mexico with Serafín; her daughter, Gloria; and the Aprista group must surely have been among her happiest. She was young and immersed in a "sensuous bath" of ideas, impressions, and enthusiasms. Their poverty was hardly debilitating and certainly not comparable to the destitution experienced by César Vallejo in Paris in those same years. A tinted snapshot taken in Mexico shows Magda, Serafín, and Gloria posed in a courtyard rinsed with white light, a red geranium on a windowsill. In another photo Magda sits on a rocky ledge with her legs dangling over a stream. She is smiling and Gloria is beside her. In a group photo we again see Gloria, small and grave in a dark coat, surrounded by future leaders of the Aprista Party of Peru.

Magda and Serafín avidly followed Haya's lecture series in December of 1927. In those twice weekly lectures and in his book *El antiimperialismo y el APRA*—which he completed the following year (the manuscript typed by Carlos Manuel Cox and Magda Portal) but which would not see print until 1936—Haya articulated his most influential ideas. Above all he explained his conception of the anti-imperialist state—a form of revolutionary nationalism—as a counterforce to the overweening power of transnational corporations. In poor countries such as their own, Haya theorized—revising Lenin—that imperialism was not the last but the first stage of capitalism, in which foreign companies would provide the capital needed to launch economic development. Only a truly sovereign and anti-imperialist state, Haya insisted, could amass sufficient power to regulate foreign investment and realize a truly progressive social agenda.

Despite his initial enthusiasm for the Russian Revolution, by 1927 Haya had distanced himself from the Soviet Union and the Communist International.

He now criticized national Communist parties as being little more than out-posts of an International that took its direction from leaders in Moscow. Those leaders, he charged, were not competent to formulate policy on mat-ters pertaining to Latin America because they did not thoroughly understand the local conditions, and sometimes they lacked even a rudimentary grasp of the geography.

Rejecting the Communists' call for a single-class political party, that is, a party representing solely the working class, Haya proposed a multiclass party embracing the three main groups he saw as suffering from imperialist incur-sion in Latin America—factory and mine workers, campesinos, and middle-class elements in the cities and hinterlands. The APRA leader scorned the idea that an industrial proletariat could lead a revolution in Latin America, dismissing the notion as preposterous—a European concept not applicable to the semifeudal conditions prevalent in Central and South America. Haya also rejected the Leninist concept of the dictatorship of the proletariat as the guarantor of revolutionary change. Whereas the Soviet Communists flatly re-jected the principles of liberal democracy, it's by no means clear what Haya's views were on this problematical issue, or by what force he envisaged the anti-imperialist state's maintaining itself in power so as to bring about truly major reforms. Haya's insistence on the need for a revolutionary nationalist movement involving both working-class and middle-class elements exerted substantial influence in many countries.

Haya's APRA—conceived in general terms as an alliance, a movement, and a party—did not, however, embrace all progressive elements. Some saw the APRA as a kind of popular front—indeed many wanted APRA to be an alliance uniting all left-progressive forces, including the Communist. But the APRA emerged as something very different—in fact, an alternative, an openly Marx-ist alternative, to Communist parties in Latin America.

SCHISM

In 1926 and 1927 Mariátegui's *Amauta* group in Lima considered itself part of a loosely allied "vanguard" coalition that included the APRA, whose points of unity the journal embraced. Indeed the *Amauta* journal described itself as an "Aprista forum." Prior to Haya's deportation in 1923, Mariátegui and Haya had worked together closely to advance the popular university movement. But any provisional sense of comradeship or confluence of aims between the two men ended abruptly in January 1928, just several months after Haya's return to Mexico—when the Mexican APRA cell unveiled a bitterly divisive document, the Plan de México.

Without consulting any of the interested groups in Lima or elsewhere, the Mexican Apristas, in a stunning initiative, announced their intent to form an Aprista-oriented Peruvian political party (Partido Nacionalista Libertador) and to put forward Haya de la Torre as a presidential candidate in elections to be held at some future date in Peru. As news of this unilateral move spread, the various vanguard groups began splintering wildly. Aprista cells in Paris, La Paz, Panama, and Buenos Aires—and Mariátegui's group in Lima—were plunged into a turmoil that ended in irreconcilable schisms. The Plan de México was written by Haya de la Torre and signed by Haya, Magda, Serafín, Carlos Manuel Cox, Manuel Vásquez Díaz, Esteban Pavletich, Jacobo Hurwitz, Nicolás Terreros, and several others.

As furious debate about this plan proceeded, Julio Antonio Mella's polemic with Haya de la Torre escalated. Expressing views widely held in the international Communist movement, Mella attacked Haya and APRA in a pamphlet he authored that appeared in April 1928 in Mexico City. Throughout this pamphlet, titled *¿Qué es el A.R.P.A?* Mella used the acronym ARPA—rather than APRA, which its leaders preferred. The Cuban activist began by charging the "ARPA" with being a petit bourgeois, populist organization and not a true representative of the working classes. Rejecting Haya's proposition that workers should unite with middle-class elements to form a revolutionary coalition, Mella reiterated Lenin's view that only a single-class political party, that is, a strictly proletarian party, could bring about the desired reforms, because the middle-class elements would abandon the workers the first moment their interests diverged. Mella also charged the "Arpistas" with hypocritically distancing themselves from the Communists while at the same time claiming to be, as he put it, "the successors of Marx and Lenin in Latin America . . . the destined saviors of all oppressed by Yankee imperialism."

Mella did not stop there: he went on to accuse the APRA leaders of relying on resonant but meaningless phrases that made it impossible to identify what class elements or course of action their movement actually represented. What was meant, Mella asked, by "internationalization of the Canal Zone?" What nations, he wondered, did the "Arpistas" have in mind as the potential administrators of the canal? What was the meaning, he asked, of such vague phrases as "united front of manual and intellectual workers" or "continental party"?

Perhaps the movement's most damning weakness, Mella said, was its lack of a mass base. The movement was a handful of people, he declared, mostly petit bourgeois intellectuals who were more at home in lecture halls than in trade union locals. These adherents, he said, were "divorced from the proletariat and from reality." Mella judged that the movement's "masters of camouflage . . . (by an exact and dispassionate count) were barely three dozen, mostly poets and students." Yet these few people—by indulging in aggrandizing rhetoric and structuring the movement into international cells with a central committee—these few, he said, managed to delude even themselves about the size of their following and the strength of their organization.

Mella also rejected the movement's exaltation of youth as a revolutionary force, insisting that it was not a question of "glands, wrinkles, and gray hairs but of economics and class struggle." He also dismissed what he saw as the leaders' absurd claim to be the only ones to have seriously studied imperialism and to have thought about how to combat it, noting their patronizing attitude toward the Communist Anti-imperialist League, which he believed to be far more effective at fighting imperialism.

Although Mella granted that some of Haya's adherents were well intentioned—he called them "ignorant dilettantes" and "naive utopians"—he condemned the movement's deference to the leadership of one man, Haya de la Torre, who, Mella claimed, suffered from a caudillo complex and sought power as a means, not to improve the lot of the workers, but to further his own personal ambitions.

Many in the Communist movement—and outside it, including some Apristas—did not question Haya's motives, believing the leader's differences with the Communists to be matters of principle and conviction. Some believed that Haya in fact sympathized with the Soviet state and the Communist project but preferred as a tactical matter to keep a distance, not wanting the APRA to be attacked for supporting Communism. Even some of the Soviet leaders, who met and were impressed by the APRA leader when he visited Russia, viewed Haya as a serious but wrongheaded comrade. Julio Mella, however, resoundingly refused to grant Haya the status of comrade.

In concluding his protracted remarks, the Cuban Communist called for the "ARPA" to be unmasked and denounced as a class enemy. It should be viewed, he claimed, as a divisionist organization that would in a short while become overtly anti-Communist and a dangerous neutralizer of revolutionary struggles.

This severe criticism hurt APRA in many quarters. Indeed, many of Mella's assertions were justified, but the partisan Mella did not accurately characterize APRA when he claimed that the movement consisted mainly of leaders, leaders without followers. Mella may not have known that Haya and his organization in fact did have a substantial base among organized labor in Peru. When Haya officially founded the APRA in 1924, "the most influential members of the Lima proletarian community promptly declared their adherence to the new organization." Haya's achievements on behalf of Peruvian labor were indeed impressive: his creation of the popular universities, at which labor leaders and rank-and-file factory workers gained tremendous educational opportunities; his organization of the Federation of Textile Workers, uniting eight unions into a single confederation; his leadership of the student movement in support of the textile strike in 1919. It was not forgotten that Haya had risked his life in that confrontation, which helped conclude the workers' battle for the eight-hour day, a major achievement in Peru's labor history.

In 1923 a group of labor leaders approached Haya with the suggestion that he organize a political party. But before anything could come of this proposal he was deported. Exile obviously distanced him from his base in Peru, but he retained his status as a leader by assiduously maintaining contact with trade union activists through extensive and very warm correspondence; labor newsletters in Lima reported Haya's activities abroad, and at union gatherings he was not forgotten: "In nearly every meeting of organized labor extensive mention was made of 'nuestro querido ausente'—our dear friend who is absent."

When the Mexican Aprista cell in 1928 announced the formation of a Peruvian political party, José Carlos Mariátegui—profoundly upset by this news—immediately wrote Haya requesting clarification. Receiving no answer, Mariátegui wrote directly to the Mexican Aprista cell. In a letter dated April 16, 1928, he acknowledged having received a letter that was signed by Magda Portal on behalf of the cell and in which, he reminded them, he was accused of having fallen under the sway of Soviet-dominated Communists in Buenos Aires. Throughout this episode Magda appears to have behaved toward Mariátegui with a surprising lack of regard. The editor of *Amauta* responded to the Mexican Aprista cell's collective accusation simply by stating that he believed his independence of mind to have been amply demonstrated. He went on to entreat members of the cell to remember their shared history and ideals, beseeching them to reverse course and avoid fragmenting the Peruvian Left.

The grab for electoral victory, he wrote, was a serious error, a departure from their cherished principles. "I oppose all equivocation," he continued. "I am opposed to an ideological movement that by its historical justification, by the intelligence and selflessness of its militants, by the nobility of its doctrine, by all rights should win over the majority in Peru . . . but instead is embroiling itself in extremely vulgar electoral manipulations." He expressed his distaste for the blatantly opportunistic campaign material produced in support of "a central committee that doesn't exist," material he described as indulging in the worst sort of "Creole demagoguery." Reproaching members of the cell for having formed a political party without first seeking the consensus of others in their vanguard movement, he implored his former comrades to return to the spirit of fraternity and mutuality he believed should govern their internal debates. He also urged them to heed the lessons of recent Italian history, having seen for himself how quickly socialist and other left movements could turn fascist. "I will not deceive you," he wrote in closing, "I am sickened by all this, in genuine anguish. I don't wish to seem pathetic but I can't hide from you that I'm writing in a fever, with anxiety and desperation."

About a month later, on May 20, Haya responded to this letter, adopting a harsh, sarcastic tone. He did not reply sooner to Mariátegui's "absurdly emotional" letter, he said, because he wanted to give him time to cool off. "Please, pull yourself together," he chided, "you really must consider your health." He denied having anything to do with the campaign literature Mariátegui denounced, and he accused his former comrade of misjudging his intentions. "Might you not have read just a bit more carefully?" he asked. "Calm yourself, friend Mariátegui! I'm no offspring of Mussolini." On the issue of whether APRA should be an alliance or a political party, Haya accused Mariátegui of failing to grasp the possibility that APRA could at one and the same time be a party, an alliance, and a united front. Mariátegui failed to grasp this, Haya charged, because no European precedent existed for such a phenomenon. "It's time to disinfect ourselves from European imitations," the APRA leader admonished, suggesting that Mariátegui "take his discipline not from revolutionary Europe but from revolutionary America." He continued his pointed remarks. "You are doing much harm because of your lack of composure and your eagerness always to seem European, always using European terms. I know you are against us. I'm not surprised. But we will carry out the revolution without mentioning socialism and by redistributing lands and fighting imperialism." Magda, as witnessed by fellow Aprista Esteban Pavletich, typed Haya's dictation for this pivotal letter of May 20, 1928. On reading it,

Mariátegui abandoned all efforts to maintain dialogue with the APRA leader. He then sent an open letter to all concerned with this debate. The editor of *Amauta* now viewed Haya as a demagogue, a would-be caudillo who manipulated his followers, exploiting their idealism and self-abnegation for his own purposes. Haya's lust for power, Mariátegui feared, would lead to a fascist backlash in Peru.

But what accounts for Magda's participation in the verbal assault on Mariátegui, her friend and mentor, the champion and publisher of her poetry? In short, she was probably acting under the influence of Haya de la Torre. At the time this schism developed she was more or less Haya's protégé, in the first flush of her association with the charismatic leader. She was almost twenty-eight but, as she herself admitted, a neophyte in terms of political understanding. Haya went to a great deal of trouble to explain his ideas, and it was not just the ideas that appealed to her and the others in the group. Haya proposed action, action based on his APRA agenda. His arguments persuaded them not just that the Communist approach was wrong for Peru but that Mariátegui's leadership was seriously flawed.

Magda and other members of the cell, including Pavletich, now saw their friend as an ineffectual leader, an armchair revolutionary who was not moving fast enough or even at all to establish a political party in Peru. It seemed to them that their friend was too much the intellectual, too involved with writing and publishing, too busy clarifying the ideas of their vanguard movement, to get on with the task of forming a revolutionary organization. The experience of living in "triumphant Mexico" intensified their sense of urgency. Magda was thoroughly caught up in the militant atmosphere of Mexico's ongoing revolutionary process—a revolution in power, however beleaguered and endangered. The members of the Aprista cell were passionately impatient for action but felt frustrated, exasperated, and in need of leadership to channel their intense energies, a leadership they did not see coming from Mariátegui. If Magda had any misgivings about the unfriendly tone of their criticism, these are not evident; probably she was simply carried by the momentum of developments and, above all, by her deference to the APRA leader. No doubt it was Haya who set the mean-spirited tone, while the others went along in a self-righteous, polemical spirit, convinced of the rightness of their views and proceeding without comradely concern for Mariátegui's feelings or for the constraints under which the leader operated in Peru.

The effort at ideological clarification of their vanguard movement's free-floating ideas now accelerated among the various groups as letters traveled back and forth across borders in a model of earnest deliberation. The schism initiated by Haya's Plan de México—and its announcement of a new political party—spurred Mariátegui to take action of his own: he began organizing his own political party, the Socialist Party of Peru, founded in September 1928, by a few people who met on a beach in seaside Barranco. To what extent this new party was a Communist party in all but name is a matter of debate, but it is quite certain that at some point this party became secretly affiliated with the Communist International.

Her poetry set aside for the moment, Magda turned her energies to research and political writing. The work *Dollar Diplomacy*, by U.S. radicals Scott Nearing and Joseph Freeman, which recently had been translated into Spanish, became a basic text for the Peruvian exiles. Magda drew on that and other sources as she drafted the series of lectures she would deliver the following year on a speaking tour of the Caribbean. These writings reveal an advance in Magda's intellectual powers, a maturing also evident in her survey of new Latin American poets, *El nuevo poema y su orientación hacia una estética económica* (The New Poem and Its Social Aesthetic).

Mariátegui and Vallejo both warned that vanguard formal experiments in poetry were not in themselves socially progressive but in fact might be offering old wine in new bottles. Continuing in that line, Magda heralded in her survey the emergence of a genuine social awareness in poetry—an approach that went beyond facile celebration of modernistic inventions (the airplane, the telegraph) to address "the ferocious absorption of man by the machine." She decried the tendency of Latin American writers to seek European precedents. The established figures of Latin American poetry—Rubén Darío, José María Eguren, José Enrique Rodó, Julio Herrera Reissig, and Franz Tamayo—she said, looked to Europe for their literary models, paying little attention to the nascent American culture. But now she discerned a new sensibility, one grounded in *mestizaje*—race and cultural mixture—but also open to international influences. The new poetry also acknowledged the austere and isolated world of the American Indian. She noted that a number of younger poets were writing amid a chaos of influences. Pablo Neruda, for example, was producing a pure, emotive poetry, as were a number of poets influenced by Vicente Huidobro's *creacionismo*, a tendency she believed produced genuinely social poems. She considered Huidobro to be truly open to social concerns.

She reserved special praise for Serafín Delmar—"the least lyrical and most thorough exponent" of the new sensibility. Since the publication of *Radiogramas del Pácifico*, she noted approvingly, "the possibilities of his art have been honed to serve a very definite objective." In keeping with her Pan-American outlook, she mentioned poets from Uruguay, Guatemala, Argentina, Bolivia, Chile, Mexico, Cuba, and Peru. Notably absent is any reference to César Vallejo, an oversight indicating a certain narrowness in her conception of the social poem, although Vallejo's most overtly social poetry was not yet written.

Magda's recent readings in Marxism were also evident in this essay. Denouncing the egoism she saw as endemic in the world of poetry, she rejected the "individualist sentimentalism so typical of bourgeois, especially ivory tower, art." There was nothing intrinsically wrong, she hastened to add, with the emergence of a distinctive voice in the process of creating poems. She proposed, however, that poets renounce striving to create a personal voice but instead attempt to identify with a larger cause. "The poem of today, with all its essential beauty, is not detached from a larger humanity, does not produce a dehumanized aesthetic pleasure. . . . Today's poem embodies the piercing restlessness of a cry for redress . . . a cry arising out of mines, fields, factories, and slums—a cry summoning us to the collective work, urging us—in the new Nietzschean egoism of sacrifice and annihilation of personality—to add ourselves as simple, anonymous elements to the central energy of social liberation." Magda seems here to view the subordination of personality to social struggle not as any diminution of self but as a kind of Nietzschean triumph, an exertion of the will to experience a larger, more abundant life. But such immersion in the greater humanity implied a difficult, perhaps impossible bridging of distances. She perceived her own generation as a precursor generation, one formed by a decadent civilization at a moment of cataclysmic transition; in this transitional moment they—the poets and intellectuals—were still isolated from both the worker and the Indian. "However deep its understanding, the intellectual class . . . cannot capture the true spirit of the masses. The world, nature, and life for the bourgeois consciousness remains utterly different from what it is for the proletarian." In an attempt to narrow this distance, writers and painters, she said, were trying to create a more inclusive American identity, one slavishly dependent neither on European models, nor, even worse, she thought, on strictly Spanish precedents. At the same time, she said, they faced another threat, an onslaught of U.S. cultural imperialism, which went along with economic imperialism and threatened to destroy the indigenous art forms of their continent. It seemed to her that while the Mexican muralists were creating an art adequate to the momentous transformations then under way, the poets were having a harder time because the written word was not a popular medium; their poems were inaccessible to largely illiterate populations. Besides which, poets of the new sensibility were still mired in bourgeois attitudes. At best, they could act as a bridge to future poets who would truly embody "the voice of the multitude."

Ediciones A.P.R.A. in Mexico published Serafín's most recent collection of poems, *El hombre de estos años* (Man of Our Time), in 1929. The slim collection is an impassioned plea for socialist revolution, invoking both Jesus and Lenin. An epigraph by Leon Trotsky closes the book: "Art is a solvent preparing future revolutions." Abounding with archetypal imageries—sun and moon, sailor and sea, mother and son—these poems convey a deeply felt sorrow for the Indian, the worker, and the bereft mother. There is also plain political statement: "We are foes of Wall Street / and its Monroe Doctrine / but Walt Whitman belongs to us."

Serafín also wrote on art and social struggle. His thoughts on these matters differed a bit from those of Magda, who seemed most concerned to draw poets out of their insular private worlds into a heightened social consciousness. Serafín, however, seemed more to fear that revolutionary leaders might not respect the integrity of art and artists. Insisting that the literary and other arts be recognized as essential elements in any revolutionary process, he called for the revolutionary poet to be politically militant yet artistically independent, "coordinating his art with—not subordinating it to—Aprista praxis."

With Serafín's example of politicized poetry close by and with Haya's negative attitude toward her poetry well in mind, it's not surprising that Magda let her poetry lapse, her muse overwhelmed by other concerns. There was also the fact that a good deal of her poetic production lacked social content of the sort she praised in her essay on the new poem. In any case, other means of expression were opening for her. Having acquired a political commitment, she wanted to communicate it as broadly as possible. To that end, she intended to lecture and write journalistic articles. Tirelessly she would promote the Aprista vision.

Augusto César Sandino's resistance to the U.S. Marines' invasion of Nicaragua received enthusiastic support from Magda's group in Mexico. But the Aprista solidarity work proceeded apart from—and hostile to—Communist-led efforts. Both Julio Mella and Tina Modotti were militants in the Communist front Hands Off Nicaragua Committee, a solidarity group that raised money for Sandino's improvised group of resistance fighters. To what extent Magda associated with the Communist-oriented Diego Rivera circle is not clear, but any ongoing connection must have been vexed by the arrival in Mexico City of Haya de la Torre, whose differences with the Communists were increasingly pronounced. Members of the original but dormant Aprista cell—Peruvians Jacobo Hurwitz, Nicolás Terreros, and Pavletich—had joined the newly constituted cell led by Haya and of which Magda was secretary. But as 1928 progressed and the APRA plunged deeper into schism, Hurwitz and Terreros moved to the margins of the new cell. Increasingly uneasy with the direction Aprismo was taking, they began working with the Hands Off Nicaragua Committee.

Associating with Communists, however, proved incompatible with continuing as Apristas. In an account titled "Why I Broke with APRA"—published in *El Libertador* in July 1928—Hurwitz claimed that he and Terreros were approached by an Aprista delegation and asked to stop working with Hands Off. They were promised leadership roles in the APRA cell if they returned to it and threatened with expulsion from the cell if they continued working with Hands Off. They were further threatened, Hurwitz claimed, with being refused entry to Peru if the APRA ever came to power there. For obvious reasons, Hurwitz said, on receiving this ultimatum he broke definitively with APRA. Hurwitz was among the first, if not the first, to break in a public manner with the APRA.

Meanwhile, the Apristas in Mexico pursued their own initiatives in support of Sandino's armed resistance to U.S. forces in Nicaragua. Haya, when in Paris, had organized a demonstration on behalf of the Nicaraguan patriot; he also wrote to Sandino's lieutenant Froilán Turcios offering their "unconditional services" as "soldiers of APRA" ready to fight under Sandino's command. Aprista Esteban Pavletich actually left Mexico to join Sandino and his army in the northern mountains of Nicaragua. There for a time he became one of Sandino's closest advisors, in which capacity he made the case for the Apristas' revolutionary nationalist approach to nation-building. But Sandino opted to draw closer to the Communists, whose fund-raising efforts provided thousands of dollars in aid, whereas Aprista donations apparently did not amount to anything. Peruvian autocrat Augusto Leguía, it should be noted, was the only Latin American head of state to declare support for the U.S. Marines' invasion of Nicaragua.

By early 1929 Mexico was no longer a haven for leftists. Government officials called a halt to the ongoing land reforms, while opponents of the revolutionary process renewed their calls for Diego Rivera's murals to be whitewashed.

Which did not happen, although gangs of counterrevolutionary students defaced murals by José Clemente Orozco and Rufino Tamayo. Acts of political violence were multiplying throughout the country.

On January 10, 1929, Cuban revolutionary Julio Antonio Mella was gunned down in Mexico City, slain by an agent of Cuban dictator Gerardo Machado. After working late with former Aprista Jacobo Hurwitz and several other comrades in the Red Aid office, Mella and Tina Modotti were walking home when several shots rang out. Gravely wounded, Mella collapsed, bleeding, in the street, cradled by Modotti. Rushed to the hospital by friends, he underwent surgery but did not survive. Although in shock, Modotti was immediately taken into custody and interrogated by police agents, who would eventually charge her with complicity in her lover's murder. Mella's assassination was described in the tabloid press as a "crime of passion."

This preposterous allegation against Tina Modotti played out in sensational hearings, involving prurient examinations of seized personal letters. The lurid press coverage is described by Mildred Constantine, in *Tina Modotti: A Fragile Life*, as "a vendetta of slander." Diego Rivera came to Modotti's defense while the tabloids blazoned Edward Weston's classic nude photos of the beautiful Italian American, who was vilified in salacious newsprint as a Mata Hari, a Communist, a "pernicious foreigner," and a slut. Eventually the police released Modotti, who remained under police surveillance.

Despite U.S. radical Carleton Beals's conciliating efforts, Mella and Haya de la Torre had remained at political odds, unable to reconcile their opposing views. But Mella's harsh criticisms of Haya and APRA did not prevent Magda from attending Mella's funeral or taking her turn in the revolving honor guard beside the slain Cuban's bier in the headquarters of the Mexican Communist Party. Illumined by candlelight, Mella's body lay in state, "with a huge red star and gold hammer and sickle on the wall behind." At a massive gathering at the Dolores Cemetery, Diego Rivera delivered the funeral oration honoring the Cuban militant, cofounder of Cuba's first Communist Party. A partisan interpretation of the presence of APRA militants at Mella's funeral is provided by Ricardo Martínez de la Torre, Mariátegui's friend and longtime comrade, who claimed that the APRA leaders shed "crocodile tears" at Mella's grave, attending his funeral only to give the lie to those who accused them of opportunistically refusing to associate with Communist Party fronts or activities.

Attacks from the right on leftists in Mexico, particularly on Communists, coincided with the increasing rigidity of the international Communist line formulated in Moscow. The intolerance of dissent was such that Diego Rivera would soon be cast out of the Mexican Communist Party. In the Soviet Union Joseph Stalin's persecution of purported enemies was now ongoing, the formerly dominant Bolshevik faction having been deprived of power. The official Soviet tolerance of avant-garde art forms had given way to intense suspicion and denunciation. Even the brilliantly innovative poet Vladimir Mayakovsky—whose dedication as a revolutionary could hardly be questioned—found himself attacked as a petit bourgeois in the Soviet newspaper *Pravda.* In a short while he would die a suicide.

When the Mexican Communist newspaper *El Machete* issued calls to take up arms and occupy lands (a stance Diego Rivera criticized as being dangerously aggressive), Mexican authorities assaulted the party's headquarters and shut down the paper. In response to this repressive development, on June 10, 1929, Magda's friend and Aprista comrade Esteban Pavletich fired off a letter in solidarity with the Communists. Appearing in *El Machete* on June 22, his statement condemned the Mexican government's action and offered APRA's full support to the persecuted Communists. What happened next both surprised and disheartened Pavletich; he hadn't consulted with his Aprista comrades before sending his letter but "counted on the support of three of the four members who constituted the Peruvian APRA cell in Mexico." But that support did not materialize. Instead Pavletich's unauthorized act led to his censure; he was also asked to resign from official duties in the cell. It's not clear which Apristas participated in this repudiation. Serafín would have been involved, but Magda by this time was traveling and lecturing in the Caribbean. Pavletich noted that among the cell members Manuel Vásquez Díaz was "the only one to oppose from the very outset the incipiently fascist measure of demanding my resignation." This incident, along with his growing reservations about APRA's political direction, led Pavletich to conclude that APRA had betrayed its revolutionary principles and could not be salvaged. He refused to retract his statement of solidarity with the Communists and instead broke with APRA.

A personal matter may have figured in the call for Pavletich's resignation. In March 1929, according to Daniel Reedy, Haya (writing to an Aprista comrade in Paris) complained of hostility toward him in the Mexican cell; he singled out Pavletich, whom he described as "another little poet who's against me." Pavletich hated him, Haya said, because he (Haya) had opposed Pavletich's attempt "to take away Serafín del Mar's woman, Magda."

Confirming a key element of this story, Reedy recounts that Pavletich confided during conversations in Lima that "his admiration for Magda went back to their university years in Lima, that the life they enjoyed in Mexico was fairly free with regard to personal relations, and that, in fact, he had fallen in love with Magda and tried to take her away from Serafín."

Some weeks after his censure by Mexico's APRA cell, Pavletich wrote Mariátegui declaring his allegiance to the newly founded Socialist Party of Peru. He admitted in this long letter of July 30, 1929, that he, along with others in the Mexican cell, had been extremely unhappy with him, believing he was dedicating too much time to intellectual pursuits while failing to move decisively to create a revolutionary organization in Peru. The absence of such a unifying organization, Pavletich went on, left them as if orphaned—"restless and avid for action but lacking any instrument that might focus and harmonize our efforts." This lack, he explained, accounted in large part for errors committed in the cell in Mexico, "a protracted series of mistakes, many of them very serious."

In February 1929 (the same month that Leon Trotsky left Russia to go into exile), the Mexican authorities abruptly expelled Tina Modotti from Mexico. She was put aboard the *S.S. Edam,* a cargo boat headed for the Netherlands. When the ship stopped in New Orleans, a port of call on the way to Rotterdam, the local authorities placed Modotti in an alien detention center. From there she wrote to *Amauta* in Lima, thanking the editors for sending her the recent issue and informing them of the grim turn of events in Mexico: political refugees were being jailed, summarily deported, even murdered. "The saddest thing," she wrote, "is that the Mexican government has completely capitulated to Wall Street.... The revolutionary spirit that attracted so many to Mexico is now no more than a legend."

Throughout 1928 and 1929, turmoil persisted in the far-flung Aprista movement. The Mexican cell proposed that Haya be replaced as leader by an international Aprista committee to be based in Buenos Aires. Pavletich had drafted a number of conceivably unifying points: (1) ceding control of Aprista cells outside Lima to a central cell in Peru; (2) repudiating the idea of the Partido Nacionalista; and (3) declaring the socialist, revolutionary, anti-imperialist character of the APRA. But nothing came of these proposals, and by the later part of 1929 members of the Mexican cell were scattered, the cell disbanded.

In Peru, Aprista groups in Arequipa and in Cuzco went over to Mariátegui's Socialist Party. The Cuzco group repudiated Aprismo's recent positions as running counter to their efforts to build a workers' movement. As one of the Cuzco leaders explained, "We protested the Mexican cell's opposition to the communist groups in Mexico when Magda Portal was secretary, and also disagreed with similar tendencies in other Aprista groups." In La Paz, the Aprista cell dissolved. In Paris, the cell split; Luis Heysen and Luis Eduardo Enríquez stayed with APRA, while Eudocio Ravines, Armando Bazin, Juan Paiva, Jorge Seoane, Demetrio Tello, and César Vallejo aligned themselves with Mariátegui. In response to this development, Haya ruefully observed that "the Apristas in Paris could all fit on a couch."

His prestige badly damaged, Haya de la Torre offered his resignation as head of the fractured movement, a resignation that—as Eudocio Ravines wrote to Mariátegui—"had little meaning, because with or without an official title, Haya will go on being the mentor of many people on the left; his views will be the views of comrades such as [Luis] Heysen, Serafín, and perhaps Magda and [Oscar] Herrera." As the year 1929 progressed, it was widely rumored that the APRA had disintegrated and that its members, en bloc, intended to join Mariátegui's Socialist Party. So widespread was this rumor that in late September, in a letter to an associate, Haya addressed the possibility of mass defections: "APRA is a continental organization that cannot be subordinated to any merely national organization. All the other sections established in America reserve the right to protest against any adhesion of all APRA to the Socialist Party of Peru. Besides which various national parties have affiliated with APRA, including among others the Unionist Party of Central America and the Haitian Patriotic Union, so that APRA is both an alliance and a great party." What APRA actually was at this point remained in dispute. Years later Magda asserted that in those days she did not think of the APRA as a political party. "Our group, dispersed in various countries, identified not as a party but as a movement. . . . We simply weren't structured as a party."

For several months the debate regarding APRA's status and doctrines unfolded in the pages of *Amauta,* with Aprista voices given substantial space in the journal. Mariátegui, however, had the last word; he concluded by rejecting the notion that APRA had ever been a substantial entity: "The too notorious truth is that APRA was never more than a plan, a project, an idea promulgated by a handful of Peruvian student groups. It was never effective as an 'alliance' or 'united front' . . . but instead played upon the Latin American propensity to be fooled by pompous letterheads." Mariátegui then announced that *Amauta* (now strictly Marxian and Soviet oriented in viewpoint) would no longer be open to Aprista voices: they had made their case, and the debate was over. He reserved the possibility, however, as he wrote to a comrade, that their Socialist Party might one day work in coalition with the "petit bourgeois revolutionary nationalist" APRA.

When the First Congress of Latin American Communists met in Buenos Aires in June 1929, representatives of Mariátegui's Socialist Party were invited. Despite their party's private affiliation with the Communists, Mariátegui and his comrades remained fiercely independent, refusing to go along with certain lines laid down in Moscow. At this major congress in Buenos Aires, representatives of the Comintern treated the Peruvian representatives with disrespect, going so far as to censure them for their deviations from Comintern positions. A particularly glaring divergence: Peru's Socialists insisted on full integration of the Indian into national life, whereas the official Communist position favored secession of Peru's indigenous peoples into independent Quechua and Aymara republics. Because of his fragile health, Mariátegui did not travel to Buenos Aires. In his absence Comintern representatives attempted to split Peru's Socialists, with the aim of replacing Mariátegui with a leader more receptive to the official positions. This attempt failed.

Whatever their differences, Haya de la Torre and Mariátegui were alike in their staunch resistance to attempts by the Communist International to impose policies that seemed to them inappropriate for Peru. Although Haya denounced Mariátegui's close ties to the Communists, in fact both men's views were formed in relation to the Communist international movement—whose policies and formulations framed the debate for all critics of capitalism. Historians have noted that Haya de la Torre, despite his sharply drawn anti-Communist profile, had a number of affinities with the Communists—perhaps as many affinities as Mariátegui had differences with his own comrades in the Communist movement. Haya's temperament, for example, lent itself to a Leninist top-down leadership style, in stark contrast to Mariátegui's democratic spirit and insistence on open debate among peers. An additional point—Haya's acceptance, however ambivalent, of revolutionary violence as a tactic to gain state power mirrored the belligerent stance of the Comintern in the late 1920s and early 1930s, whereas Mariátegui's gradualism and his concern with clarifying principles and steadily building a mass base was completely out of step with Communist urgings to move immediately to seize power by force.

Finding himself again deported, now in exile in Hamburg, Germany, Haya de la Torre kept in touch by letter with his remaining followers, who went their own ways, awaiting developments. It is at this point of maximum uncertainty regarding even the continuing existence of APRA that Magda played a significant role in helping to maintain what some saw as a defunct movement. In May

1929, she left Mexico to undertake a lecture tour of the Caribbean. Throughout this tour she vigorously promoted the main tenets of APRA, foremost among them the need to resist U.S. corporate domination in Latin America.

CARIBBEAN TOUR

We have one great enemy. Let us form one great union.
—*Aprista motto*

What is my religion? Love, not the small love, the sexual love between man and woman, but a universal love for humankind.
—*Magda Portal, Santo Domingo, 1929*

With tickets to Havana purchased with money pooled by friends, Magda and five-year-old Gloria boarded a ship that set sail from Yucatán, heading for "the emerald, island-scattered Caribbean." Starting out in May and continuing into September 1929, Magda traveled and gave lectures. Serafín remained in Mexico with plans to join Magda and Gloria later. It is not clear when or even if Magda and Serafín were ever formally married, but on this tour and later in her press interviews Magda referred to Serafín as her husband, and in a late interview she mentioned having been married twice. On her stamped visa to Colombia on this Caribbean tour, she named Serafín Delmar as her husband, also declaring that the purpose of her trip was literary and that she was not associated with any Communist or other subversive organization. These declarations were not exactly true: the document dissolving her marriage to Federico Bolaños is dated May 19, 1931 (the year divorce became legal in Peru); besides which her travels were not exactly for the sole purpose of offering literary recitals.

Despite continuing unrest in Cuba's capital, the Machado regime did not interfere with Magda's activities in Havana. Buoyantly optimistic throughout her tour, Magda believed that a radical transformation might well be imminent. In an article published in the Havana paper *El Diario de Cuba* on May 28, 1929, she insisted that the prevailing power relations—inherently instable—could very rapidly change, that the ultradynamic U.S. economy might even collapse if the countries of Latin America could unite in opposition to it. How much longer, she wondered, could the frenzied productivity of the U.S. economy be sustained? A sense of impending catastrophe was in the air as the stock crash on Wall Street loomed in the near distance.

After lecturing twice at the Lyceum, one of the largest auditoriums in Havana, Magda set out by boat (passage paid by Cuban friends), skirting the coast en route to Santiago de Cuba in the southeastern part of the island. From there she took the steamship *Guantánamo* to Puerto Rico, continuing on to the Dominican Republic and Haiti, returning through Puerto Rico, and concluding her tour in Colombia in September. Her travels were primarily financed with money paid by her lecture audiences. Her preferred arrangement in each city was to give three paid talks and three unpaid. Occasionally she lectured on social poetry and on women in Spanish American history, but typically she offered her two main talks, one on U.S. imperialism in Latin America ("América latina frente al imperialismo"), the other a defense of Mexico's revolution ("Defensa de la revolución mexicana"). Published in Lima in 1931, the texts of her principal lectures remain a cogent presentation of what in the 1970s came to be known as dependency theory, which popularized the view that poverty and underdevelopment in Latin America were inextricably linked to the prosperity of the industrialized nations. In a key text of the 1970s, *Las venas abiertas de América Latina* (The Open Veins of Latin America), the Uruguayan historian and poet Eduardo Galeano posited a general rule: the greater the natural wealth of the land, the more wretched its native peoples, both land and people being subject to exploitation by great powers.

Even though Magda enjoyed a certain renown as a poet and political deportee, the extent of her celebrity in the Caribbean—as revealed by the local press coverage of her tour—is quite surprising. Journalists were well acquainted with her dissident profile. A network of daily newspapers tracked her itinerary, interviewing her and reporting on her talks, sometimes at considerable length. Superlatives heralded her approach and were marshaled to applaud her lectures. She was welcomed as a comrade and heroine, a "sibyl of the ideal," and "the greatest, most noble daughter of America"—one of the few women "able to give luster to a continent." Her lecture on anti-imperialism was extolled as a "brilliant dissertation," her defense of Mexico praised as a "luminous synthesis."

In Puerto Rico she noted the pervasive U.S. presence and the widespread use of English. She took part in anti-U.S. demonstrations, distributing fliers and vehemently embracing the cause of the Puerto Rican nationalists, who opposed the annexation of the island by the United States. Besides offering her two principal lectures, she presented a talk titled "The Spanish-American Woman." Addressing a disappointingly small audience in the San Juan Municipal Theater, Magda directed her remarks primarily to women, who had failed to turn out to hear her in any numbers. "Perhaps another time," she dryly remarked. As journalist Manuel Rivera Matos went on to report, she also on this occasion defended "free love"—free in the sense that women, she said, should have the right to choose for themselves in all matters pertaining to love and marriage. Libertine behavior, she added, was not what she meant by free love. Puerto Rican women had just recently won the vote, and she offered her congratulations and proposed that the vote be treated as simply one more weapon in a political arsenal. Believing that women could be a force for moral purification, she urged them to resist being caught up in the corrupt electoral politics of the day. If women were simply going to accommodate themselves to the routines of an oppressive system, she said, they might as well stay out of politics. Rejecting the sort of feminism that limited its concerns to so-called women's issues, she espoused instead a feminism that embraced the most inclusive struggle for social justice, insisting that "in any authentic battle for social justice, feminism is implicit."

After spending more than a month in Puerto Rico, Magda traveled on to the Dominican Republic, arriving on the steamship *Coamo* on July 9, 1929. That nation was then enjoying an interlude of social progressivism under the leadership of Horacio Vásquez, an eight-year U.S. military occupation having come to an end in 1914. Within months, however, the country would be thrust into dictatorship: military man Rafael Trujillo would take power and rule the country as a personal fiefdom for two extended periods, lasting until 1952. For the moment, however, interested persons were at liberty to hear the lectures of the Peruvian agitator and to engage in public discussion of her call to action.

Thus, on July 14, despite torrential late morning rain and a darkened sky, the main auditorium in Santo Domingo, capital of the Dominican Republic, gradually filled with people awaiting the appearance of Magda Portal. Thunderous applause greeted her arrival at the podium, an ovation lasting two full minutes. Seemingly overnight, she explained to an attentive audience, the United States became a world power, consolidating its economic and military presence in Central America and the Caribbean, with Panama as a key dominion. She spoke of historical precedents—the annexation of northern Mexico; the occupation of Guantánamo in Cuba; the U.S. Marines' invasions of Haiti, the Dominican Republic, and Nicaragua. She detailed the notorious Platt Amendment, which designated Cuba as virtually a U.S. protectorate. She enumerated U.S. investments in the region, deploring the many loans that served as the major means of economic entrapment. Her speech "created a sensation that traveled vertiginously throughout the city."

In her talk on Mexico she called for the defense of the beleaguered Mexican Revolution, characterized in the U.S. press, she said, "as the work of bandits and desperados." She surveyed the economic and historical roots of the revolution, emphasizing the enormous power concentrated in the Catholic Church. She described the machinations of U.S. diplomats and denounced their attempts to sabotage Mexico's still-unratified constitution, particularly its Article 27, which aimed to levy fees on foreign extractors of Mexican oil. She cited Woodrow Wilson's plaintive remark "I have to remind myself that I am not an agent of petroleum interests but the president of the United States." Her enthusiasm for Mexico and its revolutionary process was unrestrained. "I would have liked to have been born in Mexico," she once exclaimed to an interviewer. She praised the Mexican muralists as "creators of a new art." Mexico, she believed, was the radiant font of a new American identity; every stage in Mexico's battle to redistribute land and to control its own resources embodied an urgent lesson for sister nations of the continent. Her entire being, more than one journalist noted, vibrated with high tension. As one put it, "She is all nerve, all action."

In a speaking style variously described as elegant, scholarly, impassioned, and serene, this proponent of Indo-American unity is reported to have neither harangued her audiences nor raised her voice in indignation. Although not perceived as a charismatic speaker, she is said to have captivated her listeners by the intensity of her conviction and by the avalanche of facts at her command. Her arguments were said to be "lean on sentimentality, advancing like soldiers in an invincible bayonet charge."

A number of critics noted the agility of her mind and the nuanced quality of her elucidations. Several commentators, however, were not impressed. In a tone of exaggerated politeness, "the Chronicler" in Barranquilla, Colombia, wondered why "the lovely Peruvian dilettante Doña Portal, cultivated, beautiful, and intelligent," left the comfort of her hearth "to tilt at the windmills of the great northern colossus." In response to her remarks on social poetry, she was accused by the same journalist of "Hispanophobia" and chided for her ignorance of Spanish literature. In fact, she would later confess to having harbored a lifelong prejudice against Spain and a reluctance to read Spanish authors, with the exception of Miguel de Unamuno, whose works were greatly valued by Mariátegui.

Another critic of her lectures is made uneasy by a certain grandiosity in her political outlook. Another regretted that she appeared to have fallen under the influence of disputatious advisors. Particularly addressing the young, Magda called upon all "who love the ideal and have blind faith in the future of our race" to unite and resist U.S. corporate domination of their respective countries. Those with a faith less blind might not have been moved by her fervent message. But many were. Her talks won adherents to her cause, and as she traveled she organized Aprista committees, some of which remained active for many years.

Although her lectures were well written and effectively delivered, the spectacular success of her tour must also be attributed to the novelty of her being a woman—a young, attractive, and sensationally modern woman, indeed "a very twenty-first-century" one. Perceived as "exquisitely feminine" she was also described as a "virile, aggressive . . . protagonist of ideas." More than a few who attended her talks were "astonished and disconcerted" by them. Certainly a number of the young (male) radicals in the Dominican Republic were, as one put it, "amazed at her knowledge of what has hitherto, we have to admit, been solely a masculine domain: political economy." One member of her audience in Santo Domingo described her effect on these young men: "When Magda Portal reached our shores, we felt torment. The poverty of our element, the lack of MEN, virile men, so greatly embarrassed us that we hesitated to shake her hand. We felt ashamed, and sad. A woman, teaching us to be men!" Despite the self-mocking tone, the chagrin expressed here may have been real, even if her enthusiasm did strike the young men as naive.

Nor did her good looks escape notice, including in some florid commentary: "Magda Portal: twenty-eight years old, slender in build . . . a high broad forehead framed with gold-blond curls, a delicious mouth with impeccable pearly teeth, empurpled lips . . . penetrating, gray black eyes pooling like lakes or glinting with metallic lights." Journalists also noted a characteristic flicker of self-derision in her smile, the same ironic smile that decades later would still be noticed.

Identifying herself as a representative of APRA—"a Marxist, not a communist"—she ignored the internal Aprista disarray to concentrate on promoting the broad points of Aprista unity. The entire United States, she maintained, operated on the principle of a gigantic trust whose director was the U.S. government itself. While the northern colossus long since had consolidated its formidable union, Latin America remained "a mosaic of small countries divided by arbitrary frontiers" and "splintered and enfeebled by internal divisions." The solution? Pan-American confederation. "Either we come together and resist, or we disappear, becoming no more than Yankee colonies."

Gloria did not accompany her mother to the Dominican Republic but stayed behind in Puerto Rico in the care of friends. An interviewer in Santo Domingo drew Magda out on this point, noting that she seemed uneasy, that something apart from politics seemed to be troubling her. "My daughter is waiting for me in Puerto Rico," she acknowledged. "I wanted to spare her the discomfort of further traveling."

In transit through Haiti on her way back to Puerto Rico, Magda was struck by "the blank stare of malnutrition" she saw on faces in the squalid slums where Blacks lived on the outskirts of San Juan. In early August, lecturing at the University of Puerto Rico, she again attacked U.S. policies in the region, provocatively insulting the U.S. flag on display near her podium. Immediately after this lecture, U.S. authorities summoned her for questioning. She recalled that the U.S. officials "insisted on speaking to me in English even though I told them I knew only Spanish. . . . One official leafed through a bulging file on his desk, every now and then glancing up at me in disgust." At the end of a four-hour interrogation, she was ordered to pack her bags and be out of the country within twenty-four hours, her sojourn on that island was at an end.

One of Mariátegui's Puerto Rican correspondents wrote him about the impact in the region of her talks. "*Compañera* Magda's campaign in Puerto Rico and Santo Domingo has been formidable. It's made a profound impression. One proof of which is that I was nearly expelled from the country myself as a 'subversive.'"

Accompanied by her daughter, Magda continued her travels, paying her respects at the tomb of Simón Bolívar in Caracas on her way to Bogotá. She concluded her talks in Barranquilla, Colombia, where she first met Rómulo Betancourt, then a student in exile and later a dedicated Aprista.

As the summer of 1929 drew to an end and her hectic tour came to its close, Magda could look back on her travels with a well-earned sense of achievement. The taking of such a bold initiative, the accolades received, the cordial receptions, the new friendships so easily formed—all this must have greatly strengthened her self-confidence. Her network of friends and acquaintances now extended over a number of countries such that she might now think of herself as an intrinsic and perhaps even a leading proponent of transcontinental struggle.

Serafín would join them in Costa Rica, where Magda settled for some months, enrolling Gloria in a San José school. Journalist Carmen Lyra's recollection of Gloria at this time suggests that her parents' itinerant and agitated lifestyle did not agree with the child: "She seemed unsettled, pale, thin;

only her lustrous black hair and dark intelligent eyes seemed to blossom." In San José Magda returned to her writing; she also gave talks and offered classes on Marxism despite what she perceived as her lack of expertise in the subject matter. Rómulo Betancourt, then exiled in San José, credits these classes in Marxism as being formative in his own political education—one day he would be president of Venezuela. The paths of these two exiles would cross many times.

Magda was befriended in San José by Don Joaquín García Monge, editor of the distinguished left-wing journal *Repertorio Americano,* in which Magda's writings appeared over the years. Her series of lyrics, "18 cantos emocionados de 'Vidrios de amor,'" completed in 1924, was first published in that journal in December 1929. Some time after her arrival Don Joaquín wrote Mariátegui with news of Magda in San José, signaling in his remarks that she had put the unpleasantness of the schism episode far behind her. "Magda Portal is with us," he wrote on October 30, 1929. "We speak of you often and with much sympathy. . . . Magda is contented here, and waiting for Serafín. They are planning to go on to Chile where they hope to see you."

In Lima, Mariátegui was living under intensifying strain, his frail health near breaking point. U.S. radical and writer Waldo Frank (author of *Our America, Virgin Spain,* and *Rediscovery of America*) visited him in Peru's capital earlier that year. An admirer of Frank's writings, Mariátegui was working with Samuel Glusberg, director of the Buenos Aires review *La Vida Literaria,* to arrange for translations of this work into Spanish. Frank found Mariátegui in an alarming state, subject to continual police surveillance, routine theft of his voluminous mail, and devastating police raids of his home. *Amauta* continued to appear, but the workers' review *Labor* was outlawed, and Mariátegui himself was under heavy attack not just for his radical politics but now also for having Jewish friends and associates. Augusto Leguía's regime now exhibited an ugly anti-Semitic streak. During a crackdown late in 1929, when police arrested Mariátegui along with other leftists, they detained the director of the Jewish review *El Repertorio Hebreo;* prominent members of the Jewish business community also experienced persecution.

Government censorship of Mariátegui's articles not only thwarted his ability to communicate but also seriously affected his livelihood. Having received word from Magda that a particular conference was being held abroad, Mariátegui wrote a friend that he would not be able to attend because of the cost. "We're working in poverty here, there are no funds for anything." Early in 1930 he wrote Waldo Frank to ask if he could possibly arrange for the *New*

Republic to pay him for some writing, mentioning that one of his articles, in translation, had appeared in the *Nation.*

Despite—or perhaps because of—his deteriorating health, Mariátegui continued working at a desperate pace throughout 1929, strengthening ties with the miners at Cerro de Pasco, La Oroya, and Morococha, leading his Socialist Party, and at the same time frenetically working to organize the National Confederation of Trade Unions (La Confederación Nacional de Trabajadores del Perú). All this in addition to editing and publishing *Amauta* and continuing his extensive correspondence. He had not given up attempting to win over those whom he felt should rightly be his allies in the socialist cause but who had fallen under the sway of Haya de la Torre. It was not clear to him where Magda stood in the aftermath of the dissolution of Mexico's APRA cell. In a letter to Esteban Pavletich on September 25, 1929, José Carlos asked him to intervene: "I hope you are still in touch with Magda and will be able to explain our position and obtain her adherence." In this letter he also issued a call, requesting that all the comrades scattered abroad return immediately to Peru if they could possibly arrange to do so. He also wrote directly to Magda in Costa Rica, inviting her to join his Socialist Party.

Her answer was no. She later reported having replied to Mariátegui that she "was already committed to the party Haya was organizing." It is not clear that the APRA was in formation as a political party but it is certain that Magda preferred the Aprista tendency. At that time it seemed to her that Mariátegui's Socialist Party "was less timely for Peru than the APRA, which was more Peruvian." A plan to meet with Mariátegui was in the works, as Magda recounted.

> José Carlos Mariátegui wrote me of his desire to travel to Buenos Aires for medical treatment early in April 1930. I replied immediately from Costa Rica. I told him that if he were going to Buenos Aires we could all plan to meet in order to have a more complete conversation. Our group would be in Santiago de Chile before that date, and he being the one who was ill, we would go to him—*anywhere in America.* Replying immediately in the affirmative, he closed with a memorable phrase: "I know you will be there wherever duty calls." With that he signed off. Our group then mobilized to send letters to friends in various parts of Europe. We wrote to Mexico, to Central America, to Buenos Aires and Uruguay.

Much had happened since the tense interchanges that spurred the 1928 schism in Peru's Left. Magda's affectionate regard for Mariátegui now appears entirely restored, her attitude recalibrated by the passage of time and also perhaps by the fact that Mariátegui never gave up on her—as he had on Haya de la Torre—but wanted her to join his Socialist Party. It seems that Haya did not plan to attend the proposed gathering—they decided to meet in Chile—but other Aprista exiles were making plans to travel. Peruvian critic and activist Luis Alberto Sánchez, then exiled in Chile, arranged for Mariátegui to give a series of paid lectures at the University of Santiago.

Carrying false passports, Magda, Serafín, and Gloria, with several Aprista comrades, set out by boat from Puerto Limón, Costa Rica. In Panama City as they awaited a ship arriving from London, they ran out of money and were forced to part with their books. Magda and Serafín routinely traveled with cartons of books, one carton containing a special edition of the works of the great poet, essayist, and Cuban patriot José Martí, a gift to her from friends in Havana. With great reluctance she offered the prized Martí along with other volumes to the local university. The proceeds of this sale enabled them to eat and to stay in a cheap hotel until their connecting boat arrived. Although brief, the stopover in Panama gave Magda an opportunity to observe the racist nature of the U.S. presence in the Canal Zone. "U.S. officials treated the Panamanians as inferiors," she reported. "Certain areas were cordoned off with chains and marked with signs: 'No Negroes or dogs.' In the city outskirts the blacks lived segregated in ghettos that they left only to go to their jobs. . . . There were bloody clashes between U.S. officials and Panamanian young people protesting the occupation."

The group continued their voyage in a small English vessel crowded with destitute immigrants from Spain. They endured suffocating heat and a nauseating stench until the ship dropped anchor at the port of Callao, in Peru. There the exiles hid below deck, successfully eluding detection. But when they arrived in Santiago, Chile, they were promptly arrested and jailed by Chilean authorities.

Being a woman did not on this occasion—as it had in Havana—exempt Magda from being incarcerated along with the men. The miserable conditions in the jail, including the awful filth, so appalled her that she refused to eat. After eight days of her hunger strike, the authorities released the Peruvian group, who agreed as the condition of their liberty to avoid all meddling in Chilean politics. Amid rumors of the imminent collapse of Leguía's regime in Peru, Magda and her Aprista comrades settled down to await the arrival of José Carlos Mariátegui.

Fig. 1 Magda, ca. 1915

Fig. 2 Magda

Fig. 3 Magda with her daughter, Gloria Delmar

Fig. 4 Seated: Gloria Delmar and Juana del Risco, Magda's maternal grandmother; *standing:* Magda and her mother, Rosa Amelia Moreno del Risco

Fig. 5 José Carlos Mariátegui, 1928

Fig. 6 Woodcut depicting Magda Portal by Pantigoso, from *Amauta,* no. 2, October 1926

Fig. 7 "To my lovely little daughter," 1929

Fig. 8 Magda, Serafín Delmar, Mariblanca Sabas Alomá, Gloria, Havana, 1927

Fig. 9 César Vallejo, summer, 1929

Fig. 10 Julio Antonio
Mella, 1928

Fig. 11 Magda with
Serafín and Gloria,
Mexico City

Fig. 12 Mexican Aprista cell (with Gloria). *Left to right:* Esteban Pavletich, Serafín Delmar, Manuel Vasquez Díaz, unidentified, Magda, Víctor Raúl Haya de la Torre, Carlos Manuel Cox

Fig. 13 Haya de la Torre, Magda, Plaza de Acho, APRA rally, 1931

Fig. 14 Magda and Gloria,
Buenos Aires, April 1939

Fig. 15 Gloria with
Salvador Allende,
Colegio Dalton

Fig. 16 Magda, Salvador Allende, front center, with Chilean Socialists, 1945

Fig. 17 Flora Tristán:
La precursora, cover,
Lima, 1944

Fig. 18 Graciela Pareja Moreno, 1946

Fig. 19 "Apristas in Zorritos Salute Magda Portal," June 1946

Fig. 20 At a country school in Lampa

Fig. 21 Magda in Iquitos, 1945

Fig. 22 "In a theater," Tumbes, 1946

Fig. 23 Frontispiece, *¿Quíenes traicionaron el pueblo?* 1950

Fig. 24 Reception, El Fondo de Cultura Económica

Fig. 25 Magda with Kathleen Weaver, San Francisco, 1981

Fig. 26 Magda with niece Rocío Revolledo, 1984

IN THE APRA:
THE "HEROIC YEARS" (1931–1944)

The Aprista struggle was all-consuming. I gave myself to it completely, to the point of forgetting my home and family, which may have been a mistake but that's how it was.
—MAGDA PORTAL

FOUNDING THE APRISTA PARTY OF PERU

The stock market crash on Wall Street in October 1929 had immediate and disastrous repercussions in Peru. The flow of credit to the country from New York banks abruptly stopped. Prices for Peru's commodities plummeted. Unemployed workers in Lima sold fruit, collar stays, or lottery tickets on the streets while hungry people scavenged in the city dump for food. Even the exclusive Jockey Club, redoubt of Peru's Anglophile elite, teetered on the verge of bankruptcy. Augusto Leguía would soon be deposed, his eleven-year regime another casualty of economic depression.

In the early months of 1930, as the depression deepened and Leguía made futile efforts to control the damage, Mariátegui's worsening health took a grave turn. Luis Alberto Sánchez recalled how he learned that his friend lay near death. Magda, Serafín, and Serafín's brother Julián Petrovick approached Sánchez after one of his lectures at the University of Santiago in Chile; Mariátegui's condition, they said, had deteriorated to the point that no recovery could be expected. Word soon came that the great intellectual and labor leader had died on April 16, 1930, after weeks of intense suffering. He was not yet thirty-six. In a massive outpouring of grief and reverence, thousands of workers and other mourners accompanied Mariátegui's casket, draped with a red flag, to Lima's municipal cemetery. The Peruvian activists waiting in Santiago had missed the chance to confer with Mariátegui about the future of their divided movement. Magda remembered how disappointed they were at the time. It seemed to her, looking back, that a crucial opportunity had been lost: "If Mariátegui had arrived, if he'd been able to meet with us, it's possible he would have united us and created a new atmosphere, with new political perspectives . . . and the course of Peru's history might have been changed."

Following the ouster of Leguía in a bloodless coup later that year, the far-flung Peruvian exiles began returning to the country. Magda returned several weeks after the collapse of Leguía's regime. "The country was in crisis," she recalled, "in total disarray. . . . The masses, especially the lumpen, were an unleashed whirlwind demolishing everything in its path. The actual time of Leguía's downfall was terrible." It was not, however, the unrest of the impoverished masses that brought down Leguía's eleven-year rule but the defection of the great landowners, who continued to demand tax breaks, subsidies, more water, and more credit, as if the country were not in the throes of economic collapse. When Leguía asked these wealthy landowners to make sacrifices, they abandoned him, opening the way for a military coup, the so-called revolution by telegram.

In August 1930, Lieutenant Colonel Luis M. Sánchez Cerro deposed Leguía merely by announcing his intention to do so. Jubilantly cheered by the very people he had once described as "the indolent and lazy rabble," he entered Lima as a liberator. Presenting himself as a champion of the people and perceived by many of Lima's mestizo residents as "a *cholo* like us," the rugged, battle-scarred military man quickly consolidated mass support by suspending evictions, abolishing forced labor on the roads, and enacting a number of other popular measures. He also granted the great landowners the favors that Leguía thought unaffordable.

Despite his relief measures, the new strongman could not control an unruly urban populace. Mobs sacked and burned the houses of prominent Leguía supporters as an emboldened press rushed to detail the corruption and despotic methods of the autocrat, in power for more than a decade. His modernizing achievements forgotten, Leguía himself was nearly murdered by an irate crowd. Arrested and imprisoned in a dank cell on San Lorenzo Island, the former ruler came to a pitiable end. Only belatedly receiving treatment for a painful prostate condition, he weighed a mere sixty-seven pounds at the time of his death in prison, February 6, 1932.

Following events from his exile in Berlin, Haya de la Torre urged his followers to return immediately to Peru and begin organizing to counter the growing influence of Peru's Communist Party—none other than Mariátegui's Socialist Party, which, after a bitterly contested name change, was now openly affiliated with the Soviet Union and the Communist International. In the final months of Mariátegui's leadership of the Socialist Party of Peru, and for a good while before that, Eudocio Ravines had played a central role as Mariátegui's confidant, all the while operating as a secret agent of the Communist International. Ravines, as it turned out, had been recruited by the Comintern in Paris, going on then to become active in the Paris Aprista cell. By his own admission, made in his memoir, *The Yenan Way,* he had worked successfully as a Comintern agent to move Mariátegui and other Peruvian leftists into the communist sphere. Decades later Ravines would denounce Communism and align himself with the anti-Soviet cold war politics of the United States.

When Magda returned to Peru after three years in exile, she was welcomed by a group of Communist women, including her friend Carmen Saco, the distinguished sculptor Magda had come to know in the *Amauta* circle. In this fluid moment, with APRA founder Haya de la Torre still in Germany, some of the returning exiles wondered if the schism in Peru's Left might still be reparable. It proved not to be. Magda judged in retrospect that the Socialist Party's name change—from *Socialist* to *Communist*—"ruled out any possible fusion of that tendency with the nascent Aprista movement." Those who identified with Aprismo went on to create their own organization. Luis Alberto Sánchez recalled the modest beginnings of the Peruvian Aprista Party (Partido Aprista Peruano, typically referred to in Peru as the APRA).

> Magda Portal, Serafín Delmar, and Julián Petrovick were in Chile, where I witnessed their extreme poverty. With their meager belongings, they traveled third class aboard a rickety boat that followed the coastline to Peru. Luis Eduardo Enríquez was just out of jail. Alcides Spelucín came from Trujillo. Aprismo was a mere handful of people. The night Carlos [Manuel] Cox and I arrived in Lima, the executive committee met, and there was Magda, eager for work and for action. We held clandestine meetings in her rooms in the Pasaje de la Encarnación. . . . We had no official gathering places, no press, and hardly any members.

The participants in these early meetings would soon become prominent leaders in Peru's APRA. Magda described the charter meeting, at which some twelve people were present. They met in a union hall with no electric light and worked by candlelight. "We could barely see to draft the founding document," Magda remembered, "or even to see each other's faces."

Luis Eduardo Enríquez was appointed interim secretary until the official founding on September 21, 1930, of a Peruvian section of the intercontinental APRA movement, at which time Carlos Manuel Cox was appointed general secretary. This organization, it must be emphasized, was initially conceived not as a political party but as a section of an intercontinental movement. Some fifty-five names, including those of Magda, Serafín, Alcides Spelucín, and Luis Eduardo Enríquez, appear on the September 21 charter. More names would be added as more exiles returned to Peru.

According to Luis Alberto Sánchez, "Magda was a woman who took charge, who started things; she was passionate, impetuous." He also found her to be "austere and self-sacrificing as a revolutionary . . . but with a certain touchiness or quarrelsomeness about her, a sometimes excessive belligerence." By the end of 1930, he avowed, "Magda and Serafín were the mandarins of APRA." Continuing his close association with Magda and Serafín was Serafín's brother Julián Petrovick (Oscar Bolaños). All three in the coming years would be imprisoned for their Aprista activities.

The emergence of Peru's Aprista organization coincided with strikes and labor violence in the central Andes. When an official of the Cerro de Pasco Mining Corporation took out a pistol and shot dead a protesting miner, mass demonstrations erupted, leading to further deaths. Violence raged throughout September, October, and November of 1930. As militants in the Communist Party of Peru, former Apristas Esteban Pavletich and Eudocio Ravines now led the miners' fight as workers occupied the mines and took hostage the U.S. manager of Cerro de Pasco. U.S. citizens were hastily evacuated from the region while in Lima a call for a general strike led to widespread work stoppages. As demonstrators thronged the streets marching and singing the Communist "Internationale," the Comintern proclaimed the imminence of the worker-campesino revolution in Peru.

Peru's new strongman had no intention of sitting back and watching the triumph of a revolution in Peru. Sánchez Cerro responded decisively—declaring martial law and outlawing the Communist Party, the APRA, and the National Confederation of Trade Unions, which Mariátegui had successfully organized. By late November 1930, Magda, along with other members of

APRA's National Directorate, including Enríquez and Spelucín, was actively being sought by police. Authorities jailed Carlos Manuel Cox, deported Manuel Seoane to Chile, and officially forbade Haya de la Torre to return to Peru.

During this brief period Magda changed houses some twenty times, often narrowly escaping arrest. Police repeatedly raided her mother's home. But no amount of police power could control the ongoing strikes and labor walkouts. In early January 1931, seven military rebellions occurred within two weeks. All fizzled, and the country remained without viable governance. Acknowledging his inability to establish civil order, would-be strongman Sánchez Cerro departed for Europe, leaving the field free for the Apristas to renew their efforts at building a mass organization, which eventually came to be seen as a political party, but not without a good deal of internal dissension regarding the aims and methods of the Aprista endeavor.

Long before Leguía's ouster, Haya de la Torre had been thinking about running for president in Peru, first in 1928 in Mexico as a candidate of the fugitive and bitterly divisive Partido Nacionalista Libertador, a party repudiated before it even existed, then later, when Haya again made known to his followers his desire to run for president in post-Leguía elections. Magda and a number of others were not enthusiastic; she recalled their resistance to the idea: "'The youngest candidate for Peru's presidency.' That was the idea put forward on a little colored flier that pictured Haya with his arms folded in a frankly Mussoliniesque pose. He sent a number of copies for us to circulate and gauge the response. Personally I thought the whole idea premature and didn't care for it. We made criticisms and argued so strenuously that Haya threatened to resign as leader, which didn't happen."

In 1931, with Leguía incarcerated and a terrific vacuum of power just waiting to be filled, Haya was determined to seek Peru's top office in elections scheduled for later that year. But some in the APRA leadership, including Portal, Cox, and Enríquez, were not happy about what appeared to be a shift away from their own grassroots orientation, as Magda explained: "Haya's wanting us to prepare for elections led to many arguments and various defections in the nascent organization. It was not a question, some of us thought, of engaging in electoral politics. It was about preparing the masses for a continental struggle against the national oligarchies and foreign imperialism." It seems that Magda was no longer the novice unquestioningly following Haya but, along with others, openly criticizing his initiatives. His divisive Plan de México no doubt taught them to be skeptical, wary now of his tendency to cast himself as the maximum leader. The very fact of upcoming elections, however, put tremendous pressure on the Aprista militants to devote themselves to winning a possibly momentous electoral victory. Its young and vigorous leaders therefore set about building an Aprista party. With painstaking attention to detail, they proceeded systematically to organize block by block, going on then to organize at the regional and departmental levels. Magda's presence at the major rallies, she believed, encouraged women to identify with the APRA and also compelled the men to yield on a number of points so as to be sure of her adherence. Her experience provided a contrast with that of the early Soviet women's leaders, Aleksandra Kollantai among others, who fought Lenin (who feared separatism) in order to win the privilege of having a distinct organization devoted to women's concerns. Such an organization, however, was thrust upon Magda: "First there was the Executive Committee.... Later the Women's Command was formed and given to me to head, although I never wanted men and women to be separated. I recall saying, 'The Party is one, there ought not to be separations.' But the men didn't understand this."

In the process of building from the ground up a national organization of Aprista women, Magda established for herself an independent power base and realm of autonomy within the Partido Aprista Peruano. As head of the Comando Femenino (Women's Command) and as national secretary for women's affairs she acquired a permanent seat on the party's National Executive Committee. APRA leader Manuel Seoane described Magda's efforts.

> She went from province to province, persisting in her work, bringing in more and more women until finally the movement became large and important. Her task was to organize the women recruits, to give direction to their specific needs and demands. She held meetings, gave classes, founded brigades to deliver social services. She overcame obstacles and resolved conflicts. She pressed forward, encouraging, leading.... She studied the problems of women, and for the first time in the history of Peru she put forward at the First Party Congress a platform of women's demands.

Drawing on lists of concerns submitted by women representing various regions of the country, the Women's Section drafted a "Declaration of Women's Rights." Composed in a radically egalitarian spirit, this document encompassed many of the points then being articulated throughout the multifaceted women's movement emerging across Latin America. The declaration called for full equality for women before the law, including the right to vote at age eighteen and the right to hold any public post. It called for women to retain independent civil status following marriage and to receive equal pay for equal work. It also proposed a number of general reforms, including the establishment of a minimum wage in accordance with the cost of living; the protection of minors in the workplace; the prohibition of child labor; the secularization of women's prisons; the guarantee of free public education; and the abolition of the diminished status imposed upon persons born outside wedlock, who at the time were forbidden by law to attend certain schools, enter certain professions, or marry without restriction.

The Declaration of Women's Rights was unanimously approved by the First National Aprista Congress. The Aprista position on the women's vote, however, would soon be compromised. Internationally during those years many progressives feared that if women had the vote, especially women in predominantly Catholic countries, they would use that vote to elect reactionaries. In response to this concern, Magda modified the Aprista call for universal women's suffrage, as she explained: "The cultural level of the Peruvian woman, her prejudices, her meek dependence on male influence, often on that of priests, suggests that the women's vote would favor conservative not revolutionary ideas." In discussions concerning the content of Peru's national charter, the Apristas called for restricting the women's vote to "married women, mothers, teachers, professional women, office workers, factory workers, the self-employed, and authors." Magda herself went so far as to declare that "the vote of the woman who works is more valuable than the vote of the woman who lives parasitically." The parasites she alludes to here were not housewives who worked in their own homes, but privileged upper-class women, whom she viewed on the whole as ignorant, indolent, and pampered class enemies.

In later years she distanced herself from this backtracking position on the women's vote, hinting that she had changed her position under duress, having been pressured by her male colleagues: "The women's vote was 'premature,' they said. It was not yet the time. . . . They said that women weren't 'prepared,' that 'first they had to be educated.'" It seems likely, however, that at the time she was persuaded that a full women's vote could threaten their radical agenda.

The Declaration of Women's Rights turned out to be one of the most controversial planks in an Aprista platform that was nothing less than a blueprint for a modern, technocratic, social welfare state. Elaborated in oddly minute detail—a sort of madman's specificity—the platform's many planks left little doubt about the party's revolutionary orientation. Central to the plan—the true cornerstone—was agrarian reform, the breaking up of the enormous haciendas (while offering compensation to owners), and the restoration of these lands to indigenous communities. In addition certain industries were slated for nationalization—an extremely radical proposal. Gold mines, for example, were immediately to be expropriated, while other key industries were gradually to be phased into the public sector. Affirming the desirability of continued modernization—few questioned the wisdom of rapid develop-ment—the platform affirmed that while foreign capital would be welcome, very welcome in Peru, such investment would be subject to regulation in the context of a rigorously anti-imperialist policy toward British and U.S. cor-porations. Also to be carried out were ambitious public works and social welfare programs, including the institution of a social security system, the introduction of progressive taxation, and the undertaking of broad initia-tives in health care and labor relations. Among other reforms, the literacy requirement for voting, which disenfranchised the majority of Peruvians, would be scrapped.

Particularly divisive was APRA's frontal and totally impolitic assault on the Catholic Church. The platform spelled out the Aprista intent to separate church and state, confiscate monasteries, nationalize the clergy, and insti-tute a comprehensive system of free secular education. This incendiary plank horrified traditional Catholics in a country that had never experienced a Protestant Reformation.

From the earliest days of the Spanish colony, the functions of church and state in Peru were very much enmeshed. Church schools flourished on state subsi-dies; church authorities appointed state administrators and were paid salaries out of public coffers. Answerable to no civil authority, high-ranking clergy were free to behave like "medieval potentates." Only by special waiver could a religion other than Catholicism be imparted in Peru, even by a parent.

In colonial days a full-blown Inquisition existed in the country. Barbaric tortures were inflicted on suspected heretics, and lesser infractions against church rules were severely punished. Even women of aristocratic lineage were subject to jailing if caught reading proscribed books. The Peruvian Catholic female ideal was far less the executive, institution-building Saint Theresa of Avila than it was the meek Saint Rosa of Lima, revered for her charitable works but equally famed for the zeal with which she inflicted bodily tortures on herself, employing metal devices rivaling those in Lima's dank, dungeon-like Museum of the Inquisition. Magda viewed the Catholic Church as a formidable obstacle in the way of women's emancipation. "Until age fifteen I was a Catholic but I broke free. I believe that religion is extremely diminishing, especially to women. The Catholic Church has held women back, reined them in, subjugated them, especially in marriage: women must 'obey the husband.' To think I was once married in a church!"

EMERGENCE OF A FEMINIST CONSCIOUSNESS

Although Magda Portal has been described as "the mother of the modern women's movement in Peru," it's worth noting that her activism was not an isolated phenomenon but part of an ongoing concern with women's rights and social betterment. Tentative stirrings of a feminist consciousness became evident in the later part of Peru's nineteenth century when a group of well-educated and generally privileged women came together in literary salons to share their writing and exchange thoughts on current issues. At salons, or *tertulias,* initiated by Argentinean writer Juana Manuela Gorriti in 1876, a typical topic for discussion might have been one or another aspect of "the women's problem." The plight of the Indian was also a concern. Clorinda Matto de Turner, a leading voice in the incipient *indigenista* movement, and Mercedes Cabello de Carbonera, another writer who used fiction to address social questions, were outstanding figures in the constellation of women that became known as the Generation of 1870, the "precursor" generation to that of Peru's early twentieth-century women activists.

In Peru, as elsewhere, the rise of a feminist consciousness coincided with economic modernization. Only with the emergence of an industrial working class—very small in Peru—did factory workers, including women, come together in large numbers to demand reforms. Peruvian women toiled in tobacco plants and in food processing and textile factories, and they were active in the anarchosyndicalist movement. Typically it fell to the women operatives to take responsibility for cultural and humanitarian work, such as setting up lending libraries or arranging assistance for ailing workers and their families. But women also took part in dangerous labor actions. In 1916 a number of women were killed in a labor strike in the port city of Huacho (Mariátegui's birthplace), and women workers, as well as wives and daughters of workers, were militants in the battle to win the eight-hour day.

Two seminal women's organizations came into being in the early decades of the twentieth century. In 1914 María Jesús Alvarado Rivera founded Evolución Femenina. With a membership of mostly professional women, Alvarado's organization fought for years to have women seated on the exclusive Charity Board of Lima, which allotted funding for social welfare projects. Finally in 1922 women won the privilege of being seated on this board, a victory considered a major advance for women's rights in Peru.

In 1924, when the Pan-American Women's conference convened in Lima, one of the main issues was the women's vote. But when María Jesús Alvarado proposed broadening the agenda with a call for women's full equality before the law, the Catholic Women's League objected with such vehemence that Augusto Leguía responded first by jailing then exiling Alvarado, removing from the scene a major figure in Peru's social struggles.

It might be expected that traditional Catholic women would be conservative on women's rights. But many others, including some progressive women, resisted calls to improve women's status. Some feared the unknown consequences of any change, while others were simply not convinced that women were intelligent enough to be able to function on an equal level with men, fearing that "their delicate brains might be damaged by the impact of ideas too large for their minds to hold."

Peru's entrenched racism presented yet another obstacle to women's rights, as observed by Francesca Miller in her outstanding study, *Latin American Women and the Search for Social Justice.* She cites U.S. suffragist Carrie Chapman Catt, who visited Peru as a representative of the Pan-American Woman Suffrage Alliance. "We had heard much about conditions in Peru before our arrival. Everyone predicted failure. The organizing difficulty was a wholly new one. . . . All the university women, doctors, etc., are not only middle class but mostly of decidedly mixed blood. The pure Castilian woman would die before she moved equally herself with those of color." As Miller concluded, "In Peru there were few claims to the sisterhood of all women."

Founded by Zoila Aurora Cáceres, another significant women's organization appeared in 1924. Membership consisted of educated women of Peru's middle and upper sectors. An outstanding figure in the battle for women's rights, including the vote, Cáceres went on to organize women workers—notably, in 1931, Lima's telephone operators and the seamstresses in state-run workshops—into trade unions. In her writings of 1933 Magda singled out for mention a number of women leaders of the recent past, including María Jesús Alvarado, Dora Mayer de Zulen, and Miguelina Acosta Cárdenas. She acknowledged Cáceres but failed to appreciate her pioneering efforts. She ignored her union organizing, choosing instead to deride Cáceres's educated followers as being "upper-class women with no ideology beyond winning the vote." This dismissal exemplifies Magda's polemical stance toward suffragists, whose single-issue concern for the vote she denounced as self-centered and insensitive to the extreme poverty of most Peruvian women. But such off-hand dismissal of Cáceres's work was unreasonable and may hint at a partisan rivalry: Cáceres's highly effective labor organizing may have competed with Aprista efforts to expand its base in the trade union movement.

As the APRA women's leader, Magda addressed her recruiting efforts to factory women, to campesinas, and to women in Peru's tiny middle sectors—teachers, secretaries, and other white-collar workers. Peru's middle sectors at this time represented a small but growing proportion of the population, by some estimates a mere 4 percent. Women in the upper reaches of these middle sectors—including those with degrees in such male-dominated fields as medicine and law—were also targeted as potential APRA members. From all these sectors would be drawn the women's base of the Partido Aprista Peruano. Magda called upon women—with or without the vote—to become actors in the unfolding drama of building a modern Peruvian nation.

ELECTORAL FRENZY

In 1931 as Adolf Hitler's Nazi movement rapidly gained new adherents in Germany, Haya de la Torre remained in Berlin. Fearing for his physical safety, some of his followers urged him to remain abroad until conditions stabilized in Peru. He apparently did not object to his Aprista comrades drafting the platform in his absence. Magda recalled his writing them, "What could be more democratic than that you in Peru should draft the platform and present it to me in completed form?" Haya planned to return, she recalled, when they had successfully mobilized a mass movement. Later that year, when Haya arrived in New York City on the luxury liner *Bremen,* purportedly he had in his luggage a silken presidential sash he had had fashioned for himself in Paris.

Finally, in July 1931, after eight eventful years in exile, Víctor Raúl Haya de la Torre returned to Peru. Wildly cheering crowds welcomed him as he disembarked in Talara on Peru's north coast, site of oil fields and refineries owned by International Petroleum, a subsidiary of Standard Oil. With tears streaming down his face, Haya reportedly knelt and kissed the ground, promising that one day they would nationalize "this great wealth of Peru. . . . I swear it, *compañeros*." From Talara Haya traveled on in a triumphal procession from town to town, enthusiastically welcomed at every stop on the way to Lima.

Haya's extraordinary charisma made it almost inevitable that a full-blown cult of personality—with messianic overtones—would become an integral part of the Aprista Party of Peru. Among an increasingly large number of devoted followers, he enjoyed the status of a demigod. As Magda recalled, Haya promoted self-magnification as a political strategy, pointing to the success of Zapatismo in Mexico. "To go up against Sánchez Cerrismo, Haya said, we urgently needed *hayismo*."

Some of the other leaders—including Magda—were wary of this personalist strategy; they were not even fully convinced that APRA should become embroiled in electoral politics. In August 1931, several weeks after Haya's homecoming, Carlos Manuel Cox, secretary-general of the Aprista Party, bluntly stated that their organization "was founded on principles considered sacred and not amenable to compromise; it was not simply a group of people united around a transitory electoral battle." Despite their differences with Haya, these leaders eventually deferred to the undisputed founder and head of the Aprista movement. As Luis Alberto Sánchez perceived it, the APRA in those early days was "a singular mix of puritanism and bohemianism . . . of solidarity and arrogant *caudillismo,* of altruism and megalomania, of humanitarianism and hardness." Never resolved but only set aside, the contradictory impulses within APRA would contribute to shaping Peru's history over several decades.

The party platform awaited Haya's signature. After reviewing it, the leader took issue with a number of points. Magda recalled the episode.

> "No, this is impossible!" he said. "You've got far too many expropriations here—even the Gildemeisters!" The Gildemeisters owned one of the largest haciendas on the north coast, covering three administrative districts. "If we go that far, agriculture will be destroyed." It seemed to him that a number of points were far too revolutionary to be put forward at that time when so many interests were united against us. He made his case to the party leaders. Any attempt to expropriate the immense landholdings, he insisted, would end in catastrophe—the powerful would resist and our options would disappear. Those of us who had drafted the program were disappointed but we weren't the majority. We had to listen to reason and leave for another day the grand ideas and sweeping actions.

Even with some of its radical points moderated, the APRA platform was generally viewed as a revolutionary program, one its framers believed could be carried out. Many thought that Haya de la Torre had an excellent chance of heading the first democratically elected revolutionary government in Latin America, a hope not entirely fanciful in that a number of military men sympathized with APRA's goals and conceivably might step forward to defend with arms an Aprista administration. At the same time, the feared northern colossus—in the grips of the Great Depression, with its bread lines and hunger marches, and facing a militant anticapitalist movement—might prove too preoccupied with its own problems to interfere in Peru.

Exponentially, the APRA gained new members. On August 23, 1931, in a major speech detailing the Aprista plan to transform Peru, Haya addressed more than thirty thousand people—one-quarter of Lima's population—assembled in the Plaza de Acho, Lima's immense bullring. According to historian Fredrick Pike, an elaborate pageantry was devised for the event. Horns honked, white handkerchiefs waved, hands in thunderous unison clapped the Aprista slogan—*Solo el aprismo salvará al Perú*—(SE-A-SAP)! (Only Aprismo will save Peru!) Following the singing of the Aprista hymn to the emotive tune of the French revolutionary anthem, "La Marseillaise," Haya appeared before the crowd flanked by his honor guard, who were "attired in blue shirts—symbolically [he was] the sun in the midst of the blue sky." Throughout Haya's mesmerizing three-hour talk the emotion in the arena was overwhelming. If, as Mariátegui believed, Peru lacked the Mediterranean spirit of luminosity and joy, it seems that Haya imported enthusiasm, a truly Dionysian exultation. This highly orchestrated spectacle transported the crowd.

During his time in the Soviet Union as well as in Germany, Haya closely observed the techniques by which great crowds were swayed, in Berlin making it a point to observe Hitler addressing his followers. Haya repudiated the Nazi leader's politics—especially his views on race purity—but he frankly admired Hitler's confident leadership style. At the Nazi rallies Haya noted the ritual elements that so powerfully moved mass audiences, later incorporating some of these features into the APRA, mingling mythic and political themes in such a way that Aprismo came to resemble a religious crusade. Even leaders who initially resisted Haya's candidacy—Magda, in any case—hastened to strengthen and spread the cult of the anointed leader.

APRA now presented itself as undertaking a momentous class struggle against a local neocolonial elite in league with foreign imperialists. As this aggressive rhetoric flooded the campaign, members of Peru's oligarchic elite looked to the other main candidate, failed strongman Lieutenant Colonel Luis Sánchez Cerro, now back in Peru. They looked to him despite their distaste for him; they did not care for the coarse manners of this career soldier who spoke crudely and was known to slap his subordinates if they annoyed him. In addition to which Sánchez Cerro was not exactly white but "a dark-skinned *cholo* who was even suspected . . . of having a few drops of Negro blood." Also not to the liking of Peru's oligarchs, Sánchez Cerro campaigned as a populist. Yet, as historian Fredrick Pike has concluded, Peru's elite had little choice but to support the scrappy colonel: "The defenders of the established order, for whom male domination and white supremacy constituted the essential and eternal order of things, saw Aprismo as the gravest menace Peru had ever confronted."

To displace rule by oligarchic elites, the APRA proposed a "functional democracy" to be organized along corporatist lines, that is, according to primary spheres of economic activity. From such natural, work-related groupings a rational rule by technocrats would then emerge. How parliamentary debate or elections might fit into this vague scheme remained to be seen and was not an overriding concern.

With Marxist terms radically peppering their discourse, the Aprista militants were widely viewed as communists, leading some APRA leaders to tone down their threatening rhetoric in the interests of winning votes. Haya himself sought out corporate and governmental leaders in London and New York and in private attempted to assure them he had moderated his views regarding Yankee imperialism. As U.S. ambassador to Peru Frederic Dearing recounted in a confidential government memorandum to Washington, Haya had informed him that U.S. interests in Peru had "nothing to fear" from the APRA. In Ambassador Dearing's judgment, the APRA was of a liberal bent and would initiate a period of stability if it came to power. If such assurances on Haya's part were known at the time to his colleagues, they would most likely have been interpreted as acceptable stratagems meant to disarm a potentially fatal U.S. opposition.

With the Communist Party banned from the race and other parties on the ballot commanding scant attention, Haya de la Torre faced off against Sánchez Cerro in the first mass electoral campaign in Peruvian history. At the turn of the twentieth century in Peru, political parties were tiny elitist concentrations, more akin to exclusive gentlemen's clubs than to the parties now emerging as authentic mass political organizations. The APRA and Sánchez Cerro's Revolutionary Union addressed their appeals to more or less the same social groups—middle sectors, factory workers, and the urban and rural poor.

For the first time, candidates for office campaigned outside Lima, setting out on strenuous trips to take their message deep into the country's hinterlands. Magda's high-profile participation in the Aprista campaign created a sensation. She acknowledged that being a woman gave her a distinct advantage as a campaigner, guaranteeing her an audience wherever she went. She no longer read her speeches from a podium, as before in the Caribbean, but spoke extemporaneously out in the open, standing in bright sunlight or in moist night air. When speaking through a translator, addressing Indians who knew only a few words of Spanish, she and her fellow Apristas, she recalled, always presented themselves as comrades, "never talking down or giving orders." Throughout this campaign it seemed to her that she was participating in something truly new and significant: "For the first time, I think, there was an opening, an opportunity to reach the people, to speak face to face. . . . I've seen the tremendous enthusiasm when we spoke to the people of their sufferings and about the promises written into our party program. The campesinos, always fearful of strangers, would run to meet us."

Her travels extended from the southern desert to remote villages in the high sierra. She visited Cuzco, Arequipa, Puno, Piura, and numerous small towns and villages along the way, traveling from Tacna in the south, near Chile, to Tumbes, near Ecuador, on the north coast—in the process becoming far more familiar with her native land. She visited hospitals and schools of indescribable squalor. She saw "sickly, neglected children being auctioned in the weekly market to be taken to work as servants in the capital." She saw local jails where country people were imprisoned with their entire families, guilty only of having been witness to the theft of an animal or some other valuable.

These extensive travels in Peru made a lasting impression on the campaigner herself, as well as on some who heard her talk. In the Valley of Paucartambo, in the mountainous vicinity of Cuzco, as a friend told her, "time is measured by the arrival of Magda Portal, who bore a message of hope for a better life." Sometimes the Indian women ran to greet her, welcoming her with their few words of Spanish: "Señor APRA, no? APRA—justicia!" Accompanied by two male campaigners, one of them veteran labor leader Arturo Sabroso, she traveled by car over primitive roads winding through hazardous mountain terrain. Magda later described her visit to Piura on the far north coast.

I spoke all over the region, with many people arrayed against us. We arrived in a town and went straight to the auditorium. A deathly silence greeted us. No applause, nothing. The socially prominent sat below. The atmosphere was tense, seething with anger. The audience included socialists as well as supporters of Sánchez Cerro. I usually went last, after a number of *compañeros* had spoken. "I would like to address my remarks to those in the balcony, not those below," I began. The poor people sat in the balcony. I spoke of our poverty and of the well-heeled politicians with money to burn on their campaigns. I talked for about forty minutes and at the end they burst into applause. I then walked out unharmed in a long line of people. Our tires were slashed but that was all.

In Cuzco she spent an entire month preparing the ground for Haya's arrival; she spoke to union groups, to crafts guilds, to all sorts of organizations, tirelessly attempting to win people to the Aprista cause. Finally they felt ready, with sufficient support to summon Haya. "I sent a telegram: 'Come now, we're ready for you.' So Haya arrived with his entire entourage and we had a magnificent demonstration. All to the good. We walked at the very front of the march. Sometimes people jeered, or a bullet might zing past Haya, but mostly the worst that happened was that people threw a few stones." As the campaign progressed, Magda and her companions became accustomed to moving about in an atmosphere of extreme tension. Although personally she encountered no real violence on the campaign tour, this electoral battle on the whole proved to be one of the ugliest and most violent in Peru's history. Sánchez Cerro became the object of crude personal attacks by Aprista rhetoricians; he was compared to an ass that aspired to become a horse; he was denounced as illiterate, neurotic, an advanced paranoiac. Nor did Aprista propagandists eschew obscene graphics, having produced a handbill depicting Sánchez Cerro's mother in sexual congress with a pig. Apristas also attacked the opposition candidate for receiving support from Lima's *cholo* street vendors, an impolitic slur against low-income mestizos that belied the party's vaunted regard for the indigenous and urban poor.

Even worse: drive-by assassins in Lima gunned down more than twenty of Sánchez Cerro's supporters. Although Haya de la Torre repudiated this bloodshed—which he blamed on undisciplined supporters—the killing did not stop. Apristas also died in the pervasive campaign violence.

Peru's elections in the past had been notoriously corrupt, with armed thugs stealing ballot boxes and intimidating election officials; the upcoming contest, however, promised to be the first fair election in Peru's history. Mechanisms were being put in place to secure a rigorously monitored vote and a scrupulous count of the secretly cast ballots. Excitement mounted among Haya's followers with the approach of election day: October 11, 1931. But when the votes were in and the results tabulated, Haya de la Torre, to the surprise and bitter disappointment of his followers, was not the victor but had gone down to defeat by a substantial margin. It was widely assumed that the count was fraudulent. Many Apristas, including Magda, were indignantly convinced and would always be convinced that this crucial election had been stolen from them. The legitimacy of Sánchez Cerro's presidency remained in doubt.

In an atmosphere of intensifying civil unrest, certain Apristas began conspiring with dissident military and police units, and a number of hastily planned and abortive uprisings took place in the weeks immediately following the October voting. Civil order further deteriorated as an agitated year drew to a violent close. On Christmas Eve in the coastal city of Trujillo, shots rang out, fired into Haya de la Torre's car as the leader arrived at a midnight political meeting. Haya escaped without injury, but Sánchez Cerro's police broke up the gathering, brutally dispersing the crowd, which included women and children, and arresting a number of Apristas.

Viewed by his followers as "the moral president of Peru," Haya was now subject to ongoing police surveillance. Daily he attended sessions of the parliament so as to provide leadership for the Aprista bloc. This group consisted of some twenty APRA leaders, including Luis Heysen, Luis Alberto Sánchez, Alcides Spelucín, Carlos Manuel Cox, Manuel Seoane, and labor leader Arturo Sabroso. The Aprista parliamentarians proposed a number of radical reforms, but they stubbornly refused to compromise or enter into coalitions with other parties—hence their ambitious program remained on the drawing board.

As the year 1932 began, the political atmosphere in the capital remained tense. The government's Christmas Eve attack in Trujillo engendered sympathy for the Apristas even as their representatives in Parliament faced increasing hostility from other parliamentarians, who viewed them as noncooperative and obstructionist.

Frustrated, provoked, the legitimacy of his presidency still not established, President Luis Sánchez Cerro now lost patience with constitutional government. In the first week of February 1932, his police agents surrounded the homes of several Aprista legislators, who made frantic calls from their besieged houses to their colleagues in the parliamentary assembly. The ensuing protests were able to stave off their arrests, but not for long. On the last day of

February, Sánchez Cerro's government ruled to expel not just some but all the Aprista members of Parliament, jailing some and deporting others. This stunning development led to partisan outrage. Within a week, in an atmosphere of crisis and impending dictatorship, an Aprista gunman committed a terrorist crime, one that contributed to plunging Peru into civil war. As Magda and Serafín were centrally implicated in this event, the episode marked a turning point in their lives.

SIXTEEN BLACK MONTHS

In the early months of 1932 Magda was working openly as head of APRA's Women's Command, while Serafín directed, the party's official journal, APRA, to which Magda contributed articles. Serafín's salary and the money Magda earned for her journalism helped maintain the household they shared with Magda's mother in the San Isidro district of Lima. This interlude of relative stability for the couple and Gloria ended abruptly when an eighteen-year-old Aprista militant named José (Pepe) Melgar Márquez shot and seriously wounded President Sánchez Cerro as he emerged from a church in suburban Miraflores. "The government," Magda said, "believed this assassination [attempt] was plotted in my home." Apparently this allegation was well founded. Graciela, Magda's half-sister, then thirteen, experienced the traumatic raid of the family apartment on Sunday, March 6, 1932: "I heard a loud knock at the door, which I opened, and some thirty to forty armed men burst in waving their pistols. They arrested Serafín and would have taken Magda, but she happened to be out. The *compañeros* found her and warned her not to go home. Later the *compañeros* came back and took away Gloria. I was left by myself. Terrified, I hid under the bed until my mother returned home." A law had recently been enacted making a number of broadly defined political acts treasonable and punishable by death—an extreme response to the escalating deterioration of civil order in the country. In the space of a week, a hastily convened court martial heard testimony and pronounced verdicts in the attempted assassination case.

As reported in the Lima newspaper *El Comercio,* Melgar Márquez stated at his court martial that on the Sunday preceding the assassination attempt, he had been at a meeting in Magda and Serafín's apartment, at which time he disclosed his intent to kill the president. Also present, he said, besides Serafín and Magda, were Juan Seoane and poet Catalina Recavarren; he specified all by name. He went on to say that Serafín had favored his plan and suggested that he (Melgar) submit a letter of resignation from APRA before taking any action. Melgar Márquez's testimony did not just amount to a confession of his own role in events; he incriminated his friends, which Serafín would not do.

As reported in the press, Serafín Delmar appeared exhausted at his court martial, his face creased and drawn with anxiety, as if he had not slept. He testified that Melgar Márquez had informed him that an assassination of the president was being plotted but without specifying who was to carry it out. He also testified that he advised Melgar Márquez to tell the would-be assassin to resign from the APRA.

Within a week the military tribunal announced their verdicts: Melgar Márquez was pronounced guilty of the actual shooting and Juan Seoane of inciting the act and providing the gun. Both were sentenced to death. Serafín, who was charged with knowing about the plot and taking no action to prevent it, was pronounced guilty of conspiracy and sentenced to twenty years. It was generally thought by Serafín's Aprista comrades that he received this heavy sentence because he refused to incriminate his friends.

The harsh sentences handed down by the tribunal were met with widespread shock and revulsion. Even those parliamentarians who had voted in favor of the death penalty for a range of political acts did not want it carried out in these cases. Apristas along with other supporters mounted an all-out campaign for clemency. From her various hiding places Magda participated in these urgent efforts on behalf of the condemned men. Sufficient pressure was brought to bear that the parliament passed a resolution urging the badly wounded president to reduce the sentences.

During their first harrowing weeks in prison, Seoane and Melgar Márquez went to bed each night fearing they might face a firing squad at dawn. Although Serafín had not been sentenced to death, his friends nonetheless feared for his life, so dire was the mood in the capital. In April 1932, the still-convalescent Sánchez Cerro emerged from seclusion to announce that the death sentences would be commuted to life terms. But Serafín's sentence remained unchanged—twenty years to be served in the bleak red-brick Panóptico, the men's penitentiary in Lima. Serafín's brother Julián Petrovick, also convicted of taking part in the conspiracy, would be sent to Satipo, a particularly feared prison in the Amazonian jungle.

Serafín began serving his sentence in solitary confinement, which went on for months with some time spent in the prison infirmary. Eventually he was permitted to receive visitors. As reported by Magda's sister Graciela, Magda's mother became the conduit for the passionate letters exchanged by Magda and Serafín, a correspondence that has been lost. Gloria also visited the prison, accompanied by her grandmother.

Vowing to "pulverize Aprismo," Sánchez Cerro launched a systematic attack on the APRA, whose leaders and other militants were forced to live on the run. Many were tracked down and jailed. Magda continued to escape arrest, taking refuge for several weeks in the home of a great aunt in Chorrillos, a resort town on the Pacific coast.

In May 1932, Haya de la Torre's clandestine whereabouts in the home of a friend in seaside Miraflores became known to authorities, leading to his arrest and incarceration in the Panóptico. The leader had been sought as a subverter of public order, thus potentially eligible for the death penalty under the draconian Law of Emergency then in force. Alarm raced among Haya's supporters, who feared that the leader might be executed at any moment. In the panic and confusion following Haya's jailing, an Aprista-led mutiny broke out aboard a naval vessel in Callao Harbor. This uprising was quickly suppressed, and eight young sailors were arbitrarily selected to stand trial. Summarily convicted, the sailors were executed by firing squad within an hour of their sentences being handed down. These highly publicized executions horrified many in the populace and greatly contributed to APRA's growing sense of itself as a party destined to produce victims and martyrs.

Held in solitary confinement in the Panóptico, in a cell with only two small vents providing light and air, Haya de la Torre began suffering stress-induced ailments, including recurrent bouts of colitis. As the strain worsened and fears for his life intensified, his supporters, including Magda, mobilized international support on his behalf. Renowned figures such as Upton Sinclair, Sinclair Lewis, Jane Addams, Waldo Frank, Miguel de Unamuno, and José Ortega y Gasset sent letters urging that Haya's safety be guaranteed. The American writer Carleton Beals drafted the protest sent by the American Civil Liberties Union. A plea even came from Albert Einstein. In solidarity with the jailed leader, the Mexican government broke diplomatic relations with Peru.

By July, as execution of the APRA chief appeared imminent, the distress among his followers became excruciating, precipitating a disastrous uprising in Trujillo. In ferocious street fighting, APRA forces seized control of the city, an Aprista stronghold on the north coast. Workers from nearby sugar plantations joined the rebellion, as did many Aprista women, who built barricades, carried munitions, and cared for the wounded and dead. Initially the government forces were overwhelmed. But reinforcements were called in, and the air force strafed the city, rapidly clearing the streets so that soldiers could move through them, quelling the insurrection.

In a chaotic retreat, the Aprista rebels murdered a number of their captives, among them high-ranking military men being held in the local garrison. The gruesome mutilation of these officers' bodies—one was castrated, another's heart was cut out—infuriated Sánchez Cerro's forces. The enraged soldiers then perpetrated a historic massacre. In a savage house-by-house search, arrests were made of anyone seen as even remotely suspicious, above all any person whose hands showed signs of powder burns. Countless bystanders were swept up in this dragnet. Transported to the nearby ruins of the indigenous city of Chan Chan, the arrestees were summarily shot, their bodies tumbling into the ancient ditches, where they remained, abandoned to the rats and buzzards. For months the stench of decaying corpses carried into Trujillo. It was too dangerous to attempt retrieval of the bodies. The estimated number of casualties ranged from a conservative count of two thousand to a high Aprista claim of six thousand dead. When Carleton Beals visited Chan Chan several years after the massacre, he stumbled upon skulls and scattered human bones. Among the participants in the Trujillo insurrection, Beals wrote, were indigenous farmers whose lands had been expropriated by the bishop of Trujillo. "The Indians, having exhausted every legal recourse, [had] refused to pay [rent on their own lands], rioted, and were put down by the army. The leading rebels were thrown off the estate, losing all their worldly possessions; the others were locked up nightly in the hacienda church and taken out each morning to toil." Among these were the native farmers who joined the Trujillo rebellion, and when it failed, Beals said, "some twenty were brought down to Chan Chan and shot by the army."

Aprista uprisings simultaneously broke out in the cities of Huaraz, San Lorenzo, and Cajamarca. Huaraz was captured, but Aprista forces were not able to hold it. Eventually every instance of armed APRA rebellion was put down, leaving behind corpses and injured participants. As Magda reported, "Women too were among the tortured and killed. Women's capacity to endure suffering culminated in those sixteen months in which a black cloud of hatred and bloodletting seemed to engulf our country." Apristas by the thousands were jailed, and Santo Tomás Women's Prison built a new wing to accommodate Aprista women prisoners.

Out of the savagery of the Chan Chan massacre and the ruthless suppression of APRA that followed, there emerged a new image for the APRA party, whose own bloody crimes were as if expiated many times over by the magnitude and ferocity of the government-inflicted violence. APRA now presented itself as a party of victims and martyrs, which indeed it was, all the while rejecting any responsibility for having themselves provoked the military repression by their own violent aggressions and noncooperation with governance. Throughout these months, support for the APRA remained widespread and highly visible, as Carleton Beals observed. "Frequent pilgrimages are made to martyr graves. . . . Everywhere houses are daubed with signs; even high Andean precipices have been carved with gigantic letters: APRA. Desert plants, set out on high arid sands, spell APRA. On the Argentinean beach I saw a lean dog branded on the side: APRA. Propaganda enthusiasm can go no further." Reorganized along lines of a strictly vertical, even military, chain of command, the APRA acquired aspects of a religious brotherhood, one identified with the early Christians in the Roman catacombs. Historian Jeffrey Klaiber suggests that the APRA embraced Christian iconography and metaphor in such a way that the movement succeeded—despite its initial hostility toward the Roman Church—in reconciling revolutionary aspirations with Catholic belief, at least for many Apristas who were practicing Catholics. This was a substantial achievement. Aprismo's use of religious metaphor, Klaiber thought, "paved the way for an emergence of a social Christianity long before most Peruvian churchmen began to think in those terms." This dimension of Aprismo indeed anticipated the liberation theology movement of later decades.

Although Magda did not participate in the Trujillo uprising, she was deeply affected by it and by the persecution that followed. She commemorated the massacre in a partisan poem titled "Aprismo," penned in a declamatory style.

> a p r i s m o
> 6,000 crosses mark your history
> your finest pages drenched in blood
> the tears of children and humble women
> engrave your glory
> a p r i s m o
> untold suffering has shaped your heroic tale
> so far you've brought us exertion and martyrdom
> yet we who believe in you therefore love you
> knowing there's no redemption without pain without Christs.

Still actively sought by the police, Magda remained in hiding, her appearance variously disguised—she dyed her hair black—as she moved from one safe house to another. Typically she stayed no more than a week in any one place. An effective organizer even in adverse circumstances, Magda as a fugitive maintained contact with the other leaders and with women's organizations. She helped mobilize Aprista women to collect food and clothing for jailed comrades. She used a portable press to print leaflets, fliers, and manifestos, as well as the party's official newsletter, which appeared on small slips of paper that passed from hand to hand.

During this episode she assumed the post of APRA's secretary general; but not even that elevated status assured her of consistent support from her comrades. She sharply criticized Aprista leaders in Cuzco who failed to arrange for her accommodation in a safe house. Once she spent the night standing motionless in a field, held at bay by wild dogs. Another night she slept in a ditch. Sometimes Aprista sympathizers among the police warned her in advance of impending raids. Sometimes she arrived at a promised refuge only to be sent away immediately, with no place to go. During these months, she experienced loneliness, isolation, even betrayal, as well as many instances of solidarity. Certain of these episodes are dramatized in her autobiographical novel, *La trampa*. Such desperate conditions, she observed (in her narrator's voice) brought out the worst in people but also the best. The Aprista women, she believed, kept the party going throughout the most grueling months of Sánchez Cerro's persecution: at great risk to themselves and their families, women opened their humble homes on the city's edge to fugitives urgently in need of shelter; these homes were also centers for the distribution of Aprista literature.

Among the individuals who risked arrest to protect those in hiding was Magda's own mother, Rosa Moreno. Following the attempt on Sánchez Cerro's life, police raided the family apartment, confiscating a number of personal items, including Magda's correspondence, which was not recovered. After the initial raid on their apartment, Rosa immediately began moving from house to house, typically spending only two weeks at a residence before Aprista comrades would appear at the door to tell her she had to leave at once. So intense was the nervous strain, her youngest daughter, Graciela, developed a persistent, uncontrollable trembling. It was reported in the press that Gloria had been tortured, her arm broken during interrogation. It is not clear, however, that Gloria was ever taken into police custody. But rumors flew. During these difficult months, Aprista friends helped take care of Gloria, and it's possible that the child was able to see her mother.

At one point Magda's family took refuge in an abandoned factory. In the basement the Apristas had installed a printing press, and late at night they ran off fliers—until the police became aware of the site and raided it. According to Magda, the entire family was arrested. "They took my mother, my married sister [Amelia], who was ill, my other sisters [Juana and Graciela], and Amelia's two children. The notorious [Damián] Mústiga, head of Leguía's political police, was still in power. At the police station the prefect ordered the release of everyone in the family except my mother, who was detained by order of Mústiga himself. She was then moved to Santo Tomás Women's Prison, jailed for the crime of having refused to reveal her daughter's whereabouts."

For six months Rosa Moreno remained incarcerated, sequestered behind the massive walls of Santo Tomás, formerly a monastery. Despite prison rules, the mother superior allowed Graciela to remain with her mother, even permitting the girl to come and go to and from the prison to attend school. When later asked how her mother coped with this situation, Graciela emphasized her mother's forbearance: "She often wept. Yet it could have been worse. The nuns were the prison guards and were good-hearted women, part of a congregation. . . . But my mother was interrogated many times. 'Where is Magda?' the police asked. She wouldn't answer. 'They will kill me,' she said, 'before I tell them where my daughter is.'"

In late August 1932, Peru found itself on the brink of war with Colombia, its neighbor to the north. A contingent of armed Peruvians—acting on their own initiative—had boldly invaded the Leticia port region, an Amazonian territory recently ceded by Peru to Colombia. Many Peruvians saw this transfer of territory as an outrageous giveaway—the unacceptable result of a botched treaty negotiation. Despite substantial pressure to send regular army troops to back up the freelance occupiers, President Sánchez Cerro hesitated. Still hiding and on the run, Magda nevertheless managed to organize resistance to this threatened war. The APRA Women's Command—"liberated from absurd patriotic prejudices"—issued a document calling for a peaceful settlement of the conflict. Circulated in the Latin American press, the statement closed with fighting words: WAR IS THE PERPETUATION OF TYRANNY! WAR UPON WAR AND TYRANNY!

The APRA maintained contradictory positions on this issue; some (male) Apristas were actually calling for war, attacking Sánchez Cerro as wanting in patriotism, accusing him of failing to act with alacrity to secure the disputed territory. But the Women's Command went its own way, defying the war-mongering calls of men in the APRA leadership. The Aprista women's position on this matter echoed that of Peru's Communist Party.

Throughout these agitated months, Magda's activism evidently did not falter. As APRA leader Manuel Seoane suggestively observed, "She also took part in conspiracies. She carried out dangerous missions. She did not rest for a minute. Until the tyrant fell in blood." Seoane alludes here to the assassination of Sánchez Cerro on April 30, 1933. At a military rally at the San Beatriz racetrack in Lima, Peru's strongman-president, having just reviewed troops about to leave for Colombia, was shot dead by an Aprista gunman, who himself was shot and killed at the scene. No evidence has emerged to link Magda to any conspiracy to commit this crime. But there is no question that she rejoiced at the strongman's death.

A distinguished and widely respected military officer, General Oscar Benavides, now took charge of the affairs of state, apparently with Haya de la Torre's blessing. The new ruler sent troops to secure the men's penitentiary, purportedly aiming to thwart a rightist plot to assassinate Haya in his jail cell. Disregarding a constitutional provision barring members of the military from holding civilian office, the parliament confirmed General Benavides as Peru's president, thereby conferring upon his rule a substantial legitimacy. Many hoped he might succeed in restoring order to a country badly disrupted by a de facto civil war.

Proclaiming his intent to establish an era of "peace and concord," Benavides declared amnesty for political prisoners. This amnesty, however, was far from universal. Haya de la Torre was allowed to go free, but not Serafín Delmar, or the other Apristas convicted in the initial attempt on Sánchez Cerro's life, or for that matter any of those convicted of fomenting the Trujillo insurrection.

As violence in the country abated, Benavides, a superbly competent and civic-minded administrator, set about instituting social reforms, many of which were set out in the APRA platform of 1931. But political dialogue in the country was still mired in old hostilities. In a letter of May 22, 1933, to the editor of *La Noche* in La Paz, Magda denounced the hostile rhetoric she saw as dominating contemporary discourse, a rhetoric of hatred that she believed would stymie attempts at reform and plunge the country once again into civil war.

> This hatred is not exactly class hatred—our social classes are too poorly defined to talk of that. But it is hatred, nonetheless, political hatred, erupting in one belligerent group after another, expressed in pseudodoctrinal articles in the daily press and in the discourse of

opposing parties. Unfortunately, the press has played no small part in encouraging this attitude, lending comfort to those who want to be at war. . . . It seems we are still attempting to wash out blood with blood. As those who propagate these hostilities know full well, such tactics are of no use in building a nation, are of no use in attaining justice, civilization, or culture. . . . In the end, recourse to violence is anathema to true democracy.

In closing this letter she called for a return to "the dispassionate rule of law . . . by whose verdicts we should all abide." In Peru, however, constitutional government had fragile underpinnings; rule by law had no aura of sanctity.

THE NEW WOMAN

What—the new woman? Does she really exist?
—*Aleksandra Kollantai, "New Woman"*

During the first heady months of political freedom under Oscar Benavides's rule, Magda resumed her public activities as the APRA's national secretary in charge of Women's Affairs. Aprismo now entered a constructive phase. The party inaugurated a number of widely utilized public services—low cost medical and dental clinics, blood banks, counseling services, community cafeterias. The party sponsored lectures, panel discussions, athletic matches, and chess tournaments. At that time, as Luis Alberto Sánchez recalled, "Magda was very close to Haya, practically his immediate collaborator, above all in 1933."

Focusing on women's education, she worked with the Women's Command to bring into existence—not just in Lima but throughout the country—a series of basic skills classes for women, providing instruction in reading, writing, and sewing. In Lima she promoted lectures on topics of special interest to women; she organized workers' cooperatives and lectured at the popular university; she helped found the League of Revolutionary Writers of Peru, whose membership included Alberto Hidalgo, Serafín, Ciro Alegría, and Esteban Pavletich, among others. As director of the party's Atahualpa Press, she published a series of pamphlets written by Aprista leaders—texts guaranteed to reflect the most current Aprista doctrine. Among these pamphlets was a slender anthology of poems, *Cantos de la revolución,* in which

Serafín dedicated his contribution, smuggled out of prison, to "my little daughter Gloria, witness to great struggles for Social Justice."

Also published in the Atahualpa series in 1933 were two texts authored by Magda Portal, *El Aprismo y la mujer* (Aprismo and Women) and *Hacia la mujer nueva* (Toward the New Woman). Fredrick Pike describes these writings as containing "the most dramatic testimony to the awakening Peruvian feminism to be found in the first half of the twentieth century." In them Magda not only projects an ideal future but also promotes an immediate, partisan goal—allaying fears that weakened support for the APRA party and fostering unity between Aprista men and women. Unity is the overriding theme: nothing is for oneself alone—all is part of a large, revitalizing effort to lift society out of its present ruin.

By means of these writings and in her activism, Magda popularized radical views concerning women's emancipation. Although generally not credited with being an original social theorist, Magda articulated her own blend of views as she adapted socialist-feminist ideas to Latin American conditions of mass poverty and exploitation. In these conditions, she said, woman should not be man's adversary—fighting a separate battle for her own emancipation—but man's teacher and equal partner in the battle for social reform.

Early in her career as an activist she defined herself in opposition to "the feminist," a term she used polemically to distinguish her own approach from that of Peru's upper-class advocates of women's suffrage. In her novel, *La trampa,* the protagonist expresses a scorn for "feminists" that mirrored Magda's own in the APRA party's early days: "Our struggles, comrades, are not based on our sex—a fight that we leave for the 'feminists'; we are fighting for justice for all, because if justice does come for our male comrades, it will come as a consequence for our children and for ourselves. . . . The Party makes no distinction. . . . Men are just as exploited as women. Social injustice weighs equally on both men and women. Hunger, poverty, and wretchedness make no distinction with regard to sex. Our battle is against a society based on privilege and which denies us the right to happiness."

Magda counseled that "the Aprista woman should put forward her ideas about justice and emancipation without hostility toward men and without attributing to men a perverse stubbornness and intolerance toward women." As a free-spirited, divorced woman, Magda might seem an unlikely defender of family values. Yet in these writings—with a newfound deference to prevailing mores—she insisted on the sanctity of motherhood and the centrality of the family as the basic unit of the nation. By no means, she said, did the

APRA encourage women to abandon their households. Any improvement in a woman's status or educational level, she held—far from undermining the family—would elevate both the family and the nation; the Aprista woman would not abdicate her traditional duties; she would only add to these the responsibilities of citizenship.

Magda's insistence in these texts that women were to act as teachers and civilizing influences within the home echoed the approach of women reformers in Peru's nineteenth century. Novelist and social critic Clorinda Matto de Turner advocated education for women on the grounds that women could more effectively teach their sons if they themselves were well educated. It was impolitic then—and remained so in Magda's day—to suggest that education for women might be an end in itself. But the time had come, the women's leader declared, for Peru's women to emerge as distinct, self-actualizing individuals: "The individual woman struggles not only on behalf of her own household, her children, her husband. She also struggles for herself—to secure that space in which her own personality, never before expressed, never before understood, might manifest itself fully, capable of great and noble actions. The struggle of women, then, is much broader and more encompassing than that of men. Women are striving not only for greater economic dignity. . . . They are battling for the right to develop their own personalities." Education—she insisted—held the key to both personal and national development. She observed that Peruvian women, including upper-class women, were miserably undereducated, the vast majority having failed to acquire even a primary education; but a good deal more was wanted than the acquisition of skills in reading and writing. "Education is of the whole person," she affirmed. "Woman's great error consists in her absolute ignorance of her true role in society. Never questioning her supposed inferiority, she blindly accepts her situation." If men behaved despotically in their households, she observed, and if women responded with servility, both were victims of demoralizing values, the heritage of colonialism. She believed that men and women working in partnership could reinvent their social roles and advance together as comrades in the battle for social reform. In this battle, women would exercise initiative in every realm, "acting not as man's adjunct but as his indispensable complement, not dependent on his whims and awaiting his instructions but participating as a conscious, active element in social struggle, with her own issues and with sufficient ability and authority to attain her goals." From their privileged position within the household, she continued, women would play a vanguard role, educating their husbands and setting in motion a revolution that would go beyond economic concerns to bring about profound changes in consciousness.

Conciliating, even equivocating, Magda's 1933 texts and her political activity trod a wavering line. Eager to promote unity, she was equally desirous of confronting social prejudices and addressing women's most urgent concerns. The Women's Command, for example, had a special committee that heard complaints against men in the party. The very existence of such a committee could only have heightened existing tensions—yet women's concerns (at least some of them) were not going to be postponed.

Magda also sought to repair the damage wrought by APRA's menacing stance toward the Catholic Church, as articulated in the 1931 party platform. APRA, she now stated, wished neither to condemn nor to compete with the Catholic Church. Being a secular movement, she explained, the party was neutral with regard to religion. Religion ought to be "strictly a matter of personal conscience, unless, that is, Aprismo wished to convey an impression of being unaware of the sentiments of the majority of its members, women in particular."

However placating she may have been on some points, Magda refused to conceal the truly radical nature of her position, the Aprista position, with regard to women, expressed in the statement "Woman is man's equal, and may even become his superior." This epigraph attributed to Socrates appears in *Hacia la mujer nueva,* in which the following rather provocative statement by Aleksandra Kollantai is also cited: "The new woman is self-disciplined rather than exaggeratedly sentimental. She appreciates liberty and independence, rejecting the submissive role and the effacement of her personality. She has renounced mindless efforts to merge with the man she loves and affirms the right to enjoy earthly pleasures, having rejected the hypocritical mask of 'purity.' Finally she has subordinated the adventure of love to a secondary place in life. Before us we have not a female, not an inadequate copy of a man, but 'an individual woman.'"

Such individuality, Magda warned, should not be an end in itself for the Aprista woman, who should never seek her own fulfillment at the expense of others but always for the betterment of society as a whole. Nor should the Aprista woman seek role models in the films and magazines of the capitalist world. The women's leader repudiated what she called the "Yankee flapper type," a sort of "feminine boy, sportive, agile, bold, unafraid, but uncertain of her direction." She went on to observe that Peru's women were so deficient in role models that they had no choice but to improvise, to reinvent themselves as best as they could under the pressure of unfolding events.

Her historical overview of women's participation in APRA acknowledged that many women suffered because of their membership in the party. Living out new and poorly defined social roles could in itself be painful: "Aprismo is a revolution, especially as it affects women. It uproots woman from one spiritual and social state and places her in another, one unlike anything she has ever known—and opposed to it." Add to that the sheer physical danger of challenging the government, with its police and military forces, and it was clear that adherence to APRA entailed considerable, even mortal risk.

Magda viewed her epoch as one of transition; the women then fighting for reform were intermediate types destined to struggle and sacrifice for the future, their lives distorted by the strain of being constantly in opposition. She might have been describing herself when she wrote the following:

> Partly masculine and partly feminine in spirit, this transitional type is only vaguely defined. She is not, however, subject to the ambivalent mental states experienced by women in decadent civilizations—women who move in the spiritual ambiance of capitalism. The transitional woman is the pure type of the social revolutionary, courageous, energetic, but not sharply delineated in her sexual identity; the feminine is as yet synonymous with weakness, gentleness. Ready to endure any sacrifice, she has no choice but to fight "like a man" and forget she is a woman. But her ambivalence is less strong than that of other modern women. Led by Aprismo, she is moving forward to realize her true place in society, in a world in which one day women will attain their authentic stature as women, and motherhood will be part of that realization.

In a coming era of restitution, she concluded, "the human pair will share the work of sustaining life, continually transcending themselves, each stimulating the other to attain higher spiritual levels, and woman will once again enjoy the status she lost centuries ago." This reference to a virtual golden age, in which women shared power equally with men, suggests that Magda embraced Friedrich Engels's conjectures about the decline of women's status with the institution of private property. Following Engels and Kollantai, Magda insisted that women themselves should assume the responsibility for improving their own situations.

In 1935, in an open letter to Cuban Aprista women, she highlighted the theme of initiative, again calling for the elimination of boundaries that separated potential allies, "whether these be differences between men and women or borders between nations." Praising the heroic efforts of Cuban women in the fight to depose Cuban dictator Gerardo Machado, she challenged women to resist passivity and cultivate impatience. Her open letter was broadcast on Cuban radio and discussed in Aprista committees on the island. She wrote:

> *Compañeras* . . . we are the authors of our own destinies, and by the same token of our own subjection. We create the tyrant. We cannot wait for some inevitable historical progress to bestow upon us the fruits of freedom. . . . We cannot wait for . . . the natural evolution of civilization to attain for us what we've not managed to attain for ourselves. We have to fight for every gain. No one will do it for us. We must start in the Aprista households—it is there we must begin to create the new consciousness that will defeat not only the external enemy . . . but also the despot within—the ignorance, the indolence, the conformity, and that great rash of small vices all of which add up to a formidable obstacle to any progress.

PRISON

Beyond all these bars
freedom awaits us
with open arms.
—*Magda Portal, "Celda no. 2"*

In 1934 Magda set out on a second major speaking tour of Peru. Aiming to recruit additional women into the party, she traveled through the southland before moving north in October into the coastal region, where she drew crowds in the northern towns Zorritos, Lambayeque, Chiclayo, Talara, and, farthest north, Tumbes, bordering Ecuador. Looking back on these travels, she commented that some of the male leaders were allotted travel budgets but that she had managed on her own. "I arrived somewhere, organized a committee, and the newly formed committee paid the fare to my next destination." Customarily, she said, she lodged in cheap hotels or private homes, sometimes very humble ones, simple shacks.

General Benavides's goal of establishing peace and concord remained elusive; the country remained highly unstable. Political parties and military factions continued to vie for power in a disquieting atmosphere of recrimination and protracted crises. Right-wing groups continued to demand that the APRA be outlawed, while Apristas persisted in mounting provocations—disregarding the dangerously volatile situation. APRA unions, for example, staged disruptive strikes while Aprista leaders repeatedly attacked Benavides for failing to schedule elections and refusing to reseat the APRA deputies expelled from Parliament by Sánchez Cerro. APRA's polarizing pronouncements and unwillingness to seek compromise were strongly criticized by those favoring a gradualist, evolutionary approach to social reform. The intensifying unrest culminated in various attempts by Aprista plotters to seize power by force.

In November and December 1934, Aprista-led uprisings took place in Lima and in the central Andean towns of Ayacucho, Huancayo, Huancavelica, Junín, and Cuzco. The Lima uprising, led by retired army colonel César Enrique Pardo, broke out on November 26. Authorities immediately put down this rebellion. Although Aprista forces captured several cities in the interior, as well as several military garrisons—to short-lived jubilation—they could not hold them; the uprisings were quelled.

In years to come, Magda—although not a pacifist—often referred to peace as a transcendent value, especially when nuclear armaments entered the arsenal of available weaponries. But the fact is she did not object in principle to the seizing of power by force, nor did she shrink from the likelihood of deaths, if the loss of life would further the cause of social justice. She even criticized Haya de la Torre for being squeamish about violence. "Revolutions aren't made without bloodshed," she flatly stated. "And Haya couldn't stomach bloodshed." Increasingly, however, she became frustrated by the poorly coordinated military coup attempts by Aprista plotters—bungled attempts that led to mass repression and the outlawing of progressive political parties.

In a late interview, and with fresh exasperation, Magda recalled these "little revolutions" that ended so badly and that she credited with landing her in jail when, as she said, "I was just talking, not inciting revolution." She claimed that those in her group were "absolutely ignorant" of any of these plots to seize power by force. Many died in this new rash of rebellions, in the actual fighting and later by execution. The democratic opening offered by Benavides now snapped shut. Within weeks nearly one thousand Apristas were arrested.

A day or so following the thwarted uprising in Lima, Magda was speaking at a political rally in Chiclayo, a seaside town some four hundred miles north

of Lima. Throughout the "sixteen black months" of Sánchez Cerro's regime
she had managed to evade capture. Now moving about openly, taking advan-
tage of the political toleration the Apristas and other activists had enjoyed
for more than a year under Benavides, she was easily arrested, on November
26, 1934, swept up in a large dragnet. For a week she was detained in a tiny,
vermin-infested jail cell. When finally brought before a local judge, she was
sentenced to five hundred days in prison under the Law of Emergency. No
charges were filed against her; no defense was allowed. Along with a number
of other prisoners she was put aboard a Chilean vessel to be transported to
the port city of Callao. From Callao she would be transferred to the women's
prison in Lima. At the start of her voyage south, as she jumped from the
launch in an attempt to board the Chilean ship—the sea was very choppy—
she slipped and took a bad fall, which gave rise to many rumors: it was said
she had broken a leg; it was said she had been shot. These rumors greatly
alarmed her family.

Once she was on board the Chilean vessel, the captain, an anarchist, offered
to hide his notorious passenger in the ship's hold when they reached the port
of Callao, then transport her on to Chile, an idea she decided against when
the captain informed her that the authorities in Callao were planning to
fumigate the ship in port, to make sure all the prisoners disembarked. "If
I'm going to be poisoned like a rat," she told the captain, "I might as well face
up to the situation and get off at Callao." So she did and, along with other
prisoners, was taken by police escort to the reception room in the former
Spanish fortress El Real Felipe.

Exhausted and clutching her small suitcase, Magda sank into a chair in a
room crowded with waiting people. The subterranean cisterns of this colonial
fortress had been converted into dungeon cells in which a number of Apris-
tas were being imprisoned, including at that time the novelist Ciro Alegría,
who had contracted a serious case of tuberculosis in the dank prison. He was
just then being processed for deportation to Chile; they acknowledged each
other very discreetly as he passed by her. Aprista leaders Luis Alberto Sánchez
and Alcides Spelucín, along with Alegría, would be deported to Chile on the
ship from which Magda had just disembarked.

As the clock ticked, an official behind a desk called out name after name
but never once looked in her direction. The entire morning passed. Finally
in a fog of fatigue Magda demanded attention. "I am Magda Portal," she
announced. Only then did she realize (with profound chagrin) that the offi-
cial had no idea who she was, that she could simply have walked out the

unguarded door and gone into hiding. Having drawn attention to herself, however, she was roughly seized by the arm and led to a back room. What a disaster it would have been, remarked the officer in charge, if she had got away from him.

Later in the day, recovering her spirits, Magda even joked a bit with her captor, who brought her a cool drink. Near midnight, she was transported to the Santo Tomás Women's Prison. There she was admitted into a bleakly lighted room in which haggard inmates, including prostitutes, some groaning, others sobbing, were sprawled on hard benches. Their faces reminded her of a painting by Goya, "each a mask of atrocious suffering." Still wearing the crumpled tailored suit in which she'd been arrested a week earlier, she was greeted by hostile stares. Common prisoners generally did not mingle with the political prisoners. "'Political, right?' said one of the inmates with contempt, since I wasn't one of them. I weakly confessed that, yes, I was a political prisoner. Another woman chimed in, 'That's right, political.' She looked at me with real disgust."

Experiences of the past week had left her badly shaken—the initial shock of arrest, the distressing fall and injury to her leg, the days in jail, then the sickening roll of the ship on the journey to Callao. The first night in prison brought a kind of relief.

> I felt better, more stable. After days of uncertainty and unpleasant surprises and demeaning treatment now I was in a bed with clean sheets, of coarse material but fresh, as if made up especially for me. My mind drifted over the last few days. . . . So much had happened and not a word, complete silence from family and friends. Did they know I was in Lima? Did they even know we'd been arrested or where we were? . . . I thought of my mother, my daughter. . . . I'd never been jailed in Peru, only wanted by the police and in hiding but now. . . . The cell was dark but through the high windows a broad shaft of moonlight fell across the bed, spotlighting my body. I couldn't relax. Suddenly a black form glided through the window—a bat! It swept down, grazing my face, then flew out the window. I screamed and unable to hold back any longer I began sobbing and the tension drained out of me. An enormous weight lifted. . . . That was my first night in prison.

For many months Magda remained in solitary confinement, forbidden visitors as well as reading and writing materials. Eventually a friend, Dr.

Bernardino León y León, a former president of Peru's Superior Court and ex-director-general of Peru's penitentiaries, used his influence with the nuns to improve her situation. Every week he brought her a book, returning a week later to retrieve it and leave another. The nuns allowed this distinguished visitor to speak to Magda without supervision. He brought news of the outside world. The dictatorship, he said, was hardening.

The prison routine included an unvarying three-in-the-morning wake-up call for prayers and an early lights-out at six in the evening. The incessant mumbling of prayers, both voluntary and mandated as punishment, greatly irritated the lapsed Catholic. Eventually the nuns allowed Magda to receive visitors and to enter the general prison population. Her mother came, bringing fresh clothing. Her daughter also visited. As a general rule only women visitors were permitted inside. The wife of one of Magda's friends reported that a nun confided to her that prior to Magda's arrival they were all warned that because of the vicious nature of this particular prisoner they should avoid any unnecessary contact with her. "But we soon realized," the nun said, "that she's a very good person. . . . If only she were not an Aprista."

The nuns also permitted Magda to offer classes to the regular inmates. She taught them songs, wrote little plays to be performed on birthdays, and gave simple lessons on the history and geography of Peru. She explained, for example, that the earth was round, a concept she found hard to get across, since many of the women were without formal schooling and some of them knew only a few words of Spanish. Hoping to improve hygiene in the prison, she successfully petitioned the nuns to set up regular bathing times at the faucet in the prison courtyard.

The mother superior, a tall, heavyset woman of about fifty (who turned out to be the sister of one of Magda's former classmates), sometimes stopped by Magda's cell to discuss politics. She even offered to pray for Haya de la Torre, and sometimes there materialized from the ample sleeves of her habit a loaf of bread still warm from the convent oven.

At a certain point in Magda's incarceration, Aprista women in large numbers began entering the prison population, arrested in the ongoing protests and demonstrations. They brought news of other arrests and rumors of Aprista uprisings that were in the works. As a general rule the political prisoners enjoyed special privileges and were treated with greater leniency than were the other inmates; but some Aprista women, by Magda's account, suffered terrible mistreatment, including beatings that sometimes led to miscarriage or even death.

In prison Magda began writing again; she returned to her poetry and other texts; she also wrote letters that reached the outside world. In a dispatch to the Buenos Aires journal *Claridad,* she expressed an unshaken utopian faith. "I believe and continue to believe that Aprismo is a direct bridge between the present and the future—a trampoline to launch us toward other possibilities, ones more radical, more leftist. Aprismo as an evolving doctrine can transcend itself and become all it is capable of becoming in a future in which class antagonisms exist no more."

Even when imprisoned, Magda generated controversy. Sordid stories circulated. Particularly vulnerable as a woman to smear by sexual innuendo, she was accused of being promiscuous, as she recounted.

> They invented love affairs. Once a newspaper published a photocollage showing me with many faces, each kissing a different party leader. I never saw this doctored photo because I was in jail. I refused to pay attention to that sort of thing. I would have gone crazy if I did, and been much less effective in the struggle.
>
> You see, in this country the first thing they do is attack a woman on sexual grounds. I have to say that even in the Party this same tactic was used to defame women of the upper classes. I disliked that and protested. "Why do we have to attack the honor of women?" I asked them. Even if the accusations were true, that sort of attack is very crude, very low. But the men replied, "The public likes that sort of thing. It wins support." Of course it also worked against us when things were said about Aprista women, especially me. But I never paid attention to what was said about me. Of course, it was also said I was in love with Haya. And not only with Haya but with all the leaders.

This kind of talk reached Serafín Delmar in the men's penitentiary in Lima, and he suffered greatly because of it. As Daniel Reedy recounts, Magda too suffered anxiety occasioned by "difficulties with her imprisoned lover, resulting from malicious innuendos and political jealousies." Throughout her mother's incarceration, Gloria remained with her grandmother. To see her parents, Luis Alberto Sánchez reported, she had no choice but "to go back and forth between prisons." Sánchez remembered one day seeing Gloria, not long before her mother's arrest: "She was playing innocently on a beach near Lima, and in her I saw all the youth of Peru, hardened by cruelties, yet gentled by the same sorrow that in hearts like those of Magda becomes fertile and will rise in new dawns."

Magda's imprisonment became something of a cause célèbre. In Buenos Aires the left-wing journal *Claridad* devoted their October 1935 issue to extolling her "exemplary rebellion" and calling for her release, even though, as one writer observed, the regime in Peru was guilty of far more terrible crimes than imprisoning "our comrade Magda." Her tremendous capacity for work was repeatedly mentioned, as comrades who knew her well chronicled the various facets of her career.

In fact Magda's treatment in prison appears to have been relatively humane compared with what many of the male prisoners in Peru were forced to endure. A double standard prevailed. Nor can Magda's persecution be compared to that suffered by women militants targeted by later regimes in Latin America, particularly in the 1970s and 1980s in Argentina, Chile, Brazil, Uruguay, El Salvador, and Guatemala, in some of which the brutalization included rape, torture with electric cattle prods, even the murder of women activists, including nuns.

Released from Santo Tomás on February 28, 1936, having served all but a few weeks of her five-hundred-day sentence, Magda joined her family in seaside Barranco, where they lived on La Bajada de los Baños, a narrow street descending to the beach. She would soon send an open letter to *Claridad,* expressing her gratitude for the support she had received during her jailing, solidarity from so many comrades all over the continent. "My freedom is not satisfying," she wrote; "in fact it's not real freedom but exists at the whim of police agents. It's even less real when my comrades are jailed, persecuted, or in exile. In countries like mine now, to be at liberty is almost shameful."

Hoping to obviate any resurgence of civil chaos, General Benavides continued to suppress the APRA. Throughout the later 1930s, Peruvian jails were filled to capacity with Aprista prisoners, many of them women. Magda observed in a newspaper article that all these prisoners "were expiating the enormous crime of wanting to live more nobly, of wanting to act more consciously, of wanting to eradicate poverty and end the people's degradation." The party's leaders were jailed, exiled, or on the run. Haya de la Torre continued to live in hiding in Peru. Luis Heysen (formerly a key member of the Aprista cell in Paris) was sought under orders that he be shot on sight. A bounty was offered for the capture of Manuel Vásquez Díaz (formerly of the Aprista cell in Mexico).

As months passed, then years, Serafín Delmar remained incarcerated in the men's penitentiary in Lima. In May 1936, *Claridad* devoted an issue to his situation, as in 1935 an issue had been given over to Magda's. *Claridad* presented a generous sampling of Serafín's poems, stories, and political texts along with tributes to the jailed militant (then in his mid-thirties) by various comrades who referred to their tall, introspective friend in subdued, even somber tones. There seemed little hope that Serafín would be out of prison before his fiftieth birthday. An admirer who had not met the jailed poet before but who managed to spend a few minutes with him under the watchful eyes of a guard came away convinced that imprisonment was inflicting incalculable harm upon the gifted writer-activist. His friends agreed that someone of his particular sensibility could not help but experience the deprivations of prison as the equivalent of being buried alive. His visitors were severely restricted because of official fears of an escape attempt. Luis Alberto Sánchez, who received permission to see his Aprista comrade only after waging a vigorous press campaign, found Serafín somewhat heavier and more withdrawn, but uncomplaining and eager for news that would either "allay or confirm his anxieties." It is possible that some of these unspecified anxieties were related to Magda. Sánchez reported that despite his suffering Serafín had not lost faith—"the faith of an illumined man." Over the years the loyal and effective Luis Alberto helped arrange for the publication of Serafín's extensive prison writings, including his Andean stories, *Los campesinos y otros condenados* (Campesinos and Other Prisoners), which appeared in Chile in 1942.

SECOND EXILE

With a limited scope for political action, yet wanting to do something on behalf of Peru's women, Aprista and Communist women joined forces in Acción Femenina, founded in 1936 by Communist militant Alicia del Prado. Aprista members included Magda, Carmen Rosa Rivadeneyra, and Carmela Yarlequé. Despite her participation in this alliance, Magda did not flourish following her release from prison. Thwarted in her attempts to find paid work, and subject to police surveillance, she continued to live with her family in Barranco. In 1938 she applied for a passport, hoping to be allowed to leave Peru to attend a peace conference, one of the many antifascist activities then being organized on the Latin American continent. When authorities detained her for a week then refused to grant the travel document, she resolved to leave the country without official papers.

In November 1938, her daughter with her, she slipped across the border into Chile, only to be immediately detained by Chilean authorities in the border town of Arica. There she waited while friends in La Paz worked hurriedly to arrange a visa for her to enter Bolivia. Deeply wearied by the trials of this journey, finally in mid-January 1939, she arrived in the Andean city of La Paz. There she was warmly welcomed by old friends but prohibited by Bolivian authorities from speaking in public—even at gatherings organized in her honor. Students protested this prohibition, to no avail. In a short while she was deported to Argentina, at the behest, she believed, of Peru's ambassador to Bolivia.

Arriving in Buenos Aires, mother and daughter were met at the central train station by exiled Peruvian friends who crowded around them on the train platform, eagerly asking news of comrades in Peru. Throughout Central and South America, left-wing cadre of all factions were acutely focused on events in Europe. In 1939 Hitler's army entered Poland, and the Spanish Republic went down to defeat by Generalissimo Francisco Franco's rebel troops, supported by Germany and Italy. Several thousand refugees from Spain's civil war would soon find a haven in Chile, their entry arranged by Salvador Allende, then a Chilean government official.

After a brief stay in Buenos Aires, Magda traveled on to Montevideo, Uruguay, as APRA's delegate to the Congress for World Democracies, a gathering of antifascist activists, including many writers and painters. In a photo taken at this congress she is the sole woman seated at a long, convivial banquet table, at the far end of which can be seen the Chilean poet Pablo Neruda. Luis Alberto Sánchez, commenting on the tension between his own moderate liberal tendency and the ultraleft persuasion to which Magda subscribed, noted that the civil war in Spain united many of them who had previously been at odds within APRA. Although Magda deeply resented Spain, her support for the Spanish Republic led her to distinguish between a Spain she loved and the despised Spain of the conquistadors and colonists. Haya, for his own reasons, refused to allow the APRA to take an official position on the war in Spain.

Following the Montevideo congress, Magda returned to Buenos Aires, where she settled with Gloria for several months, then moving on in November 1939 to Santiago de Chile, a city of refuge for Apristas and other leftist exiles. She arrived in Chile's capital with "her suitcases splashed with stickers from every hotel in America." Throughout this period of exile—which may represent the height of her fame in Latin America—she received a good deal of press attention, repeatedly lauded as an exemplary social fighter and champion of democracy. A journalist writing for the Santiago newspaper *Ercilla* described her presence: "A slender woman of great nervous intensity, Magda Portal . . . has rebellious chestnut-colored hair and expressive eyes that seem always to be seeing, sensing, comprehending something beyond the apparent. At first this penetrating gaze is unsettling; even more so is her smile, which seems ironic and perhaps is."

Gloria was described as a tall girl of fourteen or fifteen "whose seriousness made her seem much older than her years." Magda's concern at this point, as she said in the interview, was her daughter's disrupted education; she hoped to remain in Chile long enough for Gloria to complete school.

Luis Alberto Sánchez also recalled her arrival: "Magda Portal came to us with her daughter Gloria. She [Magda] was overwhelmed by sadness." Asked about Serafín during an interview that December, Magda visibly tensed, glanced quickly at Gloria, and uneasily explained that censorship made communication with Serafín Delmar impossible; she went on to say that Cuban intellectuals were calling for his release or for a new trial.

Meanwhile a new strongman had taken power in Peru. Manuel Prado Ugarteche now replaced General Benavides, providing a continuity of suppressive rule and instituting even harsher measures against the APRA. The conditions in prison were increasingly miserable, even ghastly. Haya sent encouraging letters to the jailed Apristas, assuring them that they were not forgotten and that their suffering would not be in vain. In newspaper articles published outside Peru, Magda assailed the prison conditions, as did other journalists. As reported in the Havana newspaper *Patria,* hundreds of Apristas were confined at the notorious El Frontón, the maximum-security prison where ingenious new torture mechanisms were unveiled with pompous ceremony. Among the most feared was "the Tomb," a kind of cage extended over the ocean. The dank walls of this contraption oozed salt water as icy waves sloshed through the open slats of the floor. Even a brief time in this cage could bring on dysentery, rheumatism, and fainting spells. Some prisoners were permanently debilitated by this torture, and a number died.

A new note entered Magda's journalistic writings. She now attacked what seemed to her weaknesses within the left-progressive movement. Decrying the feeble show of international solidarity among the working classes, she lamented that once again weapons dealers were profiting hugely by selling arms to all sides in the European conflict while workers were being manipulated by bellicose appeals to patriotism. "'Where, then, workers of the world, is your class consciousness?' . . . It is not enough to be against war. It is necessary to be against everything that serves as an instrument of war. . . . The class consciousness of the proletarian world is again being put to the test. And once again, it seems, it is failing to meet the challenge." This righteous antiwar, anticapitalist criticism bucked a powerful tide, as many leftists rallied to the antifascist call to arms.

In the later part of Benavides's rule, Magda had begun to appreciate the relative restraint of former autocrat Augusto Leguía. Under Prado, she observed, conditions were far worse than under Benavides; Peru had been reduced to a vast prison and cemetery, "the blackest point on the map of Indo-America." By contrast the constitutional government and democratic freedoms then enjoyed in Chile seemed to offer a superb model for her own country. All the while retaining her Aprista affiliation, Magda joined Chile's Socialist Party, then part of a ruling leftist coalition. Befriended by Socialist leader Dr. Salvador Allende and his wife, Hortensia Bussi Allende, she found a new political home and soon became active in the Socialist Party's women's section. At a tribute offered her by the Chilean Socialists in April 1940, Dr. Allende praised Magda's efforts on behalf of democratic social ideals. On another occasion the Socialist women's organization passed a resolution demanding that Peru's strongman grant amnesty to political prisoners in Peru, singling out for mention "the distinguished writer Serafín Delmar."

Magda's fascination with the brilliant nineteenth-century French Peruvian social theorist and activist Flora Tristan began during the later part of her Chilean exile, in 1944, the first centenary of Tristan's death, in France. Felicia Vargara, head of the Socialist Party's women's section, invited Magda to deliver an inaugural tribute to Tristan at the Socialist women's first national congress. At that time very few of Flora Tristan's writings were available in Spanish, and her achievements were little known outside circles of labor historians. But Magda managed to exhume the essential story of Flora's life, which exhibited striking parallels with her own: the sudden death of the father in early childhood, the consequent reversal of fortune, and above all Flora's zealous organizing in pursuit of social justice. Inaccurate in a number of details, her remarks to the Socialist women were terse and passionately admiring, indicative of her own tendency to idealize and also to identify with her subject. In this speech she made much of Flora's beauty, her talent, and the envy these incited, especially among women. Published as a tiny pamphlet that year in Chile, and the following year in a Peruvian edition, Magda's speech at that centenary tribute initiated her decades-long commitment to popularizing the life and work of Flora Tristan, whose seminal work *Union ouvrière* (Workers' Union; 1843) articulated the concept of an international organization of working men and women. Flora's call for industrial workers to unite across borders anticipated the work of her elder contemporaries Marx and Engels, who knew at least some of her writings. Her famous phrase "Workers of the World Unite" from *Union ouvrière* appeared at the close of the *Communist Manifesto*. Flora insisted that the right to work was a basic human right, analogous to the bourgeois right to own property—for what, she asked, did wage earners own if not their own labor? If they could not sell their labor, they were condemned to starve. But unlike Marx and Engels (and unlike Magda Portal), she never envisioned radically altering or even dismantling the capitalist system. Nor did she advocate that workers resort to violence, predicting that any such violence would only be turned back in greater force against the workers themselves, ultimately worsening their situation. But if workers were unified and strongly organized, she maintained, they might then—through the legislative process—win laws ensuring them a fair share of the wealth created by their labor.

Under the auspices of the Chilean Ministry of Education, Magda now enjoyed gainful employment as a radio producer, creating experimental programs using radio as a medium for mass education. Her extended exile in Chile provided an interlude of relative stability in which she returned to writing and editing her manuscripts. A collection of poems, *Costa sur* (Southern Coast), appeared in 1944, near the end of her Chilean sojourn.

This new collection reveals a substantially matured poetic sensibility. A number of poems explore complex feelings having to do with her enduring love for Serafín Delmar; their separation had now lasted nearly ten years, beginning with his arrest and jailing in 1932. In addition to addressing anxiety, yearning, loneliness, and the exhilarated remembrance of shared happiness, these poems explore a deepening sense of estrangement from the increasingly unreal lover whose silence and remoteness resembled that of the dead. Taken as a whole, the cycle of poems stemming from Magda's connection with and separation from Serafín form a substantial body of love poems, but the achievement is vexed by reiteration and prosaic stretches. As critics at the time noted, *Costa sur* is uneven in quality. Enriching the work, however, are superb lyrics such as "Reality of Being," which is a poem of ecstatic reunion not just with the lover but also with a world brilliantly freshened and vibrantly alive and young. Critic and fellow Aprista Luis Alberto Sánchez thought *Costa sur* Magda's finest work in poetry, but overall he judged that the harshness of her life, which might have raised her poetry to another level, in fact had not done so: "Magda wandered America in exile, speaking and protesting while leaving her poetry aside." Sánchez also complained that Magda held back her poems, hoarding them with a "certain inexplicable modesty" that might have come, he speculated, from "an erroneous sense" that writing poetry was somehow shameful and "detracted from revolutionary effort." Sánchez was chidingly outspoken about what he perceived as her failed promise as a poet.

> We hear people say, "So and so gave up everything for his principles, money, job, financial prospects." Few recall, however, that some have sacrificed a good deal more than that—their very personalities, which aren't so easily recovered. Among these is Magda. In addition to her material well-being, she sacrificed her poetic gift. If she'd continued along the lines marked out in *Anima absorta* and *Una esperanza y el mar*—if she'd written more and made a greater effort to enrich her inspiration and her poetic language—she would have attained . . . an indisputable position of honor."

It may be true that Magda lacked the single-minded devotion to poetry that might have enabled her to raise her work to a consistently higher level. It may be true that she lacked dedication to craft, a lack perhaps related to her limited formal education. Her temporary renunciation of poetry, her tendency to set aside her manuscripts, even to lose her manuscripts, also hints at a deep-seated ambivalence with regard to her creative writing. It is also possible that her political work allowed her in good conscience to avoid a fuller commitment to poetry, the sort of avoidance associated with suppressed fears and conflicts. As she laughingly remarked on the subject of her not being a prolific writer, "Nobody can give back to you the nights spent hiding under beds to escape arrest—in fact I never hid under a bed, but I spent plenty of time hiding in other places to escape the police. The truth is I nearly quit writing." In any case, approaching poetry as a craft or a discipline seemed hardly to interest her. Above all, she relied on inspiration.

> I think there's a moment in which one is lucid and able to write better than at other times. Sometimes I can't write at all, but sometimes interesting things emerge that later can be slightly revised by changing a

word or metaphor. But for the most part the poem remains as it first came to me. I think poetry is like that. If you keep changing a poem, first one thing, then another, nothing may be left of the original inspiration, which should, I think, remain intact as the essence, the inner voice of a poem. I don't revise much. My poetry is not highly crafted. There's a good deal of spontaneity and self-reflection in my poetry. It's always been that way.

She viewed her poetry, finally, not so much as having been diminished by her political activism, but as an essential complement and counterforce to that commitment. She experienced writing poetry as a gift, something ever flowing, like an underground river, a resource to which she turned for emotional sustenance and renewed resilience. She credited it with saving her from becoming embittered.

A DREAM DISINTEGRATES (1945–1957)

We are stagnating. Aprismo has grown old complaining.

—MAGDA PORTAL, LETTER TO VÍCTOR RAÚL HAYA DE LA TORRE

Many were now saying it: the great Aprista vision was no longer potent. Magda disagreed and passionately defended her party. Privately, however, she expressed misgivings. As early as June 20, 1941, in a long letter to Haya de la Torre, she challenged her old comrade to leave Peru and renew his contact with the larger movement that some of them felt he had lost sight of during seven years of internal exile. Ostensibly he was living in hiding all this time, but the location of the "Incahuasi" (House of the Inca)—the consecutive dwelling places of the APRA leader—was an open secret. "Everybody visited him," Magda said, "and journalists freely interviewed him. [Strongman] Prado [Ugarteche] himself used to say, 'I know perfectly well where he is and I let him alone. He's not bothering me.'" It was even possible in those days to send a letter addressed to "Haya de la Torre, c/o Lima, Peru" and in a short while receive a reply from the APRA chief. In her long letter of 1941 Magda called on Haya to reunite with the party faithful in exile and help them launch a campaign to resist the successful efforts by the United States to co-opt their long-standing call for Pan-American unity. She reminded Haya that while the United States under President Franklin D. Roosevelt might call itself the Good Neighbor, the northern colossus continued to pursue the same imperialist policies as before, lending money that could be used only to pay down debt to U.S. banks. Although Magda greatly respected Franklin D. Roosevelt, she did not believe that "the goodwill of one man" could alter the usual workings of the capitalist system. The Peruvian comrades, she told Haya, had sacrificed enough for APRA, and with the exception of a few leaders, they were tired of it.

> We are stagnating. Aprismo has grown old complaining. Everything Aprismo did over a period of fifteen to twenty years is now ancient history, forgotten. We no longer have anything to offer with our petitions and lamentations. Outside Peru people are sick of hearing about our suffering, our prisoners, our persecuted. We've exhausted the plaintive tone. Unpleasant comments are being made. In Peru you don't hear all this, but the fact is we've become like the whining beggar who at first elicits compassion, then boredom, and finally ends up being booted out the door. In all Latin America we are the only country in perpetual protest against tyranny. Why not try another tactic?

But what tactic? They needed Haya's guidance to help them find a fresh approach. Assuring the APRA leader that he would not be condemned for leaving Peru, Magda expressed in flattering yet probably true terms her personal debt to his leadership. "I have always believed you to be the quintessential Indo-American, and through you I too am Indo-American, without qualification. . . . Your traveling will not be badly interpreted. How it's viewed will depend on how we ourselves interpret it, how we ourselves explain the need for it. You are not the ancient patriarch of a tribe in decline that will perish when the leader is gone. Besides, you won't be gone for long."

Haya fired back an indignant reply to this letter, accusing the Apristas in Chile of lacking "the apostolic spirit" and of "abandoning their posts"—becoming soft as they enjoyed the easy life in exile far from the dangers of Peru's dictatorship. "Everyone [in Peru] down to the most downtrodden street child," he contended, "knows that Haya de la Torre is the only leader who has not gone into exile, hoping, like those who left, that others would boil the water so they can return and make tea."

In her letter Magda had intimated that Haya's departure from Peru might open the way to amnesty for political prisoners, the lack of which remained a sore point, as Serafín Delmar was still imprisoned. In the following year, in 1942, almost ten years from the date of his arrest on conspiracy charges, Serafín was released from the men's penitentiary in Lima. He traveled immediately to Santiago. By all accounts his reunion with Magda in Chile was a passionately joyful one. In a short while, however, as Daniel Reedy has related, the couple began experiencing difficulties. There were quarrels, disagreements.

Eventually there came an abrupt break when one day Magda returned home to a profoundly disturbing scene. In the apartment the couple shared with one of Magda's woman friends, she surprised Serafín and her friend together in bed. Shocked and desolate, she broke off the relationship. One of her friends described this incident as the first of two stunning blows that were in store for her. The second would not be long in coming.

According to Magda's sister Graciela, Serafín begged Magda to forgive him, insisting that the incident meant nothing to him, that he did not want to remain separated. But Magda was adamant. She refused to reconcile, mentioning nothing of this to her relatives in Peru. It was left to Gloria, who had just returned to Lima to attend university, to explain the situation. In a long letter expressing his unhappiness, bewilderment, and desire to restore the marriage, Serafín appealed to Magda's mother, imploring her to intervene. But nothing could be done to change Magda's decision. This was a shame, Graciela said, because Serafín was "the great love" of her sister's life.

After so many years of separation, it's not surprising that strains emerged when the two were together again. But it was truly unfortunate that the relationship ended as it did. The punitive aspect of this outcome suggests that Magda still cared deeply for Serafín. As her poetry attests, she experienced protracted anxiety because of his suffering in prison, enduring long, painful stretches when communication between them became impossible. Memories of their lost happiness had besieged her; for ten years the two had looked forward to being reunited. Yet the relationship ended without recourse, without discussion. Such a brutal severance could only have inflicted harm—upon Magda herself, upon Serafín, upon Gloria. The legendary love affair between revolutionists Magda Portal and Serafín Delmar could hardly have come to a sadder, more bitter conclusion.

Remaining in Chile, Serafín continued to send money to Gloria to help meet her university expenses. Eventually he withdrew entirely from political involvement and went into business. He never returned to Peru.

EXILE'S RETURN

Women will now demonstrate that they are neither inferior nor superior to man but simply different.

—*Magda Portal,* La mujer en el partido del pueblo

Following the end of World War II and the triumph of the liberal democracies in Western Europe, the brutal regime of Manuel Prado Ugarteche in Peru relaxed its repression, freed political prisoners, and yielded to what Magda described as a mood of "democratic euphoria." After seven years in exile, the women's leader returned to Lima in May 1945 and was quickly incorporated into APRA's National Executive Committee. She resumed her work as national secretary of women's affairs and director of the National Movement for Women's Education (Movimiento Nacional de Capacitación Femenino). Apparently optimistic about the prospects for democracy and social reform, she declared in a press interview that Peruvian women, particularly Aprista women, had proved themselves over the past twenty years and were ready to renew their participation in what she called "politics in a higher sense, as a school of civility and an affirmation of democratic consciousness."

There were, however, troubling indications that the APRA's left-wing principles had been compromised. Magda and other Apristas returning from exile were not pleased that in their absence the most controversial planks in the original party platform had been jettisoned. Even the party's name was not the same. The APRA was now calling itself El Partido del Pueblo—the Party of the People. Yet the argument was made—and quite persuasively—that something had to change or the party would remain outlawed, unable to take advantage of new political opportunities. Banned for more than a decade, the repositioned APRA/Party of the People was finally accorded the status of legality, free to participate in scheduled elections. During the first months of 1945 new members poured into the party ranks, believing it to be, Magda noted, the same organization as before, with the same fundamental concerns for social justice and democracy. With Haya de la Torre expressly forbidden to be a candidate for Peru's presidency, the APRA/Party of the People played a prominent role in a coalition of centrist-to-right parties whose presidential candidate was José Luis Bustamante y Rivero.

Having operated in secrecy for so many years, the APRA long since had instituted a vertical chain of command, which in practice meant that Haya and his closest associates simply issued decrees. Many of the Aprista old guard, including Magda, disliked the abandoning of internal democracy and hoped that a wide-ranging internal debate might now occur. Yet once again the promise of an electoral victory muted internal dissension. Whatever her misgivings, Magda expressed support for the new electoral coalition. "There is no doubt of the sincerity of this alliance, which represents a convalescence for Peru and a fresh impulse toward social progress." But an undercurrent of mistrust had been set in motion.

On May 20, 1945, just a few days after Magda's arrival in Lima, Haya addressed his followers in "one of the most emotion-charged moments in Peru's political history." Again a sea of handkerchiefs waved. Again the old slogans were deafeningly chanted. The great party roared back to life after more than a decade of being utterly suppressed. From a balcony overlooking the enormous Plaza San Martín, Haya delivered his greatly anticipated talk. Magda stood in the crowd of some 150,000–200,000 people, looking up at the formerly lean, fiery radical, now a stout, balding, conciliatory politician. In this talk Haya unveiled the party's new positions and in so doing, Magda recalled, confirmed the worst fears of the Aprista old guard.

> His speech astonished us all. One of his statements was a complete contradiction of the APRA call for land redistribution—agrarian reform— and the devolution of wealth to the state. . . . This man, among other things, then made his notorious statement: "We want to make our position clear: we will not seize wealth from those who have it but create wealth for those who do not have it." Words meant for the ears of those gentlemen of the oligarchy listening from the balconies of the Club Nacional. Haya continued, "We want an Inter-American democracy without empire." Words addressed to the United States. He had thrown overboard the original postulates of the Aprista movement and party. No mention of any struggle against imperialism. No mention of taking back the wealth controlled by the transnationals, the great companies that owned the oil, the mines, and the greater part of the huge haciendas, which is to say the patrimony of Peru. . . . This change in Haya's position frustrated us terribly. Not seize wealth from those who have it? Quite a few of us, especially among the intellectuals, were disheartened. We had lost confidence.

Refraining from public comment on Haya's speech, Magda continued her work with women, watching uneasily as the cult of personality around the party leader soared to new heights of adulation. Haya was El Cid, the Sacred Heart of Peru, the Good Shepherd. He was likened to Gandhi, to Roosevelt. Yet many Aprista veterans were troubled by the increasing presence around the party chief of the militaristic *búfalos*. Named for one of the leaders of the bloody Trujillo revolt in 1932, the *búfalos* were infamous for their ugly tactics, including violent strikebreaking on the coastal plantations, an obvious affront to the party's reform ideals. Also disturbing: Haya commanded a small personal army, the Vanguardia Aprista de Choque. Nevertheless, any intimation that APRA was in a phase of "political decomposition," as Magda would later put it, was submerged in ebullient campaigning. This new electoral battle awakened long-dormant aspirations among Apristas, summoning much the same energies—in both leaders and rank and file—as were in play throughout the notorious electoral contest of 1931. But this time when the votes were counted, the Apristas emerged victorious—a key party in the winning coalition. The APRA/Party of the People gained seats just short of the all-important two-thirds majority in Parliament. The newly elected Aprista parliamentarians, having sworn an oath of absolute allegiance to the party chief, immediately passed a law that permitted Parliament to override presidential vetoes by a simple majority. It was said that with this law in force Haya de la Torre became the de facto president of Peru. Yet the long-awaited reform measures—land reform above all—did not materialize.

Although widely perceived to be functioning as a major party leader, Magda Portal was, in fact, out of power in her party, along with others of her left persuasion. Despite her stature as a leader, she had not been chosen to be a candidate for Parliament; nor had she been offered any post in the new administration—talk of her being appointed ambassador to Mexico came to nothing. Instead she was assigned to a cramped office space in the party headquarters and subjected, as overheard on numerous occasions by an Aprista colleague, to disdainful treatment by Haya de la Torre—she was not even permitted to see the party chief without first submitting to long waits.

Despite her increasing estrangement from Haya and his inner circle, Magda threw herself into party work, devoting herself to revitalizing the women's organization, promoting literacy and general education and skills' training for women. Once again, as in 1931, she undertook a major speaking tour of Peru, traveling deep into the hinterlands. She spoke in Tingo María, Junín, Arequipa, Cuzco, Puno, Trujillo, Piura—stopping in hundreds of villages and small towns along the way. She even ventured as far as Iquitos in the Amazonian jungle. She spoke in municipal auditoriums, in university courtyards, in the open-air markets of sierran villages. For the first time she visited the ruins of Machu Picchu. Frequently photographed, she often appeared in the midst of crowds, usually engulfed in a crowd of men. In remote villages large banners blazoned her name in welcome. Although the tour was an emphatic personal triumph for Magda Portal, her party continued its rightward drift. To all appearances Haya de la Torre had abandoned APRA's anti-imperialistic, anti-U.S. policies, a shift that became noticeable during the years of World

War II. Like many of her Aprista colleagues, the old guard radicals, Magda could no longer rationalize the party's new stance. But still she made no public criticism, going about her business as before, particularly addressing women's concerns.

FIRST NATIONAL CONGRESS OF APRISTA WOMEN

In November 1946, the First National Congress of Aprista Women convened in Lima. Extending over ten days (November 14–24), the convention was the result of strenuous organizational efforts, all rewarded when women descended upon the capital from every region of the country. Aprista women in Lima opened their apartments and houses to the out-of-town guests. Magda recalled the tremendous interest generated by this gathering, as exemplified by the effort made to attend the congress by one eighty-year-old woman.

> "I'm not getting on any airplane, *compañera,*" she said to me.
> "But if you don't fly, you won't get there in time," I answered.
> She boarded a plane and flew to Lima. There was that much enthusiasm.

This congress—in which Gloria Delmar participated as a lecturer on social welfare—provided a forum in which to take stock of past achievements and to revitalize women's activism. By this time, Magda's faith in her party's promises was badly shaken, but she addressed the congress with apparent optimism. In her inaugural talk she reviewed the twenty years of women's work in APRA, paying homage to women's courage and stamina throughout the party's "fifteen-year Calvary" under dictatorial regimes. Ignoring the Aprista actions that provoked the great persecutions, she emphasized women's participation from the outset and at every stage of the party's existence—as if fearing women's presence might be disregarded if they themselves did not document it.

Prior to the congress, participants filled out questionnaires specifying their particular Aprista activities, including any arrests or incarcerations. Drawing on this information, Magda retraced the entire course of the party's history, noting key moments in which individual women played leadership roles. From the very beginning, she observed, women served on the National Executive Committee—Carmen Rosa Rivadeneyra, Josefina del Valle, and Rosa Michellini de Casas, besides herself. Repeatedly she read lists of names—

fifteen arrested in this action, twenty in another—an honor roll of activism and sacrifice. She recounted having witnessed in Santo Tomás Women's Prison some "hundreds" of Aprista women coming into and being released from the jail: Francisca Steward, Carmen Saldías, Alicia de Suarez, Jesús Evangelista, and so on. She recalled the names of numerous families that took in Aprista fugitives: Ollé, Fisher, Lizárraga, Bedoya, Perone, Sifuentes, Evans, Aldana. She mentioned that María Olivia Grados showed particular courage as an organizer. Such conscientious acknowledgments fill many pages of her speech, which was later published in pamphlet form as *La mujer en el partido del pueblo* (Women in the Party of the People).

Her own foundational activities went unmentioned, with the exception of her participation in the APRA National Executive Committee. She no doubt believed that her own place as APRA's preeminent women's leader went without saying. Such reticence contrasts with her insistence late in life on the prominence of her own role in APRA. But by that time she had lived long enough to see her participation completely ignored in some historical accounts, possibly, she speculated, because she was a woman. She recalled her first forays into political organizing. "The odd thing is that I never felt any discrimination. I simply felt that men had a certain way of behaving and that it didn't much matter to me, because suddenly I was more important than they were, because I was the central figure wherever I went. I don't say that out of vanity." For the most part it seemed to her that being a woman, far from having hindered her career, in fact had furthered it, because women activists attracted notice in a context in which few women dared speak in public, and fewer still were able to articulate their thoughts effectively. Only in retrospect, her consciousness raised by the women's movement of the 1970s, did she concede that as a woman she had experienced discrimination.

In her inaugural speech to the women's congress in 1946, Magda encouraged the attendees to become active in other branches of the party. By their not doing so, she warned, they risked being isolated in the Command for Women's Education and thereby marginalized and "deterred from pursuing their goal of attaining full equality "both of rights and of duties" with men in the party. She also observed that the practice of limiting women to proportional representation on party delegations and committees—which ensured that women remained in the minority—made no sense if the party's goal was to help women fully develop their capacities. She expressed her belief that their best hope was in the young people then joining the party, the young women who were eager to work and to learn. In their ten days together, she said in closing her remarks, they would review women's predicament and explore a range of responses, including legal remedies. She emphasized that their assembled numbers would enable their demands to be heard by the party's male leadership as a single voice, one insisting that women be accorded full standing as Apristas. Magda recalled her extreme distress at the party chief's remarks to the assembled delegates at this women's congress.

> Haya went to the podium—I stood to his right—and began speaking to women about their duties. What were these duties?—Being a mother, a wife, taking care of her husband, her children, her household.
>
> "Because women," Haya said, "have no other role in life than to be homemakers, to create a home, to reign over the household."
>
> I was outraged. "Don't talk about what you don't understand," I said to him under my breath. "They didn't come to hear this." Haya continued, his face flushed with anger, then finally he was finished, turning away from the podium in an almost violent way.

In Peru as in the postwar years in the United States, women's hard-won gains were under attack, and women who were active in the larger world, who were taking on what traditionally had been men's responsibilities, were being told they should forget all that and get back into their kitchens.

As time passed and civil order in Peru continued to deteriorate, it became clear that the Aprista bloc in Parliament did not intend to pursue a progressive agenda. At the same time—and to no clear purpose—serious acts of Aprista violence were becoming commonplace. Houses of political adversaries were attacked, rival party headquarters were firebombed, political opponents were even assassinated. When journalists denounced the new wave of violence, the Aprista bloc introduced a law calling for press censorship, and Aprista brigades went so far as to attack their opposition by dynamiting a speaker's platform, seriously injuring some student demonstrators. Haya and his small group of close associates withdrew into what Magda would later characterize as attitudes of "arrogance" and "infallibility." Even veteran APRA leader and Haya loyalist Manuel Seoane criticized the *jefe máximo* for distancing himself from the people, surrounding himself with sycophants, and looking the other way as his cronies exploited the party for personal gain. At the same time, Haya's former insistence on austere living had given way, as often happens following periods of forced deprivation, to conspicuous self-indulgence. "Living in luxury and maintaining two residences in the fashionable environs of Lima, Haya traveled about accompanied by youthful bodyguards armed to the teeth. Frequently he was accompanied also by handsome young devotees, chosen for their ideological fervor and loyalty to the chief. . . . The favorites with whom Haya surrounded himself customarily greeted him with the Aprista salute."

During the World War II years Haya shed his anti-U.S. rhetoric and began collaborating with the United States. To assist that country in its war effort, the APRA chief arranged for his associates to work with the U.S. Federal Bureau of Investigation in an endeavor to locate German submarines in Peru's coastal waters, as well as to uncover Japanese and German agents operating inside the country. For these services Haya de la Torre purportedly received payments from the U.S. Embassy. Although supposedly living in clandestinity, he reportedly took "his nightly outings in a luxury automobile bearing United States diplomatic license plates." Also during this era, as U.S. State Department documents reveal, Haya appealed directly to U.S. Embassy officials in Lima to make the case that the United States would benefit by overthrowing the regime of Manuel Prado Ugarteche (which he characterized as fascist) and installing an Aprista administration in Peru. Although the United States did not intervene as requested, Haya continued making overtures to that country in the new cold war era. In 1946, as reported to the U.S. secretary of state by the U.S. ambassador in Peru, Haya offered the services of his party as a secret informant against Communists, suggesting, as U.S. Embassy official Maurice J. Broderick reported, that someone in the U.S. Embassy might, "by maintaining contact with leading Apristas, follow up the frequent communist 'leads' that the party uncovered in its regular activities."

In 1947, the year in which U.S. president Harry S. Truman chartered the Central Intelligence Agency—thereby inaugurating the "national security state"—Haya traveled to Washington, where he paid calls on State Department officials, reminding them of his anti-Communist credentials and potential usefulness to U.S. corporate interests in Peru. The APRA had always resisted the Communists, he declared, and was still doing so, primarily by contesting Communist power in the student and labor movements. Following yet another U.S.-subsidized trip to the United States, Haya announced that "U.S. capital bears no resemblance to that studied by Marx and Engels. It is more social, democratic, populist. . . . The problem is not the vast power of great nations like the U.S., but our own inferiority complex." Many Aprista leftists found this statement indefensible. Labor leader and CIA associate Serafino Romualdi later posed an intriguing question: "[Haya] and his movement have been the strongest bulwark that successfully resisted the infiltration and capture of the social-revolutionary concept by the Communist totalitarians. Peru is now considered by competent observers off the danger list. But where would Peru be today, I ask, if Haya de la Torre and his APRA Party had not been on the scene?" Magda and her left-wing colleagues of APRA's early days might have been asking themselves the same question. What, they may have wondered, had the APRA in fact accomplished?

The APRA chief now embroiled himself in a new controversy, supporting a hotly contested plan to transfer state-owned petroleum fields to International Petroleum, a subsidiary of Standard Oil. In 1931 Haya had promised to nationalize International Petroleum. Now he promoted the reverse of his original position. Even conservative politicians viewed this transfer plan as an outrageous giveaway of Peru's patrimony to a foreign interest. In January 1947, the highly respected journalist Francisco Garland Graña, who had vigorously campaigned against this transfer in the press, was assassinated in the street. The APRA/Party of the People denied any responsibility for his death. But two Apristas were convicted of the crime.

As civil unrest intensified, the anti-Aprista forces in Parliament—angered and frustrated by the Aprista bloc's refusal to enact any legislation—shut down the parliament entirely on a rules technicality. Appalled by this self-inflicted dysfunctionality on the part of the Aprista parliamentarians, Magda and Luis Eduardo Enríquez confronted Haya, insisting that he make concessions to end the parliamentary impasse. Haya responded by telling them the matter was none of their business: "The National Executive Committee should stay out of it, should leave the matter to the National Political Bureau." To the consternation and intensifying anger of many in APRA's old guard, the parliamentary shutdown dragged on with no end in sight.

Speaking with a journalist in 1950, Magda expressed her disappointment with what the APRA had achieved. She blamed Haya and his immediate circle but acknowledged a more general responsibility: they all had failed. "A party that started out so well! I blame the leaders for these errors. They believed themselves infallible in their creole Machiavellianism. . . . Over twenty years we learned many lessons but finally when we had some power, we had no idea how to use it on behalf of the people."

GLORIA DELMAR

Sic transit gloria mundi

As the APRA/Party of the People vacillated, mired in counterproductive violence and inaction, Magda sustained a devastating personal loss. In the family apartment on January 3, 1947, Graciela Pareja Moreno heard what sounded like a window slamming shut. She went to check on the noise and discovered Gloria on the floor in her room. She had shot herself in the head with her mother's gun. Bleeding from the bullet wound, she died in the arms of her young aunt. Graciela also witnessed her sister's horrified response upon learning of her daughter's suicide. "Magda screamed and tore her hair. She was nearly out of her mind and did not want to live. Haya posted a twenty-four-hour security guard in rotating shifts of four Aprista women. They never left her alone for a minute out of fear she would harm herself."

Since early childhood Gloria Delmar's life had been inextricably intertwined with the vicissitudes of the Aprista Party of Peru, which now responded in enormous numbers to commemorate her short life. On January 4, 1947, the APRA newspaper *La Tribuna* reported her death, omitting mention of suicide.

> *Compañera* Gloria Delmar, daughter of leader Magda Portal and *compañero* Serafín Delmar, now living in Santiago de Chile, died suddenly and unexpectedly last night in Lima. She had just turned twenty-three. In early childhood she suffered the tragedy of seeing her parents jailed for their Aprista convictions. Many times she went back and forth between Santo Tomás and the Panóptico to visit her parents in their respective prisons. When Magda Portal obtained her liberty, Gloria traveled with her to Bolivia, Uruguay, Argentina, and Chile, where she studied at the University of Chile, receiving a degree in social work. . . . Always restless and eager for new knowledge, she enrolled in the University of San Marcos to study literature and be part of the reforming, democratizing action of the country. . . . Her death has profoundly grieved all members of the Party, particularly those who knew her to be good, intelligent, and dedicated.

Flower arrangements overflowed into adjacent rooms at the Lima funeral home where hundreds of mourners came to pay their respects. "I will never forget the prostrate form of Gloria, delicate and still," wrote Luis Alberto Sánchez, "and Magda standing beside the coffin, sobbing." With so many dignitaries, including diplomats and members of Parliament, in attendance, the gathering resembled a state funeral. Aprista organizations sent delegations, and Aprista students carried the casket from the funeral home for several blocks before reaching the Avenida Arequipa and hoisting it into an ornate carriage that led the cortege of automobiles to the cemetery. Representing the family at the graveside was Aprista leader Carlos Manuel Cox. On February 6, 1947, the following notice appeared in *La Tribuna*: "The Women's Command of the Party of the People begs all *compañeros* to abstain from visiting *compañera* Magda Portal to express their grief personally, for it is essential at this time to contribute to the tranquillity of our beloved comrade Magda. Letters of condolence may be sent to her at Luis Felipe Villarán 318, San Isidro."

Why did Gloria commit suicide? Over the years many stories have circulated, some plausible, others not; finally it remains unclear what motivated the young woman to end her life. Several knowledgeable accounts confirm that Gloria was involved in a love affair with a man, a much older man, connected with APRA. There is some indication that Magda did not approve of this liaison, perhaps even forbade it. It is also speculated that on the day of her suicide Gloria had run into this man in the street, seeing him with his pregnant wife, which may have deeply shocked her. According to Graciela, Gloria had a quiet, introspective nature; the family had not perceived her as being depressed. In retrospect, however, Graciela reflected, it was not just one thing but probably a number of factors, including the love affair, that conspired to bring about her suicide. Graciela mentioned, for example, that Gloria had been deeply upset by the separation of Magda and Serafín. She had also been very troubled by receiving letters from a woman who despised Magda and wrote terrible things about her to Gloria. Following her death, her university friends revealed that when she received one of these letters she went off by herself and wept.

It is also reported that Gloria had only recently (in Chile), learned from her mother that Serafín was not her biological father; if so, this new knowledge might have contributed to a personal instability, especially if she acquired it following the breakup of her parents. Graciela, however, maintains that Gloria had been told in early childhood that Serafín was not her real father but "like her father."

Magda insisted that family members, as well as friends and associates, refrain from speaking of Gloria in her presence. This prohibition remained in force for the remainder of her life, although photos and an oil portrait of

Gloria were prominently displayed in the family apartment. If in later years she herself spoke of her daughter during an interview—as she did to Esther Andradi and Ana María Portugal—it was a rare occasion. In the poem "Tristitia" she articulates the wish to substitute her own death for her daughter's. In "Balada triste," a somewhat rambling expression of grief, she touches upon the question of naming and expresses a maternal possessiveness, a protectiveness that could be exercised in her daughter's absence:

> I won't let words approach you
> I refuse to hear your name
> not even spoken in hushed tones
> for now you belong to me alone
> beyond death, beyond all distances.

Graciela affirmed that the connection between mother and daughter had been intimate and loving. "They adored each other; they were like sisters," she said. When Gloria returned to the family home in Lima, leaving her mother behind in Chile, every night as she fell asleep (Graciela recalled her telling them) she felt her mother's hands gently adjusting her blankets.

In the early pages of her unfinished memoir, Magda confided the difficulty of attaining truth in autobiographical writing.

> There is narcissism or masochism in those who relate the unvarnished tale of their lives. . . . Writing a memoir is the opposite of writing a diary. You write looking back, when the patina of time is cast over everything, and the force and truth of events has faded.
>
> Except for a general sense of what life means, or death, what remains is a mixture of fear, shame, and guilt. You write what you would have wanted to be, not what you actually were, or are. . . . Or fantasy intervenes and takes the place of truth. Dreams, sleeping or waking, carry us along on currents of imagined life.

Relatively late in her life Magda began work on an extended autobiographical narrative, "La vida que yo viví: Trazos cortados" (The Life I Lived: Interrupted Traces), a project she eventually gave up on, selling the ninety-one-page manuscript to the Nettie Lee Benson Latin American Collection with the emphatic handwritten notation on the typescript "Without corrections!" This draft memoir also exists in a somewhat different version, at fifty-one pages, titled simply "Trazos cortados." Neither version extends in time beyond 1934.

Magda once defined the greatest obstacle to autobiographical truth as "that failure to include the central thing, that which is absolutely vital to defining a crucial moment or phase, the very thing that must not be evaded but which nonetheless slips through one's fingers and isn't said." Clearly she did not want to write about certain episodes in her own life, or simply could not do so; the more personal or problematic the event, the more likely the avoidance. So it is that "central things" are excluded from her most ambitious autobiographical narrative, a document notable for its evasions and omissions. For example, there is no mention of the disastrous 1932 assassination attempt on Luis Sánchez Cerro's life, which separated her from Serafín. In fact, Serafín Delmar is virtually effaced from the story, while her first husband, Federico Bolaños, is not even present by allusion. She does offer some explanatory remarks concerning her stance in the Mariátegui–Haya de la Torre schism in 1928, but a detailed account is not in the picture. On the subject of Gloria, she tersely states early in the narrative, "My daughter was born at the end of November; she occupied an exceptional place in my life. As much as possible I want to exclude or mention as little as possible everything related to her life." In a strained effort to give at least some account of herself with regard to Gloria, she mentions her own "instinctive refusal" to give herself wholeheartedly to being a mother. "Seething in my mind were so many desires, dreams, ambitions. These fractured my life, pulling me in different directions, in particular toward social action. It's possible that my daughter was a victim of my emotional instability. I didn't abandon her, but neither did I give myself to her completely."

Magda once mentioned that her social context, or historical moment, had been a major force in the shaping of her life's trajectory. She often felt herself carried by strong currents, borne along by collective dreams, responding to these stimuli "like a sunflower to the light." It seemed to her that she had never had a long-range plan or even a clear direction but instead experienced "ever-new beginnings without continuity." That lack of continuity, that personal instability, she feared, had hurt her daughter. These few but pointed remarks indicate her sense of being inadequate as a mother, a pained and reluctant admission that her very nature and way of living had contributed to her daughter's suicide.

Following the funeral of Gloria Delmar, the guards posted by Haya remained with the bereaved mother for one week, at which point Magda left

Lima for a hacienda in southern Peru. There, as Graciela recounted, she remained for a month, alone except for the caretaker.

A prose sketch published in 1979—doubtless written much earlier—suggests Magda's state of mind following Gloria's death and the break with Serafín Delmar. Its bleak mood mingles remorse, detachment, and desolation. The protagonist is described as "not old physically but with an aged heart and nothing left to experience." From the corpselike body lying on a bed, the disembodied spirit slips mistily out the window, floats over darkened rooftops, then enters upon a brightly sunlit tree-lined avenue. The land burgeons with luxuriant foliage. Iridescent insects sip nectar from flowers. Then a child appears—her daughter, her dark eyes full of tears. The mother yearns to console her, to lead her toward "the earth's lush green, and to the sea, open to all desires." This evocation of worldly beauty and promise ends in a cry, "Oh, my daughter . . . !" Unable to touch the child, the disembodied spirit drifts on, eventually coming upon a man slumped on a bench, head in hands, his black hair mingled with silver, apparently a figure representing Serafín. "He was thinking of her, the abandoned one who abandons, . . . who fled everything, even love itself. . . . She yearned to caress him, to console him like a child, to tell him that everything, even love, which is stronger than life, comes to an end. But she couldn't speak. . . . With tears in his eyes, he said, 'Hatred has destroyed my life!'" The sketch ends with morning sunlight flooding the room, rousing the motionless figure on the bed to renewed activity.

In March, two months after Gloria's death, Magda traveled to Venezuela, where she stayed with her old friend and former Aprista comrade Rómulo Betancourt, then president of that country; the friendship of Betancourt and his wife helped sustain her at this difficult time. Interestingly, in light of the importance of oil in international politics, Betancourt a decade later, along with his minister of energy, founded the Organization of Petroleum Exporting Countries (OPEC), the oil cartel in which Venezuela partnered with Kuwait, Saudi Arabia, Iraq, and Iran. Believing that oil reserves would be depleted early in the twenty-first century, Betancourt called for investment in renewable energy sources.

Shortly after her arrival in Caracas, Magda received a letter from Haya de la Torre. In that letter he urged her to rest, to take care of herself, but also if at all possible to use her influence to promote in Venezuela his recently drafted Magna Carta, a Latin American Bill of Rights he was putting forward as an alternative to the leftism still current in Latin America. If labor or other groups were to pass resolutions supporting this Magna Carta, he wanted her to send clippings of any press coverage to the Associated Press. The APRA, he informed her, was on the verge of "sounding the alarm against the new totalitarianisms." It's unlikely that Magda acted on this request. She soon returned to Peru.

THE SECOND APRISTA PARTY CONGRESS

By 1948, internal tensions within the APRA/Party of the People were nearly at a breaking point. Prominent members began openly criticizing the party. Novelist Ciro Alegría resigned in protest, as did APRA charter member Luis Eduardo Enríquez, who noted as one of the many reasons for his break "the exclusion on Haya's order of *compañeras* in the Women's Command from meetings of the National Executive Committee."

Amid continuing calls by Peru's rightists for the outlawing of the APRA, the Second Aprista Party Congress was convened, taking place May 27–June 3, 1948. The purpose of this congress was to air grievances and clarify the party's positions. Delegates came to Lima from every part of the country. This congress represented a last-ditch effort by the Aprista old guard dissident Left to reverse the rightward drift of the party. "We thought," Magda later testified in court, "that after consulting with the party's masses, there'd be a change of direction. This didn't happen. In fact, the rank and file ratified the party's new position, which led to a number of ruptures."

The APRA's internal debates of 1946–48, according to Luis Alberto Sánchez, exacerbated Magda's intransigence: "During the party congress, in the second half of '48, she showed herself to be uncompromising and irascible." In a plenary session of this congress, Haya de la Torre decreed a new policy that surprised and outraged the women's leader, who recalled Haya's stunning pronouncement and her own protest.

> "We have come to the conclusion," Haya declared, "that women, since they do not yet have the vote in Peru, cannot be considered authentic members of the Aprista Party. Women can only be sympathizers."
> "I demand the floor!" I interrupted.
> "There's nothing under debate," Haya answered.
> "I demand the floor!" I repeated.
> "There is nothing under debate!" Haya repeated.
> He slammed shut the book of rules. He was acting like a dictator; in fact he might have been a dictator but he lacked the talent for it. . . .

We had worked, we had fought, but as it turned out we were no longer regarded as active members of the party. On the contrary, we were only sympathizers. I jumped to my feet, along with two or three *compañeras* who supported me.

"This is fascism!" I said.

And I walked out and never went back. But what a disappointment. Many in the party, including many women, thought that Haya's position might be yet another of his tactics to avoid frightening people. But we'd been in the fight too long to be worrying about that. . . . Once and for all, I withdrew from the Party.

It was said that Magda was one of the few people who could talk openly and truthfully with Haya, that she could offer criticism and be heard out. That time had now passed. It was also said that Magda was the only person in the party who could never be treated badly—because the women in the party would rise up in protest. In fact, she said, following her walkout from the plenary session, she found herself isolated. "Nobody protested. The majority stayed put. . . . Five or six women walked out with me, and a few men, and that was the end of it."

The Second Aprista Party Congress elected another woman to the post of national secretary for women's affairs, demoting Magda to the position of second subsecretary, in the process officially stripping her of her office space, although it is not clear that she actually lost access to her office. She neither accepted nor rejected this new position—which entailed no duties—and began thinking about leaving the country, so as to attain some perspective before deciding what next to do. A number of Aprista women, however, urged her to stay and advise them, and she agreed. Despite her repudiation of the party's new direction, she resumed her work on Aprista committees, in particular involving herself in setting up a low-cost pharmacy. It seemed to her that the Second Aprista Party Congress marked a major turning point, signaling the end of the original Aprista Party of Peru and helping set the scene for the catastrophic insurrection of October 3, 1948.

INSURRECTION

Parliamentary government having arrived at a hostile standoff, Haya and a number of military officers began plotting an insurrection. Aprista uprisings in the past had been notoriously badly planned and poorly executed, but this plot was to be different—meticulously coordinated in advance by seasoned officers representing different branches of the armed services. The military conspirators planned to take power as a radical Aprista junta supported by an armed populace; this junta would then set in motion long-delayed social reforms, including the all-important land reform. Haya preferred to leave the specific details of the planning to others, who carefully prepared and were finally ready for the APRA chief to give the launch command, which they asked him to do. But time passed and Haya did not give the command—until finally it seemed their plot had become known. Alternative plots began coming to light, and high-level supporters of these other plots appealed to Haya with promises of carrying out a bloodless coup. Increasingly frustrated by Haya's failure to give the go-ahead, the Aprista military men made the momentous decision to proceed on their own authority. On October 3, 1948, the insurrection broke out in Callao Harbor. By this time it seems that Magda had lost confidence that even a successful insurrection would usher in the desired social reforms.

> On the eve of the uprising I remember talking with one of the leaders, my longtime friend [Manuel] Vásquez Díaz.
>
> "The uprising will happen," I said, "because everything's ready, but I feel certain that the reactionaries will end up in power."
>
> "You're right," my friend answered, "because they're the only ones who know how to run the country."
>
> "Well, if that happens," I said, "I'm leaving the country, once and for all. I won't say anything in public so as not to hurt the Party, but I'll leave, and I won't be back."

When Magda withdrew from the Second Party Congress in protest (only months before the uprising), she was protesting not just the disrespect shown Aprista women but also the declaration by executive fiat of new rules and party positions. But she made no public statement of her grievances. Her dominant impulse—despite insult and disillusion—was to protect the party she had cofounded. She described her sense of what happened on October 3, 1948, and in the days preceding that historic rebellion.

> Three insurrectionary movements were simultaneously in progress, each on the point of exploding and each a military revolt. In one of the groups was my friend Colonel César Enrique Pardo. In another was Major [Víctor] Villanueva. Their ideas were revolutionary, very left

wing. Weapons had been stockpiled throughout the country. Lima was awash in guns. But Haya was afraid. At that point, tired of delays, Colonel Pardo with two or three other leaders went to Chosica to see Haya de la Torre. "Well, Víctor Raúl," he said, "the moment has come. You haven't chosen the time, but tonight we begin the insurrection. When we take power, we intend to convene a tribunal in which all of you will be put on trial." That's what he said. But what a mistake, a grievous political error—because immediately Haya began disarming all the sites where weapons had been warehoused, and he informed the government that an attempt to overthrow it was under way.

The uprising in Callao Harbor involved units of the army, navy, and air force. For three days the battle raged, with many, many dead. Hundreds of young men had barricaded themselves in the fortress of El Real Felipe. They were armed and ready to fight, but Haya sent orders for them to lay down their arms. They opened the gates, surrendered their weapons, and were promptly shot. Incredible as it may sound, that's what happened. I went out in my tiny car with my three secretaries, all women. The gunfire was deafening and we wanted to know what was going on. About a block from El Real Felipe we pulled over and watched as a big truck drove out of the grounds. The truck bed was piled high with corpses. Men were standing in the back. As they went by, one of them recognized me and made a sign I'll never forget—it meant that they had lost.

"That stupid thing that Haya did!" Magda exclaimed to her Aprista comrade Zoila B. Maxwell. She told Zoila that immediately after witnessing the defeat, she went directly to the office of the Women's Command and right there in the building burned the files, destroying all the names, because she knew that the revolution was lost. Magda and many other Apristas went immediately into hiding. Zoila recalled the days Magda spent hiding in her (Zoila's) family home. "Magda at this time was one of the most recognizable women in Peru; everyone knew her. We were all frightened. Lunch and dinner were taken to her room, which was my bedroom, the smallest room in the house. 'Was that Magda Portal in your room?' The servants recognized her but were quiet about it; nobody said anything. 'I hope they don't arrest the whole family,'" my mother said. But Magda felt unsafe, there were too many people in the house. She only stayed a week."

The failed revolt opened the way for yet another caudillo to take power in Peru. Taking charge of the presidential palace (without resistance), General Manuel Odría brusquely instituted a new wave of anti-Aprista reprisals. More than one thousand people were arrested immediately following the October 3 revolt. Again the APRA was outlawed and party headquarters were occupied by government troops. An estimated four thousand individuals, including many of the uprising's major planners, were incarcerated during Odría's first eight months in power.

Despite his denial of involvement, Haya de la Torre was nevertheless sought as the insurrection's principal plotter. Having managed to reach the Colombian Embassy, he was offered political asylum by the government of Colombia. Contrary to long-established custom, however, General Odría's regime denied Haya safe passage out of the country. With the embassy building surrounded by trenches and barbed wire, and Odría's machine guns trained on all exits, Haya found himself unable to set foot outside. There he would remain, a virtual prisoner in the embassy, for five years. During this time he devoted himself to writing, among other things, an arcane treatise applying Albert Einstein's relativity theory to social history. Only the most visionary observer of Haya's political trajectory might possibly have guessed that the APRA chief would one day ally himself with his persecutor, General Odría, in opposition to progressive forces in Peru.

WHO BETRAYED THE PEOPLE?

Early in 1950 a large number of accused insurrectionists were tried under martial law by a military tribunal convened at the Potao barracks in Lima. Many feared that there would be mass executions. On February 10, Magda surfaced in a surprise appearance before the tribunal. Her entrance caused a rush of excitement in the courtroom. The infamous rebel, now a dignified fifty, "elegantly attired in a silk dress with white shoes and handbag," stood before the military panel, swaying a bit and appearing to tire as her lawyer, Luis Bramont Arias, read a long statement elaborating the main points of her defense: first, she was no longer a member of APRA's National Executive Committee; second, she had no prior knowledge concerning the uprising and no involvement in the crimes charged, such as fabricating explosives, inciting to riot, and so on; and, finally, the tribunal had produced no evidence linking her to any crime.

In a statement also read by her lawyer to the tribunal, Magda affirmed that even if she were still a member of the Aprista Party's National Executive Committee it would not have mattered, since that body no longer had any power, all of which, she said, resided in the Political Bureau. Asked to name the members of that group, she hesitated: "Well, the Political Bureau, how can I put it, it's really no more than a phantom organization, a letterhead; in fact the decisions were all made by Haya de la Torre, León de Vivero, and three or four close associates of the chief."

Contrary to her statement before the tribunal (in which her lawyer asserted that she had no prior knowledge of the plot) Magda later admitted that she had in fact been part of the group that knew in advance of the plotting but that she had not participated in it. No women, she claimed, were involved. Immediately following the crushed insurrection, there had emerged another Aprista plan to seize power by force, and reportedly Magda had tried unsuccessfully to raise funds on behalf of this unlikely action. But it seems that she herself was the only one to make a monetary contribution toward this effort to Luis Conterno, head of APRA's Military Defense.

While being detained at police headquarters in the Potao barracks, Magda wrote her famous denunciation of APRA, *¿Quiénes traicionaron el pueblo?* (Who betrayed the people?). In this impassioned *j'accuse!*—a shorter version of which she read at her trial—she refused to condemn the October 3 revolt, which she viewed as an act of desperation entirely justified by a regime "that had betrayed all the people's hopes." She went on to trace the course of APRA's "slippery slide into the abyss" in the years 1945 through 1948: the party's alliances with Peru's oligarchy; its betrayal of women and of the poor; its failure "to confront with valor even one major social problem" when it might, she charged, have exercised its parliamentary strength to bring about reform without causing bloodshed. She condemned the party's obfuscating manipulations of dialectical reasoning as well as its convoluted "politics of the double face"—the practice of keeping in motion two diametrically opposed policies, a practice, she said, that confused not only the rank and file but also the veteran leaders. Her indignant recital of the party's hypocrisies continued. "The leaders promised—'Over our dead bodies will the Party be forced back into illegality'—and again the Party was outlawed, not over the dead bodies of its so-called leaders," she indignantly observed, "but over the corpses of its humble rank and file." She decried the suppression of open debate at the Second Party Congress, a debate denied on the spurious grounds that internal dissension lent comfort to the party's enemies. The greatest accomplishment of this congress, Magda sardonically charged, "was to agree to build a cenotaph in honor of the party's martyrs—male only!"

The APRA, as she saw it, had betrayed its ideals and its constituents. Utterly lacking in internal democracy; militaristic; mired in demagoguery, sloganeering, and violence, the party, she concluded, had become a neofascist organization "of the sort that afforded women no civil standing." Furthermore, the Aprista Party had failed in another respect; while formerly it was able to summon vast numbers to its great rallies, APRA no longer had a disciplined following; it had lost its mass base, particularly in the trade unions and guild organizations. As its loyal following drifted away, she maintained, the leadership obsequiously courted the upper classes, whose powerful members were not placated and continued to demand that the APRA be outlawed. It was this attempt to appease and conciliate the oligarchy, she charged, that had set the party on a disaster course.

In an impassioned conclusion to this critical statement, she affirmed her faith "in the People and in Youth, who are capable of lofty and generous actions because they are not compromised by the shameful past." She also affirmed her abiding belief in the ideals of democracy and social justice upon which the Aprista Party of Peru had been founded.

Considering the thoroughgoing nature of her condemnation—it was rumored that Haya broke down weeping when he read it—some wondered why she had not broken sooner with the APRA. As she herself admitted, members of the leadership, including herself, for too long had been "mendacious traffickers in hope," a hope that she hesitated to dispel, as she later explained: "I couldn't just leave without saying a word, I couldn't go without putting up a fight. I stayed because of the people, because I couldn't stand for them to be disappointed so soon. It was all right for me to be disillusioned, but not them—no, not yet."

In the military tribunals at Potao, the Aprista Party of Peru as a whole was pronounced guilty of plotting and carrying out the insurrection of October 3, 1948. Most of the individuals brought to trial were convicted as charged. But the widely feared executions did not happen. APRA leaders Ramiro Prialé, Carlos Manuel Cox, and Luis Heysen were sentenced to from three to seven years at hard labor. Other leaders, including Haya de la Torre, Manuel Seoane, and Luis Alberto Sánchez, were cited as fugitives from justice. The APRA was now outlawed, fragmented, and demoralized, its leaders and ex-leaders in exile, in prison, or living in hiding in Peru. Following her trial, authorities allowed Magda Portal to go free, her sentence reduced to time served in detention at the army base, under house arrest, and in hiding. Her public criticism of APRA as articulated at her trial marked her definitive break from the Aprista Party of Peru.

The October 3 debacle triggered a barrage of recriminations against the APRA and its legendary leader. Critics openly accused Haya de la Torre of weakness, corruption, and incompetence. Some wondered if he suffered from "a political death wish." Even a number of his most loyal supporters were now "disillusioned with a leadership that had brought the party to the brink of power but had somehow lacked the final reserves of talent and resolve needed to grasp the elusive prize." Haya's critics charged—with substantial evidence—that the APRA chief had betrayed the insurrectionary plotters by alerting the government to the plan, while at the same time denying his own role as a co-conspirator. The 1948 uprising failed, some believed, "because of the ambivalence and treason of the party's top leadership."

Many in the APRA as well as other critics over the years have speculated about the various causes of APRA's turn to the right. It seemed to Magda that a certain vagueness had always existed in APRA's ideological position with regard to capitalism; she noted that APRA had never rejected capitalism as a system but instead focused on denouncing U.S. imperialism and the greed of the local oligarchy. But more to the point than any doctrinal fuzziness, she concluded, was the simple fact that over time the APRA had lost touch with the impoverished majority in Peru. The party, she concluded, "had begun identifying with the upper classes, increasingly feeling closer to those in power than to those beneath; in fact, APRA had gradually ceased being a revolutionary party—that is why I left."

Some of Haya's critics have concluded that he had never been anything other than "a false Marxist" and a manipulator of his followers. Magda did not share that view. Haya had changed, she believed. Early in his career, she affirmed, Haya de la Torre had been a true radical, "in his youth a pioneer in revolutionary struggles." Magda's connection with the controversial leader was a close and complicated one. He had been her most important mentor, her friend and comrade throughout years of hard struggle and persecution. The ferocity, also the bitterness, of her denunciation of the APRA chief no doubt reflects the depth and seriousness of her personal dedication to him.

Perhaps most damaging to the APRA's progressive agenda, and any prospects of that agenda being realized, was the party's recurrent indulgence in violence, a self-defeating tendency alternately encouraged and disavowed by Haya de la Torre. Peru's nascent democratic process could not withstand such disruption. This Aprista violence—not to mention the party's stubborn refusal to compromise or form coalitions with other political elements—facilitated the rise to power of regimes that persecuted all progressive parties.

The strongmen who were empowered might go on then to institute some of the very reforms called for by the parties they were suppressing. For example, under the harsh rule of General Manuel Odría, Peru's women were finally accorded the full vote. Despite several such reforms, the basic power relations in the country remained the same; the gross inequities persisted.

In June 1950 a number of those who had broken with APRA came together in the city of Arequipa and convened the Third National Aprista Congress. Declaring themselves the sole legitimate representatives of APRA, the group voted to dissolve the organization. With Magda Portal acting as president, the assemblage denounced Haya de la Torre and declared the Aprista Party of Peru defunct—a declaration that predictably deepened the chasm between Magda and her former comrades.

In the aftermath of her trial, as General Manuel Odría's punitive regime continued in power, Magda felt unsafe. Hostility from APRA loyalists, of which there were many, envenomed the atmosphere in which she moved. Some of her former comrades believed she had turned state's evidence at her trial, effectively betraying particular leaders and the APRA in general. Retaliation on the part of Aprista loyalists toward those who had left the party could be vicious, even deadly. Magda received death threats and repeatedly experienced harassment. At one point, according to her sister Graciela, a taxi driver told Magda that Haya had issued an order to the APRA-controlled taxi drivers' union: should she ever get into one of their cabs she was to be taken to a deserted spot and beaten. "I may be an Aprista," the driver told her, "but I'm also a human being—Señora, don't take a taxi." Magda took this warning seriously.

Even outside the country, some believed that her denunciation of APRA had been too harsh, to the point of betraying the larger social cause. There is some indication that even such staunch friends as Salvador Allende in Chile and Rómulo Betancourt in Venezuela thought she had gone too far. Some of her former comrades feared for her mental stability, believing her judgment to have been impaired by the shock of her daughter's death. Others viewed her behavior as simply inexcusable. The former leader found herself ostracized.

> When I left, they said hideous things about me, it was said I'd been paid off, that Odría had given me who knows how many thousands. . . . I remember I once ran into a couple of Aprista women when I was on a bus and loaded down with groceries for the weekend.

"Traitor!" one of the woman hissed.

"That's right," I answered, "but carrying my own packages the same as you."

"Traitor," she hissed again. That was all. I was simply a traitor. These things are hazards of the occupation.

THE TRAP

"I am disillusioned with APRA and with men. I'm a romantic," the now party-less radical confided to journalist Alfonso Tealdo in an interview conducted in 1950 in the family apartment on the Avenida Arequipa. APRA's "twenty heroic years" were over, she lamented, those years in which her name had been "synonymous with APRA," years in which the leaders were "depersonalized" and in which "a spirit of sacrifice prevailed." Having confounded her identity with that of a party that no longer existed as she once knew it, she seemed disoriented, as Tealdo noted, and "caught up in a dialectic of nostalgia." She now criticized the very concept of the transcendent leader. "The epoch of the supreme leader is over, the providential, infallible leader, Hitlerian style. From now on I think it's essential that people support only leaders who act strictly on principle. Let's hope this lesson has been learned. If it hasn't, my entire youth and all my struggle and love for the people will have been in vain."

Politically shunned, harassed, and unable to find work in Peru, in mid-1951 Magda boarded a plane to Buenos Aires. Landing at Ezeiza Airport, she discovered that her baggage had not arrived. Her best clothes—and clothes mattered to her a great deal—were gone. Even more saddening was the disappearance of her accumulated manuscripts, "the unpublished intellectual work of more than twenty years." Gone were poems drafted in Venezuela pertaining to Gloria's death; gone were writings on her travels throughout Peru, as well as other works in progress. Repeated inquiries to the airline proved futile; she concluded that police agents had confiscated her suitcases. So disheartening did Magda find the loss of her manuscripts that she told friends she intended to give up writing. After staying only a few months in Buenos Aires, she returned to the family apartment in Lima.

Between Magda and her mother there had always existed a profound connection. "From her I absorbed many things, her quiet sorrow, her strength, her pride. She did not talk much, preferring to let others speak. I caused her a great deal of suffering but she never complained. During my long absences she was always there, awaiting my return. She waited. As years went by." Rosa Moreno in fact sympathized with her daughter's politics and welcomed her Aprista friends into their home; she even tolerated her daughter's break from Catholicism, which she herself devoutly practiced. Fiercely protective, she believed Magda to be an exceptional person who merited the family's utmost support. "Never, never abandon your sister Magda," she repeatedly counseled her daughter Graciela. The bond between the half-sisters was also very strong. Their difference in age, nearly twenty years, was such that Magda was not only a sister to her, Graciela explained, but also a maternal figure who saw to her schooling, helped with her clothing, and later helped her find employment.

Now Magda herself was in urgent need of a job. The need was such that she would even have taken a position with Cerro de Pasco, the U.S. mining company that still prospered in Peru's central highlands—the site of so many strikes and labor riots. As it turned out, however, as a representative of that company explained to Magda's friend Zoila Maxwell, Magda could not be hired, because her notoriety was too great. Eventually the displaced activist found work as a secretary in a German import-export firm, but a steady paycheck did not ensure tranquillity. In her interview with Alfonso Tealdo, Magda wondered what had been the point of so much Aprista sacrifice. "Why then the six thousand dead of Trujillo, why all the crosses of San Lorenzo, Huaraz, Cajamarca? All that sacrifice only to end up on the side of the reaction? Sometimes I want to go before a tribunal and talk and talk and talk. But I restrain myself. Some things cannot be said."

In need of some kind of cathartic expression, Magda turned to fiction. The avowedly autobiographical *La trampa* (The Trap), based on her own experience in the APRA, appeared in 1957. The fiction has as its setting an impoverished and disorganized Latin American country, never named but manifestly representing Peru and alluding to actual occurrences in the political life of the country. The series of vignettes that constitute *La trampa* afford insight into Magda's understanding of her own experience in the APRA. The portrayal of the women's leader—Mariel, as she is named in the revised edition cited here—is an attempt at self-portraiture that acknowledges her own complicity in failed leadership. Overall, the novel is bleak in its depiction of political corruption and personal disillusion. The story turns around the assassination of a prominent establishment political figure by a young militant acting at the behest of his political party's top command, an allusion to the 1935 assassination in Lima of Antonio Miró-Quesada, director of the conservative daily paper *El Comercio* by Aprista militant Carlos Steer. In the fictional episode, the young man is alternately flattered and intimidated into carrying out a political assassination. Immediately he is arrested, sentenced to life in prison, then abandoned by the political party that had used him to achieve its ends.

Other episodes highlight moments in the lives of individuals touched by the pervasive political violence—parents of the assassin, a jailed poet, a child orphaned by political massacre, a dissident labor leader slain by party thugs. We see the ignorance and malleability of the masses, the manipulative propaganda of the party, the machinations of the party chief and his lieutenants as they conspire to create martyrs whose deaths are used to revive the flagging ardor of the party faithful, this last an incident purportedly drawn from life. Magda claims to have been present at a meeting of the National Executive Committee when APRA leader León de Vivero announced, "We need a death, we need a death." The leadership, she alleged, then set about fomenting a labor action—she does not mention whether she herself took part in instigating this action—in which an Aprista militant would be killed. "What you have done is a betrayal," she said, confronting the leaders at a subsequent meeting. From then on she found herself shut out of the inner circle of Aprista deliberations.

In a dispassionate, highly detached tone, the women's leader in *La trampa* is described as lonely and aloof, increasingly isolated and aware that the sweeping promises made by her party would not be kept. Early in life, we are told, she had experienced a personal injustice and eventually was drawn into the working-class movement. "Passionate and vehement, she embraced the ideals of the party like a new religion, dedicating herself absolutely and truly to the cause." She realized the party was not perfect or even as radical as it initially had seemed to her, but its liberal democratic, lower-middle-class approach, she believed, would eventually lead to the more thorough changes necessary. "Or so her romantic imagination allowed her to suppose." Idealistic and loyal by nature, Mariel often found herself entangled in schemes of violence and intrigue she did not entirely understand. Persisting as a party militant long after having lost belief in the party's promises of reform, she became an inextricable part of the betrayal she deplored.

Although respected for her intelligence and tremendous capacity for work, the women's leader, the narrator dryly relates, was widely perceived as inflexible and judgmental. Unable to respond directly to political intrigues, she retreated into silence and disdain. Many men, including husbands of her friends in the party, insulted her with sexual invitations, which hurt her because "she believed in love." Holding back from romantic involvement, having experienced "three failed relationships," Mariel is also described (without comment by the narrator) as having had "a kind of physical repugnance for the act of love." She keeps aloof so as not to be misunderstood as inviting attention, and her distance is interpreted as haughtiness or arrogance. Despite her difficulties with men, Mariel preferred their company to that of women. Once when she is at a party a male comrade proposes a toast: "'Mariel, may women always curse you!'" The other guests, nearly all men, laughed heartily, but Mariel felt uncomfortable. She recognized that while her leadership in the party was uncontested, for the most part women disliked her and men were wary of her, resenting the stature she had attained—"as if women had a right to be equal to men."

The narrator also states that the party needed to put forward a female leader "so as to recruit women, so it could not be said that women in the party were all relegated to minor positions." Such a claim suggests a grim suspicion on Magda's part that from the outset she had been used.

The depiction of the party chief (representing Haya de la Torre) is caustically simplified, and it is tipped in the cold vitriol of personal attack. The chief is described as vain, sensuous, and tending to grotesque obesity because of his indulgence in luxurious dishes prepared by his personal cook. Constantly attended by subordinates, including a valet and a personal secretary who participate in major party decisions, he is described as having no use for women. As the narrator goes on to recount, the party chief surrounds himself with young men, disciples who live in his house and share his bed. "In the center of the leader's bedroom is a wide Turkish bed . . . with another at the back of the room against the wall. At least four young men sleep there, and two share the bed of the leader."

By no means was Magda the first to draw unflattering attention to the APRA chief's sexual proclivities. Even so, these fictional references to his sexual persuasion are bold, not to mention in questionable taste. Following the abortive uprising in 1948, a number of criticisms leveled against Haya de la Torre made crude references to his sexuality, which previously had been exempt from public comment. Fredrick Pike remarks on the phenomenon of Haya's sexuality: "Not only his enemies but many a devoted Aprista had little doubt that Haya was indeed a homosexual. The degree to which Haya, in spite of widespread assumptions about his sexual preferences, forged a successful political career in a culture permeated by machismo . . . stands as one of the most remarkable facets of his life."

Also criticized in *La trampa* are the party slogans, salutes, banners, symbols, insignias, and emotive songs, all seen as mind-numbing devices intended to inspire as well as manipulate an uneducated populace. "A party can't sustain itself without an all-encompassing symbolism. The masses need these symbols to help them keep their faith. A social doctrine, straightly stated, leaves many openings through which doubt can slip, as well as fatigue and ebbing confidence. Symbols distract. They dull the minds of the people, especially a people so innocent and uneducated. What would the rank and file do if it couldn't sing songs, or make little red-and-yellow flags, or draw the party's totem bird, or the five-pointed star?" The thousands pouring out to attend a major rally are described as a monstrous force, terrifying in its animal vivacity but amounting in the end to an aimless, dissipating crowd, leaving behind in the great plaza only scattered political fliers and other garbage. When a local gathering is dramatized, we see the party chief in full political regalia accompanied by the woman's leader in her usual supporting role. The meeting hall is bursting with people who explode in thunderous chants as the chief bounds up a flight of steps to the speakers' platform. Mariel nervously waits her turn to speak. "Great crowds always overwhelm her. Her mouth is dry. She takes a few sips of water and reminds herself—her usual childish recourse—that the people are simple, that she must make clear points, that in the end she has studied more than those who will hear her, even more than many of the leaders. But the 'chief'—he knew more than all of them, he stood above them all, and she felt afraid." Once at the microphone the women's leader is warmly applauded and is soon speaking easily, her voice musical yet strong, hardly in need of amplification. Concluding her remarks, she steps back and the party chief approaches the podium. At the highest pitch of excitement, the crowd cheers. The leader speaks in resonant platitudes. "'For centuries the people have borne the yoke of feudal-bourgeois exploitation—the same elite class has always benefited from the backbreaking toil of the people—the campesinos, our Indian brothers. . . . We want freedom, and more, we want bread, we demand bread and liberty! . . . *Compañeros*, the future is in your hands!'" Abruptly concluding, the leader turns and runs out amid a phalanx of bodyguards as an agitated group of women crowds around Mariel. "'My husband gets drunk and beats me, *compañerita*. . . . Do you think things will ever change?'" Mariel answers with encouraging lies and vague promises. As she heads for a bus stop she thinks of all the problems, and also of the many favors given out by high party officials, jobs that do not go to the poor who have sacrificed for the party but "to friends of the leader, or opportunists who have just joined the movement." What then, we may wonder, is *the trap* signified by the novel's title? Is it a snare woven of inexperience and blind enthusiasm? Is it simply the human condition, mired in self-delusion, stupidity, and corruptibility? We are left to speculate.

When *La trampa* appeared—"the book they wanted to kill me for writing"—a hefty portion of the print run disappeared in transit to the bookstores. Magda assumed that the shipments had been hijacked and destroyed by political enemies. Not until 1982 did a second edition (revised and augmented by new chapters) become available. The original publication had infuriated Aprista loyalists; it was rumored that the APRA (again free to operate and embarked on a course of Machiavellian alliances with Peru's oligarchy) wanted the renegade author dead. Three men wearing gloves attempted to enter the family apartment—Colombians sent by Haya to kill Magda, or so the family members feared; it also occurred to them that the intruders were just common burglars. In any case, they lived in considerable anxiety for their safety, but no physical harm ever came to them. Five months after the publication of *La trampa,* the Aprista assassin, whose fate had provided inspiration for the fiction, was released from prison after serving twenty-two years. He came to see Magda and—still faithful to the APRA—reproached her for having left the party.

As the 1950s wore on, the left-progressive forces in Peru remained in a state of retreat and disarray, eventually to emerge in new configurations. Now openly allied with Peru's oligarchy, Haya de la Torre, at the head of a still-powerful APRA, refused to condemn the CIA-sponsored overthrow in 1954 of the Jacobo Arbenz reform government in Guatemala, whose programs threatened the profits of United Fruit corporation. Power brokering in 1956 with retiring dictator Manuel Odría—the very same who had forced him to spend five years as a prisoner in the Colombian Embassy—Haya backed the presidential bid of former strongman Manuel Prado Ugarteche (whom he had previously characterized as a fascist). Haya by this time was consistently allying himself with rightists, to the extent that when in 1962 he himself ran for Peru's presidency against a resurgent Odría and other candidates, the former dictator Prado Ugarteche endorsed the APRA leader as just "the sort of conservative we need in Peru." Many leftists believed, as U.S. radical Carleton Beals reported, that Haya was "the chosen CIA candidate and getting the support of U.S. money."

The APRA chief carried the general election but with insufficient votes to accede to the presidency without a runoff contest. Oddly, rather than proceed to runoff and possibly capture the long-coveted presidency of Peru, Haya bowed out of the race and threw APRA support to his former nemesis Manuel Odría, with whom he had entangled himself in a secret power-sharing agreement. So controversial was Haya's deal-making in this episode, so widespread the suspicion of electoral fraud, that a group of concerned military men intervened. Declaring the election null and void, they proceeded to act as a caretaker government until new elections could be arranged, as they soon were. When the reform-minded Fernando Belaúnde won Peru's presidency in 1963, the APRA joined with Odría's conservative party to thwart the agrarian reform plan of the highly popular Belaúnde. No longer could there be any doubt—the APRA had abandoned its reform agenda and become part of the problem, having joined forces with Peru's oligarchs.

Traveling abroad frequently in his later years, Haya expressed admiration for the Scandinavian welfare states, praising what he saw as the convergence of capitalism and Communism in the democratic socialism he saw exemplified in their social systems. Consistently maintaining that he had never changed his essential views—still calling for a middle way between totalitarian Communism and rapacious corporate capitalism—Haya retained a large, even adulatory following and continued to play a significant role in Peruvian politics until his death in 1979. Following her break with APRA, Magda Portal remained on the far margins of political power, still vitally involved in public life.

6

LATER YEARS (1958–1989)

The relative insignificance of our powers in time and space is too much for us to grasp. Instinct rescues us from sterile doubt. Each strives for what he can and should hope to accomplish: a good day's work.

—JOSÉ CARLOS MARIÁTEGUI

A BOOKSTORE

In 1958 Magda accepted a most welcome offer to establish and then manage a bookstore, as a branch in Lima of the prestigious Mexican publishing company El Fondo de Cultura Económica. Originally established by a group of intellectuals in Mexico in the 1930s, the nonprofit El Fondo had as its aim the publication of high-quality books to be sold at popular prices throughout Latin America. This idealistic mission mobilized Magda's executive energies. Now reinventing herself as a businesswoman, she built from the ground up a successful retail operation that soon became an important cultural center. In the bookstore, which took the name of the publishing company, Magda hosted author readings, panel discussions, and book exhibits. Writers, including figures of international renown, presented new works in the attractive space in colonial Lima situated on Lampa Jirón Block 8. In a photograph of this era Magda can be seen urbanely presiding at a book reception. Bespectacled and well into middle age, she is attired in a black cocktail dress and pearls. In another photo Víctor Villanueva and César E. Pardo—the principal conspirators in the failed insurrection of October 3, 1948—can be seen leaning against a table, contemplatively leafing through new books.

This bookstore work renewed her earlier concern with literacy, education, and mass dissemination of culture. As manager of this enterprise, Magda enjoyed nearly twelve years of personal stability, prosperity, and intellectual edification as a purveyor of high-quality books and director of a vital cultural institution.

In 1965 Magda published at her own expense a collection of new and selected poems, *Constancia del ser,* a title that is ambiguous in meaning. The phrase, which might be translated as "signs of being" or "evidence of existence," suggests both the act of writing poetry and the poems themselves. Within it resonates the idea of constancy, the intimation of a steadfastness, a hope, perhaps, that a life can bear witness to itself and achieve coherence despite changeability, instability, and the threat of disintegration. This collection made Magda Portal's poetry available to a new generation of readers and confirmed her place as a significant figure in Peruvian letters. This volume would be her last in poetry, although she continued to write poems and be published in magazines.

Also in 1965 a new director of El Fondo de Cultura Económica (in Mexico City) set about reorganizing the international publishing and bookstore operation by firing employees and shutting down bookshop franchises in a number of Latin American countries. When an economic downturn in Peru in 1967 led to a drastic currency devaluation, Magda's store became unviable. Books ordered at one rate of foreign exchange had to be paid for with greatly devalued Peruvian currency. Bankruptcy loomed.

Around the time Magda began managing the bookstore, her half-sister Graciela gave birth to a daughter, Rocío Revolledo Pareja. Magda had insisted on carrying her infant niece out of the hospital, thereby assuming the active role she would play in the child's upbringing. In 1967, even as the bookstore faltered, Magda purchased a small two-bedroom apartment in seaside Miraflores, one of the most desirable residential districts in greater Lima. The three-generational family of women, Rosa Amelia, Magda, Graciela, and Graciela's daughter, Rocío, then nearly ten, moved into their new home on the top floor of a small, four-story, American-style apartment building. From the tiny narrow kitchen as well as through the spacious picture windows of the living room–dining room, they enjoyed a sweeping vista of the Pacific Ocean. As the years passed, however, and the waterfront became increasingly commercialized, casinos and exclusive high-rise enclaves sprang up, fronting the sea; these dwarfed the smaller buildings and eventually obliterated the ocean view from the apartment. Frequently in her later years Magda would walk out to a small neighborhood park that overlooked a precipitous drop to the ocean and a stretch of sandy beach.

Nearly every Sunday in the bookstore years Magda drove her mother, sister, and niece to church, La Iglesia San Pedro, in colonial Lima. While her relatives attended mass, Magda would sit reading in her car, or would drive to the bookstore to catch up on some work. Several times a month after the church service they brought flowers to the Presbitero Maestro Cemetery. Located in the family plot was Gloria Delmar's grave, the space above her coffin reserved for the remains of Rosa Amelia Moreno, whose health by the late 1960s was in decline. At Magda's behest Graciela quit her job to stay home and care for their ailing mother, who died in 1971.

In that same year Magda's bookstore went out of business, bankrupt as a result of the poor exchange rate with Mexico. Despite the store's profitability for so many years and its indisputable value as a cultural center, Magda's eloquent pleas for consideration went unheeded. Refusing to negotiate easier payment terms, El Fondo's director sued her for monies owed and demanded that she return outstanding inventory; the bookstore was then liquidated.

The livelihood provided by this enterprise had been essential to the family economy. Retirement was therefore out of the question. Magda needed another job. But doing what? To continue making payments on the newly purchased apartment, Graciela sold property of her own and the sisters began disposing of possessions. Her niece Rocío recalled Magda's selling a diamond ring, the proceeds of which allowed them "to eat for a number of months." Fortunately, at more than seventy years old, Magda remained in vigorous health; she began using her small German car as a taxi, driving daily from 8:00 A.M. to 1:00 P.M., carrying as many as four passengers at once along the Avenida Arequipa from Miraflores to downtown Lima. Over a period of months, her car, parked at night in a carport beneath the apartment building, was repeatedly spattered with eggs, urine, mud, and other filth flung through the protective wrought-iron fencing. Magda attributed these assaults to Aprista taxi drivers, older ones, she thought, who had not ceased resenting her for denouncing the APRA and who also disliked competing with a female driver for fares. She decided it was not possible under such circumstances to continue as a *taxista*, and she sold the car to help pay for a secretarial course for her niece—who recalled that it was around this time that her mother and Magda sat her down to explain that she would not be able to attend university, "because they had no money." She should plan, they told her, to seek work immediately to help them meet household expenses.

Soon thereafter, Rocío began earning a salary and the financial crisis receded. Magda also found paid work writing, above all for *Ojo*. Besides editing a Sunday literary page for *Ojo*, she was a regular columnist, reviewing books and writing opinion pieces on a range of municipal, national, and international concerns. Appalled at seeing the city center suppurating with garbage and overrun with rats, she decried the deterioration of colonial Lima and drew attention to the plight of street children who vied with rodents for scraps of rotting food. In other columns she lamented the overfishing in Peru's coastal waters, the polluting of the ocean, and the objectification of the female body in commercial advertisement. "I wrote on everything," she said, "from cancer to architecture."

During the years when Magda Portal remained preoccupied with the bookstore, violent conflicts were erupting in Peru's hinterlands. As historian Daniel Masterson has observed in his comprehensive study *Militarism and Politics in Latin America: Peru from Sánchez Cerro to Sendero Luminoso*, "at no time in this century, prior to the 1930s, had Peru experienced such large-scale rural unrest as it had in the period 1959–1965." Impoverished campesinos were desperate to acquire land, even as governmental attempts at land reform were being thwarted and vast haciendas continued to dominate the highlands. An agricultural census taken in 1961 revealed that five high-sierran haciendas covered as many as three-quarters of a million acres each, while another twenty were each one-quarter of a million acres. Frustrated campesinos were taking matters into their own hands by illegally occupying vast tracts of privately owned territory. At the same time, the miners were in rebellion at the Cerro de Pasco and La Oroya mines.

In 1962 the revolutionary Movimiento de la Izquierda Revolucionaria (MIR) appeared on the scene. Formerly known as APRA Rebelde, this militant group—which carried out armed actions—was made up of dissident Apristas "who sympathized with the revolutionary objectives of the militants who led the Callao revolt of 1948." The other main guerrilla organization, Ejército de Liberación Nacional (ELN), had its roots in the Communist Party of Peru. Ideologically at odds and unable to coordinate their rebel operations, these two groups undertook various armed assaults in 1965. Responding with extreme force, the Peruvian military, aided by the U.S. Central Intelligence

Agency, unleashed its full counterinsurgency arsenal, which included napalm. In addition to a ruthless take-no-prisoners policy, these decisive measures swiftly debilitated the nascent guerrilla movements.

The death of Peruvian guerrilla fighter and poet Javier Heraud in a 1963 ELN action contributed to the romantic mystique of armed struggle, which gained further currency when Cuban revolutionary Ernesto (Ché) Guevara was murdered in Bolivia five years later.

The violence and instability in Peru's countryside led some officers in the country's armed forces to conclude that only by seizing power themselves and instituting major reforms could the mounting threat of civil disorder be eliminated. In 1948, when socially progressive Aprista officers had plotted insurrection, their uprising had failed miserably. But activist tendencies persisted in Peru's armed forces. By 1968 a substantial consensus existed within the officer corps in favor of an interventionist role for the military. Many officers feared that if Peru's extreme social inequities were not effectively addressed, the country would be torn apart by guerrilla warfare.

On October 3, 1968—twenty years to the day after the failed insurrection of 1948—a group of progressive army officers led by General Juan Velasco Alvarado seized state power in a bloodless coup. Within days of this major development the Standard Oil subsidiary International Petroleum—a legendary symbol of U.S. domination of Peru's resources—was nationalized without compensation. Also nationalized was the notorious Cerro de Pasco Mining Company. The military rulers also instituted a far-reaching agrarian reform, actually breaking apart Peru's vast haciendas with the aim of radically altering the country's economic and social structure. A number of the greater landholdings, including the huge agribusiness plantations on the north coast, were either divided into individual plots, reorganized as agrarian cooperatives, or restored to indigenous communities.

In its scope and in many of its details the junta's agenda mirrored the revolutionary program formulated in 1931 by the Aprista Party of Peru. The military government also shared the early APRA's opposition to U.S. foreign policies. Velasco denounced the U.S. war in Vietnam and established friendly relations with Cuba, Communist China, and the Soviet Union, while the USSR approved the sale of military equipment to Peru at subsidized prices.

Generating jubilant enthusiasm and expectation among left-wing Peruvians in the country and abroad, the junta's actual and proposed reforms seemed to augur nothing less than Peru's long-postponed revolution. Magda expressed support for Velasco's administration, writing in her column in the newspaper *Ojo* in defense of the controversial law that nationalized the press and restricted a number of press freedoms. The junta's programs—inexpertly, even incompetently, carried out (some thought) and at the same time extremely threatening to powerful interests—triggered overwhelming opposition. A rash of disruptive strikes, along with APRA-led street rioting and an abrupt cutoff of U.S. aid, led to the collapse of the Velasco regime in 1975. Under pressure exerted by the World Bank and the International Monetary Fund, the military junta's progressive experiment was scrapped.

The long-anticipated breaking up of the enormous haciendas in fact created new problems and fostered new resentments. Not even the eagerly awaited land reform could put an end to Peru's intractable rural poverty. So blighting and deeply rooted was this poverty that campesinos and others who despaired of peaceful means to improve their lot remained vulnerable to recruitment by guerrilla organizations. Especially effective at recruiting campesinos was the guerrilla army of Sendero Luminoso (Shining Path). This organization, like the ELN before it, had its roots in Peru's Communist Party. When that party (in accord with Moscow's line in those days) renounced the tactic of armed struggle, some members disagreed, and a dissident faction called Bandera Roja (Red Banner) emerged. This faction splintered off and became the Shining Path (its full name was El Partido Comunista del Perú en el Sendero Luminoso de Mariátegui). Led by middle-class intellectuals, this dynamic movement appeared on the scene in 1974, just before the demise of Velasco's progressive rule. Maoist in tendency, quasi-religious in its sense of mission, and terrifically bloody in its tactics, the Sendero rapidly gained adherents, recruiting from the ranks of the poorest and most disaffected campesinos, including many indigenous and many women. The Sendero, at least in certain of its aspects—"its messiah-like leader, its secretive and rigidly disciplined organization, and its single-minded conviction that only Sendero Luminoso [could] save Peru"—has been compared to the APRA movement in its early days. Convinced of the urgent necessity for an all-out war against the state, the Sendero in the 1980s carried out savagely destructive assaults, including wanton killing of people, and even of their animals, in remote mountain communities. With strongholds in high-sierran and Amazonian provinces, the Sendero's boldly orchestrated guerrilla actions severely disrupted Peru's economy. Also operating in urban zones, the Sendero terrorized a large part of the country.

A NEW AFFILIATION

From now on my country will be humanity.
—*Flora Tristan*

Following her break with APRA in 1950, Magda tried unsuccessfully to launch a new political party. From then on, as she put it, her political activity was "optional." She would never again devote herself single-mindedly to a political party. Over the years, however, she had been courted by a coalition of left parties as well as by the Communist Party of Peru, which she finally joined, as she recalled the date, in 1967. After her two decades of competing with that party as an Aprista, what now accounted for such a move on her part?

For one thing, her earlier resistance to Communism had emerged in a very different historical context and under the potent influence of Haya de la Torre. With that context gone and Haya's spell inert, Magda no doubt preferred the relative stability of Peru's Communist Party to being associated with a shifting coalition of left-wing parties. Furthermore, Magda's early objection to Communism had never been as thoroughgoing as Haya's, as indicated by a conciliating article she wrote for the official APRA journal in 1931. In that piece, which appeared in June, before Haya's return to Peru, she affirmed that Aprismo was not anti-Communist. The APRA, she wrote, "was neither with communism nor against it." This was not exactly Haya's view. Joining Peru's Communists late in her life may also have afforded her the reassurance of again being part, not simply of an established party, but of one that officially bound her to the Marxist principles she had never rejected, and to the hope-filled world of Mariátegui and the *Amauta* circle of her youth. Magda's new affiliation also situated her in formal opposition to the still-powerful APRA, which had not stopped competing with Communists for the loyalty of workers in the trade union movement.

In a manuscript version of a talk she delivered on the occasion of her inception into this party, she defensively anticipated certain questions regarding her Aprista past. Did she regret her sojourn in APRA? No, she had no regrets. "What happened in APRA," she explained, "is part of my own human situation, part of my personal burden and my fate. I don't believe in guilt." Besides which, she continued, "the APRA, with all its faults and heresies, had performed a positive function. It had readied the ground, it had raised consciousness, it had created conditions for a leap ahead. . . . My trajectory through APRA was the great adventure of my life. . . . As part of that party I came to know at the nearest possible range a wealth of people, situations, events, and facts that became part of Peru's history." Her immersion in APRA had allowed her, she declared, to encounter "deep Peru"—a realm experienced on a voyage of discovery that was its own reward.

Finding in Peru's Communist Party a congenial world of like-minded comrades, she became associated with Jorge del Prado, head of the party, who as a very young man in the 1920s had been a comrade of Mariátegui's. In this new context Magda became a defender of the Soviet Union, then perceived in such circles as the great bulwark against U.S. expansionism and unbridled corporate power. The USSR's material support of Cuba, along with its ties to the Velasco military government, no doubt further disposed her to sympathize with the Soviets.

In an opinion piece dated in manuscript February 25, 1980, Magda defended the Soviet occupation of Afghanistan, viewing the remote south-central Asian country as torn by a strife typically experienced by impoverished countries struggling to develop their own resources and attain modernity. "Afghanistan has opted for freedom, independence, and control of its wealth," she wrote," but has felt itself endangered by the powerful allies of deposed dictators." She noted that "Pakistani and Chinese mercenaries were massing on borders, a situation that led Afghanistan to call for the Soviet Union to come to its aid, invoking Article 51 of the United Nations Charter." Sanctions imposed on Afghanistan by the United States would only make matters worse, she said, "increasing tensions in the world and leading to arms proliferation."

Many leftists at the time defended the Soviet incursion into Afghanistan as a righteous battle for modernization and secularism in opposition to a reactionary and fundamentalist tribalism. Persuaded by this partisan view, Magda could hardly have guessed at the time that the invasion—and in response to it the CIA's support of Osama bin Laden and an Islamic fundamentalist mujahideen—would have incalculably far-reaching effects throughout the region and beyond, well into the coming century.

Her new party affiliation opened the way for Magda to travel as an official guest to the Soviet Union and countries in the Soviet bloc—Cuba, Czechoslovakia, and Bulgaria. In 1985, as a guest of the Cuban government, she attended a major conference of nonaligned nations, whose representatives had come together in Havana to discuss third world debt and to issue an urgent call for debt forgiveness. On that trip she received medical attention from Cuban doctors.

RECOGNITION

That day when woman will take her place alongside man in complete equality and
mutual respect, the most transcendent revolution of all time will have been
accomplished.
—*Magda Portal, Chile, 1940*

In the 1970s a new generation of women became politically active in Peru, a
phenomenon that could not have been more timely for Magda Portal. She
greatly appreciated the recognition from younger women, Peruvian feminists
who esteemed her efforts and who, following her death, would express their
debt to her, honoring her as a foundational figure in their battles. They would
see in her "the symbolic figure who opened the way for them, one equal in
importance to Flora Tristan." When asked by a journalist in 1983 if she now
considered herself a feminist, Magda did not hesitate. "Of course!" she re-
plied. Three decades earlier, in Valparaiso, Chile, she had expressed her con-
viction that over thousands of years women had indeed made progress in
their struggle for emancipation, which she described as an authentic revo-
lution, one all the more extraordinary in that it was being accomplished
"without cataclysmic bloodshed."

Magda worked closely in these years on many projects of concern to
women. In 1977 as president of the Center for Peruvian Women Writers, she
developed programs to help women advance their literary efforts. She sup-
ported Acción para la Liberación de la Mujer Peruana (ALIMUPER), also
promoting the women's publishing venture La Equidad. She responded read-
ily to interview questions, though she could only laugh when asked by Sara
Beatriz Guardia to discuss her erotic experiences. In an unusually frank and
extensive interview by Esther Andradi and Ana María Portugal (published in
1979), she shared thoughts on motherhood and on abortion.

> Abortions? Not one, but several. This is a serious problem for women
> because now it seems that abortion is used as a method of birth con-
> trol. In my time? Yes, definitely, most were done secretly. When I was
> married I had my tubes tied. I was very young and the doctor asked:
> "But won't you want to have more children in the future?" "No, doctor."
> It seems the tone of my voice convinced him. The operation was illegal
> but he was my friend.
>
> I understand that a woman who marries and wants children should

have them, three at the most. That is the human, the manageable thing. But women need to have better conditions; they should not just be mothers. Having one baby after another, no, not that. Being a house-wife, tending to the husband, doing only that, no! That reduces the woman to nothing, to an entirely effaced being. These were some of the things I was thinking when I decided to have no more children. In fact, I never wanted more children and avoided having them. Having a child is a sacred thing; I would not abandon a child. But [if I'd had more children] I would not have been able to do the other. That which came from my deepest self and was my path, my vocation.

In 1981 Magda accepted further acclaim for her life's work, having been designated an Escritora de las Américas (Writer of the Americas) by the Fourth Inter-American Congress of Women Writers, convened June 3–6 in Mexico City. As a recipient of this award and coguest of honor (along with Spanish poet Carmen Condé), she traveled to Mexico City to take part in the congress along with women from various countries in Latin America, North America, and Europe. Daniel Reedy of the University of Kentucky delivered the keynote address in homage to her career. From Mexico City she went with Professor Reedy to Lexington, Kentucky, giving several public readings before going on to San Francisco, where she stayed with her former Aprista com-rade Zoila Maxwell. During that visit she participated in the 1981 interview so often cited in these pages.

From 1981 to 1986, in her capacity as president of Peru's prestigious National Association of Writers and Artists (ANEA), she worked with a scant budget out of a pleasant but deteriorating building in old Lima. Focusing on limited goals relating to cultural affairs, she drafted a bill and lobbied (with-out success) for legislation to provide social benefits for writers and artists. She also organized panels, readings, and various commemorative events hon-oring Peruvian writers. These occasions gave rise to lectures and articles on distinctive individuals she had known in the earlier part of the century, among them Alberto Hidalgo, Ciro Alegría, César Vallejo, José María Arguedas, Ale-jandro Peralta, Gamaliel Churata, and above all José Carlos Mariátegui.

Her remarks on the novelist Arguedas reveal her mature sense of the dangers of living in constant confrontation with authority. "The principal task of the writer in our time is to denounce," she had once declared. Yet to dwell upon evil, she observed, refusing to turn away from the most unfair, the most misshapen, things in life, can debilitate, even destroy, the social fighter.

In his inordinately sad novel *Los ríos profundos* (Deep Rivers), Arguedas—who had been a militant in the APRA—depicted the bleak world of the indigenous in Peru. He died a suicide. As Magda wrote, "The injustices he lived and witnessed penetrated his neurons so thoroughly as to distort reality. . . . He felt very small in a world created on the scale of his accusation." She believed that his own hatred of injustice had overwhelmed him, along with his sense that despite their immense exertions, nothing had changed, or would ever change. She cited his despairing words: "I am sick with disappointment, rebellion, dissatisfaction, sick with the things we all die of, as life slips through our fingers like a light rain."

Magda too excelled in denunciation, relentlessly criticizing individuals, groups, and social realities she deemed unjust. Repeatedly she affirmed the need to remedy the great disparities between wealth and poverty not just in Peru but throughout the world, an ideal she had acquired as a young woman in Lima. She did not, however, question the immensity of this ideal, or entertain the possibility that to promulgate such an ideal, let alone strive to enact it on a grand scale, might—as Albert Camus supposed—amount to hubris, a failure to recognize humanity's limitations. Although she never repudiated this monumental aspiration, she seems to have resigned herself to the failure of their large plans. "There is only one real social idea," she wrote, "and that is justice, justice without compromise, justice that liberates the great national majorities from their poverty, their frustration, from the evil in which they find themselves: that justice which is spoken of by everybody and practiced by nobody." Described by Luis Alberto Sánchez as "the protagonist of a broken dream," she withstood potentially debilitating failures, both political and in her personal life. In advancing age, she cherished her sense that a number of young people truly understood the principles that her great contemporaries José Carlos Mariátegui and César Vallejo had advanced. Her faith in the young people—along with the indisputable ascendancy of the women's movement—heartened her as her own powers declined.

In the four decades since her first talk on Flora Tristan in Chile in 1944, Magda had frequently lectured on the life of the nineteenth-century writer and activist, predecessor of those who promoted socialist internationalism. She believed that women needed a history that not only recorded "the shameful past" of venal compromise, blunder, and betrayal but also embodied the ennobling theme of humanitarian exertion. Magda frankly revered Flora as an illustrious "precursor" who would always exist for her on an exalted level, in the company of "a few stellar spirits whose names defined epochs." Magda's much revised talk on Flora Tristan's life provided the starting point for a book-length study, titled *Flora Tristan: Precursora*, which appeared in 1983, the result of a collaborative research-and-writing project undertaken by Magda and five other women. Satisfying a need in Peru for a contemporary presentation of Tristan's life and work, this study would be hailed as "the bedside-table book of Peruvian feminists."

In April 1984, Magda boarded a plane for France, accompanied by her niece Rocío Revolledo. In Paris they placed flowers on César Vallejo's grave at Père-Lachaise Cemetery; from Paris they went on by train to Dijon, where Magda spoke at the First International Colloquium on Flora Tristan. This trip marked the culmination of her decades-long interest in the French Peruvian activist. In her remarks at the colloquium Magda reviewed earlier Peruvian commentary on Tristan and charged those early critics with ignoring Flora's graphic depictions of industrial misery in London, as well as her major tour of the industrial zones of France. She noted that these critics appeared to have little interest in Flora's seminal writings in aid of an internationalist union of working men and women. Instead, she observed, they focused on Flora's dramatic sea voyage from France to Peru and her complicated relations with men, ultimately viewing her as a beautiful seductress in search of a fortune—Flora had hoped to become the heir to her deceased father's vast landholdings in Peru. As Magda indignantly noted in her talk, one commentator even went so far as to defend Flora's Peruvian uncle Don Pío, who refused his niece's claim to her father's great wealth in land—her father had died without leaving a will, and his church marriage to Flora's mother had no status under Spanish law.

Magda greatly sympathized with Flora's protracted difficulties, which were indeed extraordinary; for one thing Flora was shot and seriously wounded (nearly murdered) by her estranged husband. She also endured serious poverty, illness, and official persecution as she worked to organize French workers into trade union organizations. Frankly admitting that she identified with Flora, Magda noted that she did not wish to be seen as putting herself on an equal level with the legendary French Peruvian. She would have been honored, she said, alluding to her own organizing travels in Peru, to think she had been doing something similar to what Flora had done in France. Along with other papers read at the Dijon colloquium, Magda's talk would appear in *Una reserva de utopia*, published by the Flora Tristan Women's Center in Lima, an organization with which she became closely associated.

Well into her eighties Magda remained uncommonly active. Twice she ran for public office—in 1978 for National Assembly as a candidate of Partido

Acción Revolucionaria Socialista, and in 1985 for a municipal post in Lima as a candidate of the Partido Mariáteguista por la Liberación Nacional. Both efforts proved unsuccessful. She remained, however, an undeterred supporter of progressivist causes, helping organize a committee in solidarity with the Sandinista government in Nicaragua, which came to power in 1979 only to be undermined by CIA-funded attacks by *contra* forces. She also served as president of the Peru-Cuba Friendship Association.

During these years she enjoyed an elaborate social life, one closely related to her cultural work. Her niece Rocío recalled that Magda frequently went out to meetings, lectures, and formal dinners at embassies, occasions on which she enjoyed dressing elegantly—sometimes (before animal rights became a concern) even wearing furs, appearing in a leopard-skin coat, or a white coat with a blue-fox collar. In a late interview Magda confessed that she did not relish looking old and preferred not to mention her age, acknowledging that she had never been able to shake "that female vanity that is the legacy of being a woman in our time."

In 1985, for the first time in the APRA party's long and controversial history, an Aprista candidate, Alán García, won Peru's presidency, only to be accused when his administration ended of having neglected every aspect of governance while enriching himself and his cronies at public expense. Inflation soared astronomically on his watch, while Sendero Luminoso guerrillas—allied with coca-related narco-trafficking groups in the mountains—had expanded unchecked in the interior. Fleeing the bloodletting inflicted by the Sendero and by government forces combating them, refugees from the hinterlands poured into Lima. Magda lamented the accompanying transformation of Lima's historic colonial center as thousands of street vendors took over the sidewalks each day to peddle an unaccountable jumble of wares throughout the downtown area, returning at nightfall to the city outskirts—where shantytowns known as *pueblos jóvenes* were proliferating. Voluntary grassroots, self-help organizations continued to spring up throughout these makeshift communities. The communal kitchens and health clinics were often overseen by women, who petitioned the government for urgently needed social services. One of these *pueblos jóvenes* would take the name Magda Portal.

Shortly after the APRA succeeded for the first time in winning the presidency, a delegation of Aprista wives approached Magda to ask if she might want to return to her old party. "Definitely not," she replied without hesitation. "I'm going forward, forward, I don't go back." In this brusque retort we can hear not only her stubborn adherence to a progressivist vision and its rhetoric but also perhaps, as she confronted late age, a hint of the need to bolster her own personal courage. In fact, Magda did not always endure her final years with the equanimity and optimism she typically exhibited in her public persona. In her late (mostly unpublished) poems, a disquietude is felt, an ominous sense of solitude and eerie stasis, as in the following lines:

> Perhaps my final words will go unheard
> and only the sea will gather in my voice
> and night will be one with day and time
> eternal night with its glassy moon.

In May 1985, in her eighty-fifth year, she boarded a jet and flew to a world peace conference in the Soviet Union—whose abrupt disintegration she would not live to see and could not have imagined. In Leningrad (now St. Petersburg) she visited the memorial dedicated to the million dead in the terrible siege of that city by Hitler's forces in World War II. In an article commemorating the anniversary of the siege, she recalled walking the length of the tree-shaded memorial promenade; awed by the heroism of the Soviet resistance, she felt equally moved by the magnitude of the carnage. Agitated by a phantasmagoric crowding in upon her mind of war scenes, she could not, she wrote, restrain tears. Should anyone have noticed her there, overcome with emotion on the tree-lined promenade, she must have appeared a very small, somewhat frail old woman. This trip would be her last abroad.

FINAL DAYS

> Bear me away, sea, carry me
> along an endless road
> lull me in the last
> ecstatic dream.
> —*Magda Portal, "Sea Thirst" (Sed de mar)*

By 1987 Magda Portal was losing her mind and knew it. Her recurrent mental lapses horrified her. First she was diagnosed as having arterial sclerosis, then Alzheimer's disease. Her condition deteriorated until she could no longer adequately care for herself. Not wanting to be a burden to her family, she insisted on entering a hospital. After a brief stay in a private establishment that the family could not afford, she was admitted, on December 20, 1988, into the Guillermo Almenara Social Security Hospital for Workers, a refuge for patients without the means to pay. Graciela and Rocío took long bus rides to spend time with her at this facility, whose services were very spare. It would be up to family and friends to provide nursing care; bed linens; and other essential supplies, including costly medications, and not all of these needs could be met. When friends in the APRA government learned of this unhappy situation, minister of health David Tejada offered assistance, an offer that greatly agitated the former leader, who did not want to accept anything from the party she had repudiated. She relented only when assured that it was not the APRA but the Peruvian government that wished to help; a private nurse was then assigned to care for her twelve hours a day. Drifting in and out of an agitated consciousness, she steadily declined, eventually lapsing into an irreversible coma. Death came at 1:45 the morning of July 11, 1989.

Following months of suffering in the most humble circumstances, her death brought posthumous honors and recognition. Her body lay in state in the great hall of the University of San Marcos. Jorge Campos Rey de Castro, rector of the university, delivered the eulogy, praising not only her "exemplary rebellion" but also her efforts as president of the Union of Writers and Artists of Peru to gain recognition and social benefits for Peruvian cultural workers. A profuse outpouring of obituary tributes appeared in Lima newspapers and magazines. Repeatedly she was hailed as "a woman symbolic of an epoch." Among Magda's belongings Graciela discovered an envelope containing a photo of Gloria. Written on the back in her sister's bold hand were the words "Incinear la imagen conmigo" (Incinerate the picture with me).

Her remains were cremated in an austere ceremony at the Británico Cemetery. In attendance, besides family and close friends, were representatives of Peru's women's groups, who came "to pay their final respects to one who has now entered the history of women's struggles in Peru." In accordance with the request of the deceased as adumbrated in "Clamor" (Clamor), a poem of the 1940s, read in memoriam, her ashes would be scattered in the sea.

As reported in the Lima daily *La República,* at 8:30 on the morning of July 13, 1989, family and friends of Magda Portal assembled on the docks at Chorrillos. Again present were representatives of Peru's major women's organizations—the Manuela Ramos, the Flora Tristán, and the Aurora Víver. As waves audibly lapped at the sand, the silent mourners boarded boats that took them to the coastal waters just off Barranco, Magda's seaside birthplace. The ocean was shrouded in mist as Graciela Pareja Moreno, her face bathed in tears, stood up shakily in the small boat and scattered her sister's ashes over the water. Also tossed into the sea were white flowers that "pooled in a circle where, just moments earlier, the ashes of the former secretary general of APRA had disappeared." The following lines from "Clamor" affirm Magda Portal's lifelong yearning for union with something far larger than herself. The poet addresses the sea.

> Your voice shall be mine
> in the vast night of the desolate earth
> I'll exist no more   the sea-
> shell blossoms of my dreams
> rising to cold stars
> will splash the clouds with foam
> . . . .
> Reclaim me, sea, with your love
> free of complications
> dissolve me in your waters
> forever distant from the land
> exile I will endure in you.

SELECTED POEMS

Nocturnos

Mi corazón me pesa
como una enorme piedra
y me rinde y me abruma y no me deja
levantarme. . . .
      oh, la Noche
tan larga que me resta
donde mi insomnio crea sombras
que en torno a mí pasean

Sombras que cuentan los latidos
de mi entraña tremenda
sombras que desbaratan mis cabellos
y hunden sus largos dedos en mi idea

Y en tanto da su son hondo y rotundo
mi corazón que vela
reloj que duele dentro el pecho
implacable reloj   siempre con cuerda

Por él mi alma no sueña
Atenta vive a su tic tac tirano
porque cuando se duerme
con un brusco latir   él la despierta!

Me pesa el corazón como una piedra
Y no puedo acallarlo
y no puedo dejarlo en un rincón
como un trasto cualquiera . . .

Nocturnes

My heart is heavy
like an enormous stone
subduing me, obstructing me
not letting me get up. . . .
            oh, the night
nowhere near ending
insomnia flickers
in wheeling shadows

Shadows that count the beats
of my swollen womb
shadows that twist my hair
and sink long fingers in my mind

As the deep round beat continues
I'm wide awake
clock that hurts   tightly
wound clock

I can't rest
Alert to this tyrannical tick tock
if I start to fall asleep
the brusque beat awakens me!

My heart's heavy as a stone
I can't quiet it
I can't toss it in some corner
like an old toy . . .

Cuando era niña

cuando era niña
      cómo recordarás
a la página blanca de mi frente
enmarcada en su oro matinal

cuando era niña
      y me llamabas "mía"
confiada

sin intuición
para mirar el rojo sol
que hoy me tuesta la pálida frente

sin intuición
para los viajes del Espíritu

tan largos — tan inaccesibles
      oceanos de distancia

Con mis líneas profundos

con mis líneas profundos — amanecí —

estaba la mañana fresca recién bañada
      oliente a humedad
qué dulce azul el cielo — los picos de los Andes
los árboles — la vastedad del panorama —

sobre los techos de las casas acurrucadas
se abrían cóncavos los cielos
como si les dijera: pequeñas
      id a campo a retozar

When I Was a Child

when I was a child
        you remember
a matinal amber tinged
the white page of my brow

when I was a child
        you referred to me as "my"
intimately

with no premonition
of the vermilion sun
today scorching my pale forehead

with no sense
of the journeys awaiting me
travels of mind

far and inaccessible
        oceans of distance

Lines

with deep lines—I awoke—

the morning cool, rinsed
fragrant with moisture
how soft the blue sky—
the Andean peaks—the trees
the panoramic landscape

over the roofs of nestled houses
an arch of skies
someone seemed to call to them: little ones
        go play in the fields

pero ellas no se movían
      su trágica inmovilidad

a m a n e c í a   y o

la lluvia refrescó mis neuronas
e igual a la mañana
estaba dulce — sin memoria — y pálida

      como convaleciente
y deseosa de derramar mi sol — perdón
como la mañana
sobre las trágicas palomas acurracadas

sobre la mala Vida
      que todo melo niega
llena de absurdos
      hasta afilarme el alma

      Yo — y luego?

la mañana tan fresca
      y tan sin sol

y en lo recóndito
la dulce voz que besa el alma
      como la lluvia

M A D R E   L L E N A   D E   L Á G R I M A S

yet their tragic immobility
     did not change

I   a w o k e

my mind cleared by the rain
so too the day
I was gentle—without memory—and pale

like a convalescent
desirous of pouring out sunlight—forgiveness
like morning
over tragic huddled doves

and malevolent life
which denies me everything
senselessness
    grinding down my soul

        I—and beyond that?

the day is damp
    overcast

hidden away
a soft voice caresses my soul
     like rain

   M O T H E R   Y O U   A R E   W E E P I N G

Oración al mar

Este dolor y este deseo de viajar
¡oh Mar!
Este deseo de entregarme
a tu ruda y magnífica aventura
alegre y triste
con la emoción que imprime la
grandeza
de tu perfecta soledad
y de tu ancho camino —

Engarzar en mi espíritu
el rubí tornasol de tus crepúsculos
y la esmeralda ilusionada de tu cielo —
Y al pasar por los puertos
sentir el ansia de llegar —
Y no llegar. —

Oh Mar
y descansar
un día largo
en tus brazos abiertos
como una alga dócil
a merced de la danza de tus olas. —

Canto proletario

"la vida es de los felices"
amanece en todos los pregones callejeros
rueda la mañana sobre el asfalto de
la tierra ululante y caliente

Prayer

Excruciating desire to travel
O Sea
such yearning to surrender
to your rough
and magnificent adventure
joyous and sad
the emotion aroused by the
grandeur
of your perfect solitude
and open road—

To clasp in my spirit
the ruby sunflower
of your dusks
the ephemeral emerald of your skies
To pass through ports—
such yearning to arrive
and not arrive.

O Sea
then to rest
one long day in your open arms
like a docile seaweed
at the mercy of the wave's dance.

Proletarian Song

"Life belongs to the lucky"
dawns in the scrawled slogans of the street
morning wheels over the asphalt
of screeching hot earth

al extremo de la ciudad
los árboles saludan al obrero
con sus ramas estremecidas
por la alegría del viento vagabundo
        el gran libertario

Como un dolor sigue la sombra
la silueta del hombre
que desemboca en la ancha
puerta de la fábrica
allí el humano acecido de las máquinas
el gemido de las poleas
bajo la presión del pensamiento humano

balcones a la eternidad
los ojos siguen la labor constructora
y toda la fábrica es una sola
maquinaria de empuje formidable
como un titánico organismo
que mueve "el motor maravilloso"
de los cerebros de 100 hombres unidos
el hermoso espectáculo del cerebro
y el músculo en acción

el sudor les decora la cara
como otra sonrisa
que se tuesta en los labios apretados
de anhelo
la fábrica lo es todo

      la ESPERANZA y la CÁRCEL

todos los días son MAÑANA
para el obrero que los lleva apretados
al corazón
      como la imagen de la madre

Trees at the city outskirts
salute the worker
with branches tossed
by the gaiety of the vagabond wind
    the great libertarian

Like pain a shadow tracks
the silhouette of a man
entering the broad
factory doorway
inside: the human pant of machines
pulleys groan
under the weight of human thought

balconies onto eternity
eyes follow the constructive labor
the entire factory is
one surging mechanism
a titanic organism
powered by "the marvelous motor"
of the brains of 100 united men
the beautiful spectacle of mind
and muscle in action

sweat decorates their faces
like a smile
playing on lips
tense with concentration
the factory is all things

HOPE and PRISON

Every day is Tomorrow
for the worker who keeps them
near the heart
    like a mother's image

LIBERTAD
estandarte del hombre

el Sol espera la salida de la fábrica
desde el horizonte sus anchos brazos de luz
saludan el dolor del obrero
vencedor de la Vida

Mi soledad aguaita

mi soledad aguaita
las esquinas vacías de la Noche

aquí estoy apretada
en las paredes del silencio

la duda me hace signos
desde el alféizar de su sonrisa

gatos neurasténicos pasean
en los tejados del recuerdo
las lucesitas de sus ojos
como automóviles de cita

oh   CIUDAD!
cuando te agarrarán
los remolinos de mis ojos
para que te hundas definitivamente

creo en el arco iris de la alegría
en los mil faroles eléctricos
que decoran la catedral de tu cuerpo

LIBERTY
                    raised ensign of man

the sun waits at the factory exit
broad arms of horizon-light
salute the suffering worker
                        conqueror of Life

Translated with Allan Francovich

Alert Loneliness

my loneliness
keeps watch in the night

deserted street corners
oppressive walls of silence

doubt beckons
from the windowsill of a smile

along rooftops of memory
neurotic cats parade
tiny headlights of their eyes
like lovers' cars

oh   CITY!
                when will the whirlpools
of my eyes seize
and engulf you absolutely

I believe in incandescent happiness
in the thousand electric lights
decorating the cathedral of your body

honda que arroja piedras a los pájaros
juventud cazadora de emociones
pero allí está la FUERZA
sobre los rieles del deseo

allá
　　　　las torres más altas
lucen reclamos para los habitantes
de los otros planetas

Pacific Steam

recién noche vientre negro de fiera amaestrada
tus pasillos se encienden con luciérnagas de sueño

arrinconada está la flor de mis veinte años
como una niña de cabellos largos

mar del color del jersey de la mañana
balanceo embriagante
sin palabras　　　armonía de lo silencioso

cortando el transatlántico el presente
enarboladas manos de adiós
　　　　　　　gritaban las gaviotas
pañuelos inútiles　　　sin respuesta

el rojo capitán obeso y el japonés
de ojos tatuados de deseo
flechas tiradas al azar　　　las siluetas de las
pasajeras
　　　　　　la pianola es un grito destemplado
el corazón del mar abrazado de oscuridad

sling hurling stones at birds
youth stalker of emotions
but this is FORCE
rushing along rails of desire

in the distance
        skyscrapers
beam advertisements
to the inhabitants
of the other planets

Translated with Allan Francovich

Pacific Steam

Last night black womb of a domesticated creature
your corridors spark with dream fireflies

pressed flower of my twenty years
girl with long streaming hair

sea the color of morning's blouse
intoxicating roll of the waves
speechless   harmony of the silent

steamship cleaving the present
hands unfurl good-byes
        seagulls shriek
handkerchiefs wave   unanswered

the obese red captain and the Japanese
with desire-tattooed eyes
haphazard arrows   passengers'
silhouettes
        a pianola's dissonant wail
the sea's heart embraced by darkness

viajeras pálidas   ojos anestesiantes
hombres que fuman cigarrillos de recuerdo

por las claraboyas de la noche
se asomó la mañana

EN SUS MANOS TRAÍA LA COSTA

Amistad

AMISTAD   eje cercado de distancias
polo norte a donde llega el Sol cada seis meses
todos tus osos blancos gruñen hermosamente

yo soy salvajemente hermana
como los vientos cálidos que soplan de los trópicos
para envolver en sus anillos
las ciudades dispersas del globo

intercontinental   cosmopolita y amargamente huraña
mis ojos lentes zeiss de ultrapotencia
impresionan múltiple y cósmica la Vida

AMISTAD   terciopelo de lujurias suaves
vanidad de chiffones
expresión de mujer del siglo XIX

yo soy como los yodos y las sales del mar
de vastedad jadeante   donde recién se sabe el
vértigo

ASÍ
          donde todo es posible

pale women   anesthetizing eyes
men inhaling memories like nicotine

through the skylights of the night
morning shone

BRINGING THE COAST IN ITS HANDS

Friendship

axis   circled by distances
north pole where every six months
the Sun arrives   all your white bears
growl beautifully

I am savagely sister   like hot winds
out of the Tropics   enclosing in their rings
the scattered cities of the globe

intercontinental   cosmopolitan and bitterly shy
my eyes ultrapowerful Zeiss lenses
register multiple and cosmic life

FRIENDSHIP   velvet of soft luxuries
vanity of chiffons
expression of the nineteenth-century woman

I am like the salts and iodines of the sea
gasping immensity   rush
of vertigo

NOW
        when all is possible

Todas las naves emisarias de la alegría
inflan sus velas en mis vientos

para no asirme a nada
abrí los brazos en el signo más amplio
también el mar tiene los brazos abiertas

mentira sus sirenas de encanto
los hombres no aman el mar
sino los caminos del mar

por eso yo que nunca fuí mendiga
devuelvo lo que absorben los remolinos de mis ojos
impregnado del radio de mis cavernas cerebrales

Y como el mar   surcada de veleros en viaje hacia
los puertos del Futuro
          sin gaviotas de amor   trayectoria de soles en
el sistema de la Vida
esta noche que la luna echa sus anclas en mi indiferencia

          m e   s i e n t o   s o l a

AMISTAD
          todas las distancias tienden sus paralelas
al infinito para no tocarse jamás

LOS ÁNGULOS SON HERMANOS

Poema

fumando mi cigarro de spleen
quiebro la frágil humarada del recuerdo

el caracol del mar adormece mis nervios

All the ships emissaries of happiness
fill their sails with my winds

to be tied to nothing
I opened my arms in the broadest sign
the sea too has open arms

its sirens of enchantment   all are lies
men do not love the sea
but the paths across it

that is why I could never beg
my milling eyes give back all they absorb
transmitting the radio waves of my humming brain

Like the sea   furrowed by ships
full speed toward future ports
       love's seagulls are absent   trajectory of suns
through Life's universe   tonight when the moon
anchors in my indifference

          I   f e e l   a l o n e

F r i e n d s h i p
       parallel lines extend into infinity
so as not to touch

ANGLES ARE BROTHERS

Poem

smoking my cigarette of spleen
the fragile haze of recollection dissipates

the ocean's swirling spiral lulls my nerves

todas mis costas están bañadas con la
sal de tus besos

mi voluntad lleva sus transatlánticos
hacia la China
pasando por la esclusa
que abrió en la entraña de la tierra
el deseo de los hombres

paisaje color de té
los amarillos descubrieron que eran hombres
con farolillos de papel encendiendo kilómetros

de pie en las astas de la vida
guardo un equilibrio imposible

trepidante alegría
locomotora sin frenos   mis nervios
fósforos encendidos   se derriten sobre
los dos abismos claros

horizonte bordado de esperanzas
sin dibujar

mañana reventarán los cohetes de mi dolor
incendiando los cien pisos del presente

En el cristal del agua

en el cristal del agua
cortaron los paisajes su alegría
y todas las estrellas
lloraron lágrimas de luz

your salt kisses lave
my coasts

my will propels its steamers
toward China
passing through canals
dug through earth
by men's desire

landscape the color of tea
yellow races discovered their humanity
with paper lanterns kindling kilometers

upright on the masts of life
I keep an impossible balance

wavering joy
locomotive without brakes   my nerves
lighted matches   stream
over two transparent chasms

horizon blurred by
nebulous hopes

tomorrow the rockets of my pain will explode
and set on fire the hundred-storied present

Translated with Allan Francovich

Lens

in the water's lens
landscapes curtail their happiness
all the stars
blink tears of light

mañana emigrarán los pájaros
al más lejano mapa
los trenes tiran su modorra
y echan su gran serpiente
a caminar sobre las pampas doradas

   ¡los trenes!
ahora que está lejos el mar

Yo resuelvo el problema de mi angustia
con el boleto del pasaje

Allá cómo se expande al infinito
el horizonte
cada mañana llega con su equipaje de esperanza
que resulta vacío
anochece
en el cinema de mis ojos
ya no se filman más paisajes

Enormes tiras blancas de papel

enormes tiras blancas de papel
la nieve trae mensajes del cielo
con la firma dorada de los rayos

el viento silba una tragicomedia
celestial

    que acompaña el bárbaro
jazz-band de los truenos

el escenario del cielo de los cerros
de las casas enmudecidas de neblina

tomorrow birds will migrate
to the farthest map
trains will shake off their stupor
and launch their tremendous serpent
on shimmering yellow plains

       —the trains!
already the sea is far behind

I solve the problem of my anguish
with a railway ticket

In the distance   how the horizon
expands into infinity
each day arrives with its baggage of hope
which turns out to be empty
in the dusk
my aperture eyes
stop filming

Voluminous White

voluminous white flurries of paper
the snow brings news from the sky
signed by a gilt flourish of the rays

the wind sighs a celestial
tragicomedy

       accompanied by thunder's
barbarous jazz

the stage of the sky   of the hills
of the fog-silenced houses

tiene los tonos clásicos de las grandes
tristezas:
            el gris en todas las variaciones
del mercado

los papeles blancos de la nieve
nos arrojan programas a la cara

más tarde

            el telón multicolor del
arco iris   finaliza el espectáculo
y se abren los visillos de las nubes
para que el Sol salga a sonreír

El mandato

habrá necesidad de domar a las fieras
y sujetar al muro de la Vida
las más fuertes cadenas

Y no soñar

Durante un lapso grande
ser un cerebro y una VOLUNTAD

Abrir los ojos como dos receptores
y aprisionar la Vida
redondamente en la mirada
Y ser por los que nunca han sido
como el Sol por todas las noches
como el Agua por las sequedades

Así ha de ser este HOY
Porque el HOY es la Vida

has the classical tones of the great
sadnesses:

        the gray of all the stock market's
jitterings

sheets of snow
hurl programs in our faces

later
        the multicolored drop curtain
of the rainbow ends the spectacle
and plush draperies of cloud draw back
to let in beaming sun

The Command

Our animal spirits must be broken
—fastened to the wall of life
by iron chains

All reverie suppressed

For a good long time
be a brain and a WILL

Opening our eyes
like radio receivers
to capture life in our gaze
To be for those who have never truly lived
like sunlight at night
like water during drought

It can't be otherwise
because Today is everything

Porque el Mañana está detrás
de las fronteras de la Vida

Así HOY
Este HOY majestuoso y terrible
al que se debe todo:
           hasta la muerte

Este Hoy
         que está gritándonos:
              CUMPLID!
como si todo hubiera sido estéril
y quisiera vernos rehabilitar
las horas vacuas
que como ramas tristes se arrancaron
de su árbol
           y le faltan

El mar distante

los barcos van al norte van al sur
tristeza de tus ojos que van hacia
el mismo centro de mi espíritu

Los barcos hijos de la Angustia
ellos mismos la Angustia
con su cargamento de esperanzas
inútiles   anclan en los puertos
mendigos portadores de oro
recogen dolor y dejan dolor

Oh   miradas de los viajeros donde el
mar puso la trágica ansiedad de sus
sirenas míticas
De los viajeros que no logran llegar

Tomorrow is beyond
Life's frontiers

TODAY   This majestic
and terrible present
to which everything   even death is owed

This Today
              screaming at us:
                    DO SOMETHING!
as if all our efforts had so far been in vain
and time wanted back
all those wasted hours
like sad branches torn from its tree
and which it misses

Translated with Allan Francovich

Distant Sea

ships steam north steam south
sadness of your eyes as they approach
the very center of my spirit

Ships children of anguish
Anguish itself   with its cargo
of futile hopes
they drop anchor in ports
beggars hauling gold
loading and unloading sorrows

Oh   the searching eyes of travelers
where the sea pools the tragic anxiety of its
mythical sirens
Travelers who never arrive

Miradas que desfilan por los muelles
vacíos donde no está quien las espera
Miradas como las algas   frías
Lívidos farolillos de colores que
pasean su procesión fantástica sobre
la fantasía del Mar

El viajero de todos los mares

yo era triste
como los pájaros de media Noche
acostados en las tinieblas

      Como las punas sin árboles
de frente a los vientos fríos de
la Costa —

      triste como los fuertes
y como los vencidos — cuando em-
pieza la muerte anticipada de la
        I n d i f e r e n c i a

A M O R — yo estaba triste —
se ensangrentaron mis costados —
— se murieron mis peces de colores —
y la perfidia número UNO bamboleó
mi equilibrio
      a la atracción del abismo

Y los pájaros de media noche
rondaron el naufragio de mi
Corazón — en las arenas abandonadas —

PERO LLEGASTE —
     TÚ — para quien mis brazos

Gazes shifting over vacant wharves
where no one is waiting
Gazes like seaweed   cold
Glowing lanterns of color
gliding in fantastic procession
over the sea's phantasmagoria

Sailor on Every Sea

I was sad
like nocturnal birds
nested in mist

Like treeless plains
scoured by icy winds of the
coast

sad like the strong
and like the vanquished—at the start of
the anticipated death which is
                I n d i f f e r e n c e

L O V E—I felt sad
my sides bled
—my colored fishes died
and the perfidious numeral ONE
unbalanced me
            drew me to the abyss

Midnight birds
circled my heart's shipwreck
            —desolate sands

BUT YOU CAME—
            You—my arms opened

se abrieron en cruz —
y las arañas del sueño tejieron
la seda infinita de la amnesia —

TÚ — conquistador ilusionado
de mis tribus salvajes de tristeza —
donde llevaste la religión de una
Alegría — nueva como los aeroplanos
sobre las selvas vírgenes —

Hoy el traje de nuestros almas
es el arco iris de la sonrisa —

Noche

qué grandes suenan las voces de los perros
ladrando a los ecos

Pero mi cerebro tiene todos los ruidos
que se han perdido en la Noche

Estoy lejos de la realidad
como en un baño de espacios

Yo llegué al último círculo
y sobre mi corazón flotaba
              T U   N O M B R E

La mañana está lejos
c o m o   T Ú
con puentes de oscuridad

eternidad de la Noche
              y de tu ausencia

in a cross for you
dream-spiders wove
amnesia's infinite silk

Eager conqueror
of the savage tribes of my sadness
you imposed the religion
of joy—new like airplanes
skimming virgin forests

Today our souls
grin iridescence—

Night

explosive yapping of dogs
barking at echoes

My brain retains every sound
that vanishes in the night

Far from reality
as in a bath of space

I've attained the last circle
and floating on my heart is
            y o u r   n a m e

Tomorrow is far away
like you
beyond spans of darkness

eternity of night
        and your absence

Mis lágrimas iluminan mi cara en sombras
donde se ha zincograbado
tu última mirada

Pero oye
               todos los ruidos se vacían
de mi cerebro y se reparten en los
rincones profundos de la Noche

y sólo quedan sobre el telón oscuro
de mi conciencia las luces de ben-
gala que dibujan el reclamo de
               t u   n o m b r e

Puentes

SI   VIDA
Mi blasfemia cortada
y dispersa en el dolor de mis células
cerebrales   como vidrios rotos
tiranizados
por una alegre puñalada de luz
riéndose en su arco iris de colores

H o y   e s   l a   n o c h e
que desnuda mis nervios

Y la montaña de mi deseo
se hunde sobre mi corazón
e s t r e p i t o s a m e n t e
hasta dejarme
               sin deseo

Arriba la señal roja de la amenaza
por venir

Lustrous tears illumine my shadowed face
where your last glance
is zinc-engraved

Listen
        all the noises stream
from my brain and seek their place
in deep recesses of the night

nothing remains on the black curtain
of my consciousness but flashing lights
rippling in the electric billboard of
        y o u r   n a m e

Bridges

Yes   life
My blasphemy slashed
and dispersed in the pain of
cerebral cells   like shattered panes
tyrannized
by a merry fistful of light
its shimmering laugh of colors

T o d a y   i s   t h e   n i g h t
that strips my nerves

Mountainous desire
breaks in my heart
a n   u p r o a r i o u s   c r a s h
and I am left
      desireless

Up goes the red signal of future
danger

Mañana   Hoy

pero hoy no vivo
la Vida me da las espaldas
y del Ayer salta al Mañana

Hoy es tan sólo una laguna fría
que no calienta ni sus besos
y en donde tristemente naufraga
       sobre rojos gladiolos campesinos
la rubia y verde mariposa de mi
    e s p e r a n z a

          A Y E R   M A Ñ A N A
A veces
parece que la Vida me resucita
por las noches
mientras alumbran los cristales verdeamarillo
de sus ojos sin   v o z

Ah
si supieran hablar
su extraña música hermanada a mi corazón
Sin la traición amarga de
mi carne — mármol

     Pero NO

Canto 5
〜

como otra vez tu sonrisa se hermana
a la de los panoramas idos
allá   sobre las frágiles agujas
de nuestro amor aventurero
     brújula cerebral

Tomorrow   Today

but today I'm not alive
Life turns its back
Yesterday leaps straight into Tomorrow

Today is an icy pool
which even his kisses cannot warm
and where the blond
and emerald butterfly of my hope goes down
sadly wrecked against the
      crimson gladioli of country fields

Yesterday   Tomorrow

Sometimes it seems
that life revives me
in the night
while the yellow green crystals of its
s p e e c h l e s s   eyes grow bright

Ah   if only they could sing
their strange music   twin sister to my heart
Without the bitter treason of
my flesh—marble

but NO

Song 5

Like old times your smile recalls
the glow of vanished landscapes
far away   under the delicate needles
of our errant love's
      cerebral compass

en los cuatro lados totales:　　a b u r r i m i e n t o
con el pálido Sol abrigado entre sábanas
y los vidrios de colores empañados　　iguales
abajo la alharaca del río
y el campo miserable
para los ojos desorbitados de deseo

la soledad en medio de tanta gente
siempre somos extranjeros en la tierra

la inútil campana del corazón
que anuncia el arribo de alguien
que siempre resulta　　n a d i e

　　　　celuloide ahumado
frutos del trópico
　　　　alegría de los pájaros
la luna ha barrido todas las estrellas
hundida en su baño de leche

la luna　　decadencia anacrónica
del panorama sideral

como los poetas clásicos y los románticos
en el panorama de los nuevos artistas
sumergida en un baño de spleen
quisiera cerrar los ojos y estar
a　　l a　　v u e l t a　　d e l
　　　　m u n d o

in all directions: b o r e d o m
with a pallid sun screened by sheets
and tarnished windowpanes   it's all the same
under the racket of the river
and the stony field
to eyes disoriented by desire

solitude amid so many people
always we are strangers on the earth

the useless bell of the heart
tolls the approach of someone
yet no one ever   a r r i v e s

        smoky film
tropical fruits
            exhilarated birds
the moon has swept away the stars
afloat in her milky bath

the moon   anachronistic decadence
of the celestial panorama

like the classic and romantic poets
in the landscape of modern artists
submerged in a bath of spleen
I want to close my eyes and be
o n   t h e   o t h e r   s i d e
    o f   t h e   w o r l d

Translated with Allan Francovich

Film Vermouth

tristes lagunas
para bañarse los luceros fríos
Yo estaba enferma de mi propia
incertidumbre

La duda ablanda a martillazos lentos
Y tu duda de mí
me hace dudar de mí

Con mis ojos atravesados de aceritos de miedo
en el crepúsculo final de mis ojeras
— media hora para la procesión de la Noche —
temblando de mi misma
y pidiendo socorro contra mí

Y TÚ eres todo
ilusionista en mi teatro de guiñol
La cuerda tesante de la última prueba
se pasaría con serenidad
si tus ojos terribles no anunciarán que voy
a caer —

Ah equilibrista de la Vida
Yo quisiera gritarme
          "cáete de una vez"
y pavonar de sangre las baldosas
bajo tus ojos centinelas
bajo tus manos que poseen la central
de mis nervios

ilusionista de mi angustia

YO TE BESO LAS MANOS

Film Vermouth: Six O'Clock Show

sad lagoons
bathing icy stars
I am sick
with my own uncertainty

Doubt's slow hammering unnerves me
your doubt of me
makes me doubt myself

Pinpricks of fear dilate my eyes
in the final dusk of my eyes' dark circles
—half hour for the promenade of Night—
trembling
asking for help against myself

YOU are all
master of my puppet theater
Tightrope of the ultimate test—
I'd walk it calmly
if your terrible eyes
did not predict my fall

Ah high-wire acrobat
I want to scream
          "fall, get it over with"
spatter the paving stones with blood
under your sentinel eyes
under your hands that own the
electrical grid of my nerves

magician of my anguish

I KISS YOUR HANDS

Translated with Allan Francovich

Realidad del ser

Vuelves a mí desde el azul remoto
de tu muerte sin muerte, inencontrado
todo pasado se tornó presente
todo presente desde siempre ha estado.

Vuelves por el camino intransitado
queda distante de los dos la muerte
árbol de hondas raíces engarfiado
al más allá y al más acá y al siempre.

No ha descendido el tono de la rosa
sigue vertiendo luz la misma estrella
y canta el mar en la lejana costa.

Ahora posamos en la cima enhiesta
sin atadura el ala presurosa
renacido el anhelo y la promesa.

La voz y la canción

Ah soledad   mundo lejano y mío
ah distancia y olvido y no saber
pájaro de alas tenues
sabor de huerto nido
flor abierta
corola del amanecer.

Gota a gota menuda cae la lluvia
sobre este corazón atardecido
vibrante son de una canción perdida
voz del tiempo — su voz — hiere el oído.

Reality of Being

You return to me from the distant blue
of your deathless death, undiscovered
all past is suddenly present
the present has existed always.

You return along the unwalked road
death remains distant from us both
tree whose plunging roots entwine
this world, the other, and eternity.

The vibrant crimson of the rose endures
the same star still pours down light
the sea chants on a distant coast.

Now we alight on the soaring peak
the rushing wing unfettered in the sky
—promise and desire are reborn.

Voice and Song

Loneliness   distant world and mine
distance forgetfulness unknowing
frail-winged bird
fragrance of orchard nest
full flower
dawn's corolla.

Drop by minute drop
rain falls on my laggard heart
a lost song's vibration
time's voice—your voice—hurts the ear.

Todas las flores son la flor primera
deshojados los pétalos del sueño,
algas de luz flotando
en la atmósfera tibia de la espera.

No hay ayer ni mañana
sombra y luz de esta hora que aprisiono
sabor de miel sabor de hiel a veces
y el insaciable corazón despierto.

Actitud

Estoy callada   así   tercamente callada
frente a la noche   frente a la muerta luna y a los astros
y frente al mar   estoy callada siempre
¡le tengo tanto miedo a las palabras!

Salen atropelladas como torrentes salen
las palabras azules   las rojas   las violadas
y vuelcan su tormento y oscurecen auroras
y se abren como heridas desangradas.

Un secreto pavor me turba pero cómo quisiera
poder decirle a alguien esta muerte anticipada
decirle mas no huirle camino andado y desandado
pregunta sin respuesta mirada desolada.

Ronda de pasos leves pero seguros pasos
¿a dónde me conducen vuestras visibles huellas?
si ni piden mis manos ni se afanan mis ojos
mi desbordada angustia todavía se aferra.

Mundo redondo y solo te daría la vuelta
llegaría a los seres por cuyo amor aún vivo
tomaría su ritmo y su ingenua inocencia
y la sonrisa volvería al rostro mío.

Every flower is the first
plucked petals of dream
algae of light floating
in the tepid atmosphere of waiting.

Neither yesterday nor tomorrow exists
chiaroscuro of this interred hour
taste of honey taste of iron sometimes
and the insatiable alert heart.

Stance

I am quiet   stubbornly so
at night   under a dead moon and planets
surveying the sea   I am silent
so deeply do I fear words!

But words emerge   trampled torrential
scarlet indigo and violet words
their torment twists   darkening dawns
opening like wounds bled white.

Dread haunts me. How speak of this
sense I have of death's nearness? Speak of it yes
but not escape the long-traveled untraveled road
answerless question desolate glance.

March of soft yet definite steps
where are these footprints leading?
my hands no longer beckon
anguish overwhelms.

I'll make the rounds of solitary earth
approaching those for love of whom I live.
I'll absorb their rhythms, their ingenuous
innocence, and smile because of that.

Pero me voy sintiendo cada vez más ajena
más lejana y ausente y presintiendo que se acerca
no más dolor ni más amor ni más angustia
sino el que ya no más me sentiré extranjera.

Como el reencuentro de uno mismo
o como el despojarse de todo lo superfluo
la inútil vanidad y el deseo y el miedo
y el amor y la dicha y la ambición y el sentimiento.

Y así limpia de trabas de ataduras y lastres
ascender liberada como en un sueño sin ensueños
noche de alas plegadas alumbrarán los astros
mi última hora de destierro.

Cuadro

Un cielo opalescente   nacarado y azul
a trozos con nubes como espumas
un mar inmóvil   terso que se quiebra en oros
salpicando la luz —
gaviotas aventureras dando gritos de espanto
solitarias   vagando hacia la noche
como mi alma sin paz.

La tímida silueta blanquecina
de un bote pescador
portador de esperanzas
con el tono del mar y del cielo en los ojos
de sus hombres oscuros   dolorosos
castigados por todas las tormentas
y alumbrados sin duda
por una sola estrella.

Yet daily I grow more distant, more absent still.
Now something approaches
—not pain not love or grief
but that which finally will not exclude me.

It will be like a discovery of myself
a casting off of superfluous things
vanity, desire, fear,
love, happiness, ambition, and emotion.

Free then of all entanglements
I'll ascend as in a dream without imagery
while night folds its wings
and the stars illumine my final hour of exile.

Painting

Opalescent sky   mother-of-pearl and chalky blue
foaming clouds
smooth immobile sea   shattering in golds
spilling light—
errant gulls shrieking in fear
solitary   drifting nightward
like my restless soul.

The modest whitewashed silhouette
of a fishing boat
hope-ballasted
somber tones of sea and sky
in the eyes of its dark sorrowful men
lashed by every weather
and lighted by one star.

Tarde   minuto estático   plenitud de silencio
viento frío   delicioso frescor
que bate las mejillas con su ruda caricia.
Paisaje — arenas finas y onduladas
húmedas cálidas aún amorosas.
Las piedras verdinegras con sus leyendas trágicas
esqueléticas y altas,
y el camino   el camino   al borde   sin distancias.

Alma tenue que flotas impalpable y presente
como el perfume áspero del mar y las rocas
inmensidad del marco que no cabe en los ojos —
y mi silueta — motivo gris   pequeño —
erguida como un cirio sin luz
recostada en el fondo del paisaje.

Vientos

Vientos del Norte
vientos cargados de esperanzas
y de sueños y de vida vivida
vientos del Mar Caribe
encrespados sobre las islas prisioneras.

Vientos del Golfo mexicano
silbantes y rugientes
hechos caricias
sobre la verde costa altiva.

Vientos del Sur — Arauco —
cuchilladas en blanco — nieve
y ceniza — viento de pájaros
oscuros de sol lívido.

Dusk   ecstatic moment   oceanic silence
cold wind   delicious chill
buffeting the cheek with a rude caress.
Landscape   fine undulating sands
damp   hot   still amorous.
Greenish-black stones with their tragic legends
skeletal   aloft
and the road   the road at the edge   beyond distances.

Tenuous soul drifting intangibly present
like the raw odor of rocks and sea
immensity of the frame no eye can hold—
and my silhouette   tiny gray motif
poised like an unlit candle
at the landscape's vanishing point.

Winds

Northern winds
charged with hopes
with dreams and with experience
Caribbean winds
gusting over prisoner islands.

Winds from the Mexican Gulf
their hiss and roar
transformed into caresses
over the high green coast.

Winds from the south
white lashings   snow
and ash   dark-birded wind
of a livid sun.

Vientos del largo litoral de nuestra costa
con mar pizarra   espeso y desolado
violador de nubes   creador de dunas
voz que se oye a distancia
alarido
voz que asusta a los niños y a los perros
creador de fantasmas

Vientos del Este
— pampa verde y árida —
Buenos Aires   La Paz   Montevideo
sin esperanzas   vientos
de presagios y atisbos
y de miedos.

Reencuentro de caminos
dislocación de rutas
y un sabor acre entre la boca
y cansancio.

Vientos de los caminos recorridos
vientos de todo mar y todo cielo
— aviónicos deseos de llegar
        de llegar
y no llegar
de estar en todo sitio
y de no estar.

Nostalgia del salobre viento marino
batiendo la curtida cara de sueño
viajando — ¿hacia qué puerto?
        sin destino
igual que el viento a todas partes
y a ninguna.

Viento del Río de la Plata
color de barro
color de vida turbia

Winds from the long shore of our coast
over a sluggish slate-colored sea
cloud-violator   dune-creator
voice heard in the distance
howling
frightening dogs and children
shaper of phantasms.

Winds from the east
—the green and arid pampas
Buenos Aires   La Paz   Montevideo
empty of hopes
winds of signs and omens
and of fears.

Crossing again of roads
diverted routes
an acrid taste in the mouth
—fatigue.

Winds of worn paths
of every sea and every sky
—aerial desires to arrive
                to arrive
and not arrive
to be everywhere
and nowhere at all.

Nostalgia for the brackish ocean breeze
rushing against the leathery face of dream
moving—toward what port?
      without destination
like wind itself everywhere
and nowhere.

Wind of the Río de la Plata
color of clay
color of turbid life

VIENTOS
saturados de pólenes de vida
amanecidos en mi América
sembradores   cómplices
de la roturación de la tierra
en el Gérmen y el Acto.
Cartel ilusionista:

"La esperanza viene en alas del Viento"

La hora de la rosa

La tarde va camino de la tierra
por entre cerros descendiendo faldas
como gotas de sangre   las estrellas
se encienden y se apagan.

La rosa empieza su nocturna ronda
de suavidades y fragancias
por encima del mundo el sol orea
los relieves azules de las casas.

Sobre el mantel de la invisible mesa
el vino del silencio se derrama
ningún atisbo de sonoros ecos
ni cálices de llamas.

En la mística hora del crepúsculo
es cuando vierte el corazón su lágrima
y abre la rosa la corola púrpura
mientras se cierran todas las ventanas.

WINDS
saturated with the pollens of life
born of my America
sowers   accomplices
in breaking new ground
in seed and in realization.
Mesmerizing billboard:

"Hope comes on wings of Wind"

Hour of the Rose

Dusk flows over the earth
flooding valleys descending hills
a crimson wash   the stars
appear and disappear.

The rose begins its nightly round
of fragrances and gentleness
above the world the sun exhales
above blue-silhouetted towns.

On the cloth of the invisible table
the wine of silence is poured
no hint of music lingers
no cup of fire brims.

In the mystic hour of twilight
the heart lets fall a tear
the rose opens its violet corolla
and all the windows close.

Ritmo del mar

Toda la playa brava y desafiante
de rojos monstruos y huidiza arena
la inmensa playa pródiga y distante
de oro de sol y de silencios plena.

Mar en declive de arriscadas olas
y despeinada cabellera de algas
jardinero de lirios y amapolas
y domador de embravecidas galgas.

Sobre esta mesa de mantel bruñido
el silencio oficiaba en nuestra cita
todo el azul del cielo contenido

en el templo de bóveda infinita
sin voz   ni gestos   ni ánima contrita
cabe al ritmo del mar y a su latido.

Tristitia

Tú reinas sobre todo todavía
con tu dulce presencia silenciosa
estás en el perfume y en la rosa
y en lo más puro de mi poesía.

Van pasando tus ojos en teoría
siguiendo el vuelo de la mariposa
y posando su luz en toda cosa
como la luz cuando amanece el día.

Estás presente por doquier aún cuando
nadie te nombre ni te siga amando
ni te brinde sus ramos ya la vida.

Rhythm of the Sea

Fierce defiant beach
freakish reds and shifting sands
far prodigious shoreline
burnished with sun-golds and silence.

Sea in a pour of craggy waves
flinging strands of algae
gardener of lilies and poppies
master of raging rock.

Above this table of glinting cloth
silence presided at our meeting
all the blue of sky therein contained

in the temple of the infinite vault
voiceless   beyond gesture or contrition
the sea pulses . . .

Tristitia

You have died yet dominate all things
your quiet gentle presence
reigns in fragrance and in the rose
and in the purest of my poetry.

Your eyes theorize
tracing a butterfly's wings
their light alights everywhere
like the first light of day.

You are present in all places, even when
you are no longer mentioned
no more loved
—your laurels all taken back by time.

Y yo quisiera por volver a verte
no sólo dar mi vida por tu muerte
sino darte mi muerte por tu herida.

Sueño

¿Cómo negarle al sueño su viejo privilegio
de recorrerme en su carroza por los innumerables paisajes
claros de luna u hórridos de espantos
donde la calva calavera hace su mueca eterna
y los pétalos juegan sobre el cristal de la mañana?

El no-dolor tiempla sus cuerdas suavemente
y todo es espectáculo grávido de aconteceres simultáneos
y el rosa-lila y el azul-violeta
visten mi alma desnuda
frágil e ingenua.

Lejos   lejos de la raíz que me enreda a la pétrea tierra
lejos de su lívido sol   de su aire enrarecido
de sus costumbres cotidianas   de sus afanes de hoy
la sola suma de mi angustia total.

Lejos de la certeza de esta piedra que rueda
inexorablemente hacia la nada.

Ah   por eso
cuando se abre la amapola violenta de la noche
yo me entrego.

How I long to see you again. Not only
would I give my life for yours
I would give my death to cancel your suffering.

Dream

How deny to dreams their usual privilege
of bearing me again in their carriage
through countless landscapes
softly moonlit or hideous with apparitions
where the bald skull scowls an eternal grimace
and petals sport under the glassy dew?

Oblivion suavely attunes its chords
and everything is solemn spectacle
of simultaneous events
and rose-lilac and blue-violet
clothe my naked
frail and ingenuous soul.

Far   far from the root entangling me in stony ground
far from the livid sun   the rarefied air
of daily habits   passions of an hour
the entire sum of my total anguish.

Far from the brute fact of this stone
wheeling inexorably toward nothingness.

That is why
when the violent poppy of the night opens
I go in.

Un domingo cualquiera

Hoy es domingo aquí   en Buenos Aires
amaneció lloviendo
lento caer del agua sucia de hollín   de tierra
sobre las veredas
sobre el asfalto o el adoquinado

Domingo   un domingo cualquiera
¿también será domingo en otras partes?
¿habrá lluvia o habrá sol?
¿barnizará la tierra su silencio
de chimeneas humeantes
de casas grises de gestos sin elocuencia?
¿Caerá la lluvia detrás de los cristales
royendo el hierro o el cemento?

¿Habrá risas y gritos de muchachos
como campanas de luz?

Habrá las avenidas del recuerdo
los caminos de tierra   con hierba humedecida
y los perros de ojos lacrimosos
que dan ganas de decirles "hermano"

Pero aquí en Buenos Aires no hay ni eso

Domingo con cinema
con paseos con olor a mar aunque haga frío
¡La pequeña ciudad sin artificios!

Aquí la soledad puebla todos los ecos
los rebalsa con su agua salobre
aquí el atardecer no pinta incendios
el sol no alcanza a trepar los rascacielos
y la línea lejana del crepúsculo
se hunde en el río inmenso

A Sunday Anywhere

It's Sunday here in Buenos Aires
day dawned raining
drizzle of sooty water
over sidewalks
over asphalt and paving stones

Sunday   any Sunday
Is it Sunday elsewhere?
Is it raining? or clear?
Does earth gloss over
its silence of smoking chimneys
houses gray with ineloquent gestures?
Does rain fall beyond windowpanes
corroding iron or cement?

Can there be laughter and children's cries
like bells of light?

Do the avenues of memory still extend
those pathways of the world   with wet grass
and bleary-eyed dogs
eliciting such a rush of fellow feeling

Here in Buenos Aires there is only this:

Sunday with cinema
long walks in the ocean air despite the cold
Little city without artifices!

Salt loneliness saturates
every echo in this town
sunset trails no scarlet wash of fire
skyscrapers loom in shadow
and the far line of twilight
sinks in the vast river

Los árboles prisioneros
uniformados por el humo
no tiemplan la guitarra de los pájaros

Hay un grito sin voz que rasga el tiempo
y que se pierde sin destino

Hay un deseo atroz
de amurallarse el alma
en el gran sueño

Canto viajero

mar ancho hasta el horizonte bordado de belleza
                estriado asfalto verde
caen las olas   abanicos de plumas
pienso en tu palidez
          y en las líneas oblicuas de nuestros caminos

TÚ HACIA LA MUERTE
       YO HACIA LA VIDA

como una ancha boca roja
con mil voltios de locura   proa feroz al futuro
donde todo el pasado
quiebra su inútil cristal

    t ú   h a c i a   l a   m u e r t e

proletaria mujer sin esperanza
cilicio adherido a tu carne triste
tú vacía de anhelo
como una cuerda bajas al pozo de la muerte
sin custodia de lágrimas

Trees in their prison uniforms
of smoke
strum no guitar of birds

A voiceless cry scratches at time
fading without significance

An atrocious desire
to shut the soul
in a stupendous sleep

Traveling Song

Open sea to the horizon laced with beauty
           scalloped green asphalt
waves break   feather fans
I think of your pallor
      and the oblique lines of our roads

Yours toward DEATH
      mine toward LIFE

like a full red mouth   prow ferociously future
with a thousand volts of madness
while all the past
shatters in useless spray

        y o u   t o w a r d   d e a t h

proletarian woman without hope
a hair shirt clings to your sad flesh
drained of desire
like a rope you descend
into the well of death   beyond
the protective custody of sobs

NO   LLORAR

tras el dique de nuestra rebeldía
están las lágrimas acumuladas

m a ñ a n a

aquí es que desemboca el ansia proletaria
regarán rojamente los caminos del mundo
estas lágrimas que hoy no salen por ti

       p r o l e t a r i a

mar ancho

       mosaico de ciudades miserables
donde el hombre olfatea la tragedia del hombre
como perros las heridas
hacia ti desemboco también
y los mil reflectores
de tus ciudades miserables
latiguean mi sombra

pero tú   lejana
no verás nunca este cartel
que ya mecen las manos de la aurora

EL DERECHO A LA VIDA

d r y - e y e d

the barricades of our rebellion
stanch hot tears

t o m o r r o w

      proletarian yearning will plunge into the sea
will redly splash the pathways of the world
these tears you cannot shed today

      w o r k i n g   w o m a n

great ocean

mosaic of wretched cities
where man sniffs at his own tragedy
like dogs at a wound
I also flow toward the sea
and the thousand searchlights
of your miserable towns
lash my shadow

but you   are far away
you'll never see this billboard
already cradled in the hands of dawn

THE RIGHT TO LIVE

Páramo

Si roca   el mar quiebra su furia desatada
sobre mis ríspidos costados
y el sol azota a plomo en las horas más tórridas
pero siempre es la noche
la que cobija mi tristeza
bajo su amplio ropaje.

Roca en la costa más inhóspita
roca donde se posan los pájaros salvajes del espanto
lanzando sus quejidos pavorosos
alza su arista dura al cielo sin clemencia
en la más vasta soledad.

Me rodean abismos
me golpean las enfurecidas olas
y ni una perla anida
en mis ásperos brazos.

¿Cuál mi destino en esta encrucijada?
¿en dónde la paloma del olvido?
¡me rechaza la vida   me rechaza
y yo sigo soñando con un cielo de estrellas!

Ah   corazón   páramo desolado
íngrimo de ternuras
insomne corazón
sólo te es fiel la muerte   denodado.

Abres tu rosa de sangrientos bordes
cómo bebieron ávidas mil bocas
y te diste sin tregua
tu medida es la curva de la tierra.

Sea Cliff

Yes granite   the sea's unleashed fury crashes
against my rock flanks
the sun beats down in torrid hours
but it's always night
night enfolding sadness in its ample cloak.

Desolate cliff
where shrieking birds alight
terrible birds on the hard rock face
lifted to a pitiless sky
in sheer loneliness.

Chasms surround me   furious
waves lash
and not one pearl
nests in my rough arms.

What is my destiny at this crossroads?
Where is amnesia's dove?
Life thrusts me back   back
but the dream of starred skies returns.

Ah heart   bleak outpost
alone with tenderness
insomniac heart
death alone keeps faith   intrepid death.

You open your blood-edged rose
a thousand avid mouths   how they drank
you gave yourself incessantly
your measure is the curve of earth.

César Vallejo

César Vallejo se nos fué muriendo
todos los días   poco a poco
Se moría a pedazos

Primero se murió en Santiago
de Chuco   luego en Trujillo
y después
        se murió tras los barrotes
de una cárcel de aldea

La madre   las hermanas
y aquella dulce Rita
        de junco y capulí
y el padre   hacedor de sus huesos
y nada más
        todos fueron muriéndolo
y antes y siempre
la roja llaga del Perú
        sangrándole
por todos los costados

No podía vivir así

Apurando sus hieles
se fué   a París   a España
Hambre de ser
de ver el Sol desde otros horizontes
los paisajes   los hombres
sus ansias de vivir sus sueños

Hambre de   pervivir
        de vivir y sufrir
por quienes   y por todos
Hambre de recrearse aupándose
sobre sí mismo
hambre de hombre integral

César Vallejo

César Vallejo was dying to us
each day   a little more
He was dying by pieces

First he died in Santiago
de Chuco   then in Trujillo
then
behind the iron bars
of a small-town jail

Mother and sisters
and that gentle Rita
              of rushes and cherry trees
his father also   knitter of his bones
but of no more
         all were dying to him
and before and always
Peru's red wound
bled from his side

He couldn't go on like that

Leaving behind this bitterness
he went to Paris   to Spain
Such hunger to exist
to see the sun from other horizons
from different landscapes   to know others
their intense desires to realize their dreams

Hunger to survive
         to live and suffer
for them   for everyone
Such yearning to renew himself   to rise up
beyond himself
Hunger for the integral man

Nadie sabía mucho de Vallejo
apenas los amigos   algunos
los poetas tal vez
                que es otra forma de amistad
tal vez los enemigos
¿tenía acaso César enemigos?
pero él seguía con su muerte a pausas
              a retazos
moría diariamente sin esperar el día

Cuando dejó el Perú
se fué tras de su muerte

Quizá pensó convalecer de su diario morir
        y nada

Vino el hambre   las noches frías   el destino
el no tener mantel ni mesa ni cigarros
ni sírvete
el hondo río de la muerte atrás
la gran ciudad sin compasión tragándolo
ajena a su tristeza

Vino el amor y el desamor

Y él con su terco gesto acuchillado
con su bastón para espantar las moscas
se seguía muriendo

En España murióse un poco más
          España contra España
como Perú contra Perú
            caínitas
                pero en Perú todavía amanece

Luego se fué a Moscú
        y regresó a París

Nobody knew much about Vallejo
not even his friends   a few knew him
the poets perhaps
          but that's another kind of friendship
perhaps his enemies knew him
but did César have enemies?
he went on pursuing his piecemeal death
dying daily   not waiting

When he left Peru
it was to follow his death

Perhaps he thought he might recover
          from that daily dying   the emptiness

Then came hunger   freezing nights   and that destiny
of having to do without
tablecloth   table   cigarettes
and that kindly maternal "help yourself"
death's deep river lay behind
the great compassionless city dragging him on
foreign to his sadness

Love came and indifference

With the set grimace of experience
with his stick to shoo away flies
he went on dying

In Spain he died a bit more
          Spain clutching at the throat of Spain
like Peru against Peru
          little Cains
          except that in Peru dawn always comes

Moscow
          Paris again

Traía nueva luz en las indígenas pupilas
traía la auroral resurrección de un pueblo
que se ponía a andar a toda marcha
por los caminos de la Vida
roto el cordón umbilical del miedo

La herida del Perú
volvió a vibrar su rojo caracol

    ¿algo se puede hacer desde París?

N a d a

    César Vallejo sólo pudo
brindar su muerte como ofrenda
su holocausto más puro
un corazón clavado al mástil
de su vieja protesta
su voz herida
su lloro para adentro
y el ancho caminar
de sus pies peregrinos
que es otra forma de morir

Un jueves santo
      (dijo un viernes santo)
se acabó de morir
¡estaba tan cargado de su muerte!
con lluvia y lejos
todo él lleno de Perú
de paisajes andinos
de provincias de pobres
de caciques y látigos sonándole
de banqueros y petroleros yanquis
de caudillos a sueldo
de revolucionarios de bolsillo

His indigenous eyes bore raw light
the auroral resurrection of a people
setting out at full speed
along life's roads
severing the umbilical cord of fear

The red shell of Peru's wound
echoing

      could anything be done from Peru?

N o t h i n g

      César Vallejo
had only the dedication of his death to offer
the purest holocaust
heart nailed to the masthead
of its old protest
his hurt voice
and inner cry
the broad travels
of his pilgrim feet
Such wandering is another form of dying

A holy Thursday
          (I'd call it Holy Friday)
he finished dying
so burdened with his death!
with rain and distances
all his being weighted with Peru
Andean landscapes
provinces of the poor
political bosses cracking whips
bankers and Yankee oilmen
generals on the take
pocketsize revolutionaries

Quien sabe otros
        lo pensó en voz baja
o t r o s
       quizás

Y así se nos murió

      César Vallejo

ya del todo   en París

     con aguacero

Sin tiempo

Que se hiciera la luz
urgió tu anhelo
para mirar la imagen
su brillo   su medida
su resplandor intacto
y el fulgor de sus ojos
y su sonrisa
     siempre
Musitaste   "exquisita"
como un sabor a fruta
o un viejo vino compartido
la voz apenas pronunciada
murmuraste "ya dura demasiado"
queriendo detener el momento
sin embargo
     el pasado se agolpa
el amor lacerado
     desandando el camino
y el amargo sabor
     de lo que fue un momento

Who knows what others
      he thought of beneath his breath
o t h e r s
        perhaps

Thus died to us

    César Vallejo

part now of totality   he died in Paris

    in a blinding rain

Timeless

Let there be light
     impelling my desire
to know sheen and dimension
intact splendor
his flashing eyes
and persistent smile
"Exquisite," you murmured
almost inaudibly   as if describing
the taste of fruit
or a fine wine shared
you whispered under your breath
     "this is going on too long"
nevertheless you wanted
to detain the moment

now
     out of the past
images throng   lacerated love
retracing steps
and the bitter taste

una mano en la otra
   cálida palpitante
y el fuego amaga su corriente
   sin tiempo
. . . . . .
Ya no podrá ser más
ya no habrá espera
caracolas de sueño
   sonando
     su marina canción
      sus ecos
. . . . . .
Hay más mirar
   que pronunciar palabras
dejar que corra el agua
del río del recuerdo
viendo pasar las horas
y sonreír apenas
para no deshacer
su encantamiento
. . . .
Y todo fue sin culpa
sin apenas quererlo
nube fugaz
nube de fuego
. . . .
       mayo 1981

Tarde de lluvia en Praga

Y ver caer la lluvia
  con su sabor a tierra
   y los pájaros locos
    huyendo de la lluvia.

of what lasted but a moment
wrung hands
   warm pulsing
while fire hints
  at a timeless current

. . . . . .

It's not possible now
to be anything more
there's nothing left to wait for
dream seashells
    echo ocean's song

. . . . . .

There's more
to life than words
let flow the river of memory
observe the parade of hours
and smile but barely
so as not to break the spell

. . . . . .

and everything was without guilt
and nearly without volition
fleeting cloud
cloud of fire

May 1981

Dusk Rain in Prague

Seeing the rain
  its pungent earthen odor
   agitated birds
    dart to cover

Sentir que corre el tiempo
y los árboles tiemblan
y la tarde agoniza
bajo la luz de plomo

    y el sol hecho pedazos
   rompe la nube tenue
  y se siente la angustia
de saberse tan lejos

Lejos de todo   lejos
   del espacio y del tiempo
     en un limbo sin nombre
       tal entre nubes rojas

Adherida en el aire
danzando sobre el viento
más allá de los árboles
más cerca del silencio.

    y la ciudad en calma
   mientras llueve el recuerdo
  y se duerme la tarde
con los brazos abiertos.

Praga, junio 1983

Sensing time's flow
trees shudder
in the agony of dusk
its leaden light

shards of sun
pierce a tenuous cloud
while the anguish
of distance intensifies

Far from everything   far
from space and time
in a nameless limbo
as in scarlet clouds

Aloft in air
high-stepping on the wind
beyond trees
and nearer silence

the city barely moves
as memory rains down
and dusk drifts off
with open arms.

Prague, June 1983

AFTERWORD

I first learned of Magda Portal through her poetry, when co-editing *The Penguin Book of Women Poets,* an anthology compiled in the context of the resurgent women's movement of the 1970s. Wanting to represent her poems, I learned through the tenacious efforts of Irene Vegas García that she was living in Lima. The initial contact made, Magda readily granted permission and also (in response to my expressed interest in her work) went to some trouble to send a substantial packet of materials, including out-of-print pamphlets, books, and other writings in photocopy, all of which remained dormant in my possession for many years. So began our connection, which became a friendship.

In 1981 I had the unexpected opportunity of meeting her, in San Francisco. At the invitation of Professor Daniel Reedy, Magda came to the United States to give readings at the University of Kentucky in Lexington. Professor Reedy, whose researches on Magda's life were well under way, had been with Magda at the Fourth Inter-American Congress of Women Writers in Mexico City. From Lexington she traveled to San Francisco to visit her friend and former Aprista comrade Zoila Maxwell. Based at her friend's apartment in San Francisco, Magda spent a number of days in late June and early July with Janet Rigg, myself, and Allan Francovich. Magda greatly appreciated that her poems were included in the Penguin anthology alongside those of the most celebrated women poets of South America. Because of that we met on cordial terms, and our shared repudiation of Ronald Reagan's policies strengthened an easy rapport.

Eighty-one then, she appeared to be in good health, not evidently hindered by her age. I remember her walking ahead of me—she was dressed in a pale-blue polyester pants suit—briskly covering the nine blocks from Fulton and Ward streets to the University of California–Berkeley campus, where in the recording studio of the UC language lab she read a selection of her poems for archival preservation. She was deeply pleased by the interest in her life and work that she encountered in Berkeley. In those quiet, midsummer days she seemed very relaxed and easygoing, displaying a demeanor, I was later told, that was not characteristic, as she tended to be work oriented and very demanding of herself and others. I was also told that she sometimes appeared aloof, particularly in situations in which she felt mistrust. But when she felt herself among friends, as her friend Zoila Maxwell explained, she was accordingly relaxed, as she was with us, content to be shepherded about—she spoke no English—to various tourist destinations: to San Francisco, the Golden Gate Bridge, the ocean at Point Reyes. She happily took part in the many activities planned for her, including meeting with Milt Wolf, the last commander of the legendary Abraham Lincoln Brigade in Spain's civil war. Responsive and good-humored, she quietly listened, much more than she talked, and was quick to laugh a lighthearted, musical laugh. I also observed her slightly ironical smile, the one mentioned by interviewers in the early decades of her career.

Over the course of two afternoons in the first days of July we conducted an interview. Seated beside a large plate-glass window in Janet Rigg's hillside apartment in San Francisco, looking out over a seemingly perpetual bank of fog, we filled four large reel-to-reel tapes with her commentary and reminiscences. Had I known then what only later I would learn concerning the many problematical episodes in her life, had we asked tougher, more probing questions, she might have become guarded and defensive. Instead our questions were general, as dictated by our limited knowledge of her life, and meant to elicit a narrative. In that frankly admiring atmosphere, Magda spoke easily, revealing her wry humor as well as flashes of the indignation that had driven so many of her political choices. As advised by Professor Reedy, we avoided any mention of her deceased daughter, Gloria Delmar.

We parted at the San Francisco International Airport in early July. In that visit she seemed to me a thoughtful and loveable person. Our friendship continued by correspondence until it became too difficult for her to go on with it. I am sorry to say she sometimes expressed concern about my lapses in replying to her regular letters and postcards. She sometimes sent books or recent poems and never once did she ask if I had made any progress toward publishing her poems in translation, as she had given me permission to do. Her written consent on that score was noncommittal: "I have no objection." The project did not seem to engage her, or perhaps she did not want to ask when I was absorbed by other things. In a letter of 1988 she apologized for the many errors in her typing. Her letters were always meticulously typed, and signed with her distinctive bold hand. "Thank you, thank you for everything," she wrote in that last letter I would have from her. She knew better than I then how seriously her health had been compromised, in fact had begun its rapid descent.

Only following Magda's death in 1989 did I begin in earnest to translate her poems and research her life with the intention of offering a biographical sketch to introduce a selection of her poems in translation. With no less regard on my part for the poetry, the present biography evolved as I took to heart our friend Eduardo Galeano's admonition that Magda Portal's contribution to the Latin American social struggle should be considered the foremost part of her legacy.

KW, Berkeley 2008

NOTES

ABBREVIATIONS

BENSON: The Nettie Lee Benson Latin American Collection at the University of Texas at Austin
DAEMP: Documentos/archivo de Magda Portal, the Estate of Magda Portal, Lima, in the care of Rocío Revolledo Pareja.
JCM: José Carlos Mariátegui
MP: Magda Portal
MPP: Magda Portal Papers

PREFACE

xiii *"You? Magda Portal?"*: "Magda Portal in San Francisco," B 10–2 MPP, BENSON. The typescript, in Spanish, of this interview is corrected and augmented by MP. Page citations correspond to the transcription from four tape reels (A, B, C, D) now lost. Unless otherwise indicated, in the present volume all translations from the Spanish are my own.

xiv *"a surging river could be contained"*: Zamora, "El espíritu colonial en los gobiernos de América."

CHAPTER 1

1 *Pedro Pablo Portal Ortega:* Pedro Pablo Portal Ortega's antecedents were French Huguenots who fled to England to escape religious persecution in France, later coming to Peru. Graciela Pareja Moreno, interview by the author, assisted by Rocío Revolledo Pareja, Lima, August 15, 1993.

1 *"preferred to marry":* "Magda Portal in San Francisco," A 3, MPP, BENSON.

2 *May 27, 1900:* Magda perpetuated confusion about her birth date (as on the typescript "Datos biográficos" that she sent me, in which it is written "born 1903.") I've now seen a copy of her birth certificate, provided by Rocío Revolledo: born 1900, in Barranco, her given name Julia. At some point she went to court to make official her preferred name, Magda Portal.

2 *"astounded, completely dazzled by the marvel of the sea":* "Magda Portal in San Francisco," A-2, MPP, BENSON.

2 *"was no doubt attracted by the large meadow":* MP, *Trazos cortados,* 7, memoir, fifty-one-page (shorter) version, DAEMP.

2 *Phantoms loomed:* MP, "La vieja casa y sus fantasmas," MPP, BENSON.

3 *"I'm going to have to send her to law school":* "Magda Portal in San Francisco," C 23, MPP, BENSON.

3 *"This child will do something in life":* MP, *La vida que yo viví: Trazos cortados,* 9, MPP, BENSON. The manuscript's title page has these handwritten notes by MP: "Sin corregir!" (Without corrections!) and "Primera copia del Libro Autobiográfico de Magda Portal hasta la página 92"

(First copy Autobiography to page 92). Note: neither this nor the fifty-one-page version, titled simply *Trazos cortados,* treats years after 1934.

3   *"Papa, it's me, Julita":* Magda Portal in San Francisco," A 3–4, MPP, BENSON.

3   *"This was my first experience of death":* Ibid., A 4.

4   *"I have to confess":* Ibid., A 5; see also MP, *La vida que yo viví: Trazos cortados,* MPP, BENSON.

4   *Juana de Portal, Magda's sister:* Teresa Milic (Juana de Portal's daughter), interview by Rocío Revolledo Pareja, Lima, February 1997.

4   *"How many times on those lonely days":* MP, *La vida que yo viví: Trazos cortados,* 4–5, MPP, BENSON.

5   *"I was seven, my brother four":* "Magda Portal in San Francisco," B 2, MPP, BENSON.

5   *"inept at earning money":* Andradi and Portugal, "Yo soy Magda Portal," 212.

6   *Magda would later decry:* MP, *Trazos cortados,* 20, memoir, fifty-one-page version, DAEMP.

6   *the young mother would give birth to five:* The Pareja Moreno children were Eduardo Guillermo Pareja Moreno; Carlos Alberto Pareja Moreno; Juan Fernando Pareja Moreno, born 1913, died at eight months; Oscar Fernando Pareja Moreno, who worked as a sailor, died in 1944 when his ship exploded; and Rosa Graciela Pareja Moreno, born March 25, 1918. The Portal siblings were María Amelia, born about 1898, Julia (Magda) born 1900; Felix Alfonso, the third Portal child; and Juana de Dios. Graciela Pareja Moreno, interview by the author, assisted by Rocío Revolledo Pareja, Lima, August 15, 1993.

6   *"I was very vain":* "Retrato de una mujer," 16.

6   *"This worried my mother":* Ibid., 14

6   *"in the too-austere atmosphere of our household":* Ibid., 14.

6   *were frankly irritated ; "la letrada":* Teresa Milic, interview by Rocío Revolledo Pareja, Lima, February 1997.

6   *"I always felt harassed":* MP, "Resonancias alrededor de una época," 2, MPP, BENSON; see also "Magda Portal in San Francisco," A 7, MPP, BENSON.

6   *"physical need to write":* MP, "Resonancias alrededor de una época," 2, MPP, BENSON.

6   *"It seemed to me that my writing was so naked":* Ibid., 2.

7   *"I was never frivolous":* "Retrato de una mujer," 14.

7   *"My most urgent desire':* MP, *La vida que yo viví: Trazos cortados,* 9, MPP, BENSON.

7   *"I adjusted to this new way of life":* MP, *Trazos cortados,* 17, memoir, fifty-one-page version, DAEMP.

7   *a novel by Angélica Palma:* Basadre, *Historia de la República del Perú,* 5th ed., vol. 9, 4187.

CHAPTER 2

9   *"We shared an idea":* MP, "Resonancias alrededor de una época," 4, MPP, BENSON.

9   *"Every day as I walked home":* MP, *La vida que yo viví: Trazos cortados,* 11, MPP, BENSON.

10   *university reform movement:* See Martínez de la Torre, "La reforma universitaria en la Argentina."

11   *a handkerchief doused with ether:* "Magda Portal in San Francisco," B 5–6, MPP, BENSON.

11   *"furtively withdrew":* MP, *La vida que yo viví: Trazos cortados,* 14, MPP, BENSON.

11   *"We were close, like brother and sister":* Levano, "Una mujer de pelea," 62.

11   *"The inhabitants of the town retain":* Hays, "The Passion of César Vallejo," 4.

12   *unjustly imprisoned:* See Eshleman, introduction to *César Vallejo,* xxi–xxiii. See also Smith, "Vallejo's Book of the Abyss," vii–viii.

12   *"the dawn of a new poetry in Peru":* JCM, *Seven Interpretive Essays,* 250.

12   *"the precursor of the new spirit and new conscience":* Ibid., 257.

12   *"a poet without poems":* Hernández Novás, "Vida de un poeta," LXVII.

12   *told his friends that he felt ashamed":* "César Vallejo en el tiempo," 7, MPP, BENSON.

13   *"seemed always to be giving you patronizing pats":* "Magda Portal in San Francisco," A 11, MPP, BENSON.

13   *to be reminded of the mountain rain:* Hernández Novás, "Vida de un poeta," XXVI.

15   *"four cents a day":* Werlich, *Peru,* 17.

15   *Torn from the Nest:* Matto de Turner, *Torn from the Nest.* See also Berg, "Clorinda Matto de Turner," 303–15.

16   *"indigenous women led troops":* See Guardia, *Mujeres peruanas,* 2nd ed., 41–49.

17   *given over to a British company:* As David Werlich explains, the British concern represented Peru's British creditors, who assumed the country's 50 million pounds sterling debt, thus offsetting the huge incentives. Werlich, *Peru,* 20.

17   *"will be given facilities and opportunities":* Cited in Stein, *Populism in Peru,* 53.

17   *$10 million to 100 million:* Pike, *The Modern History of Peru,* 229.

18   *"a dirty, miserable little hamlet":* Cited in Stein, *Populism in Peru,* 55.

19   *"put off by the turmoil and threat of arrest":* "Mis recuerdos de José Carlos Mariátegui," 9, MPP, BENSON.

19   *"To be white of skin":* Pike, *The Politics of the Miraculous in Peru,* 32.

20   *"A young man—whose name":* MP, *La vida que yo viví: Trazos cortados,* 25, MPP, BENSON.

21   *He subjugated his listeners:* Castro, *Haya de la Torre,* vol. 2, 14.

21   *He surrounded himself with poets:* Wolfe, *The Fabulous Life of Diego Rivera,* 132.

21   *the most significant revival of fresco:* Wolfe, *Diego Rivera,* 183.

22   *Chichén Itzá and Uxmal:* See Hurlburt, "Diego Rivera."

22   *Indo-american:* Haya would elaborate the Indoamerican concept, emphasizing racial and cultural fusion, honoring locality, and insisting that the term *indigenous* did not refer strictly to the original inhabitants, cultures, or products of the land but to all presently native to the continent and profoundly connected to a place. For a related view of the American native, see Williams, "The American Background."

22   *a design Diego Rivera helped create:* Castro, *Haya de la Torre,* 22.

23   *"three poems collectively titled":* The title "Nocturnos" probably alludes to the poetry of José Asunción Silva, whose work MP credits as an early influence. Her submission included "Cansancio," "Temor," and "Posesión."

23   *"alongside Juana de Ibarbourou":* "Juegos Florales de 1923." For more on Mistral and Ibarbourou, see Virgillo, "Gabriela Mistral," and Irving, "Juana de Ibarbourou."

23   *not certain that a woman actually wrote:* See Johnson, *Women in Colonial Spanish American Literature,* 178. See also Sabat de Rivers, *Estudios de literatura hispanoamericana.*

23   *"was a device used to conceal":* Luis Alberto Sánchez, cited in Johnson, *Women in Colonial Spanish American Literature,* 178.

23   *writing went on in such cloisters:* See also Lavrin and Loreto, *Diálogos espirituales.*

23   *Sor Juana:* See Cruz, *A Sor Juana Anthology;* for more on Sor Juana, see Johnson, "Sor Juana Inés de la Cruz," 272–81.

23   *Generation of 1870:* See Villavicencio, *Del silencio a la palabra,* 114.

23   *"Peru's first poetess"; "important in Peru's literature"; "spiritually emancipated"; "Poetry, grown old":* "Literature on Trial," in JCM, *Seven Interpretive Essays on Peruvian Reality,* 263.

23   *in print in Lima's Mundial:* Magda's writings initially appeared in *Mundial* under the pseudonym Tula Soavani. For commentary on Portal's early short fiction, see Reedy, *Magda Portal: La pasionaria,* 38–51; see also Unruh, "Ad-Libs by the Women of *Amauta,*" 173–75.

24   *"18 cantos emocionados de 'Vidrios de amor'":* For insightful discussion of this important poem sequence, see Reedy, *Magda Portal,* 70–78.

24   *"Magda Portal's soul is a landscape":* Meza, "Magda Portal."

25   *"I don't believe I understood much":* MP, *La vida que yo viví: Trazos cortados,* 17, MPP, BENSON.

25   *The auditorium of Lima's Municipal Theater:* Herrera, "Magda Portal."

25   *"I asked the master of ceremonies":* MP, *La vida que yo viví: Trazos cortados,* 18, MPP, BENSON.

26   *the inaugural issue's "Prologue-Manifesto":* MP, "Prólogo-Manifiesto" (MP and Federico Bolaños) reprinted in Castañeda Vielakamen, *El vanguardismo,* 95–96.

27   *"tormented lyricism":* "Alfonsina Storni," *Flechas,* 3, reprinted in Castañeda, ibid., 131. For more on Storni, see Salgado, "Alfonsina Storni," 501–12.

27   *"inwardly disturbed"*: Sánchez, *La literatura peruana*, 1538.

27   *confiscating the salary his wife earned:* Remarks and opinions attributed to Graciela Pareja Moreno in this narrative all derive from interview with the author, assisted by Rocío Revolledo Pareja, Lima, August 15, 1993.

27   *characterized Federico as controlling:* See Reedy, *Magda Portal: La pasionaria*, 97.

28   *in the Lima review Variedades:* MP, "El poeta de los espejos iluminados."

28   *"I had a revolver":* Andradi and Portugal, "Yo soy Magda Portal," 229.

29   *"From the very moment I took Gamaliel's hand:* MP, "Los hermanos Peralta."

29   *"an inveterate romantic":* Sánchez, *La literatura peruana*, 1511–12, 1539.

30   *"geometrically raised to new powers":* Cox, "Luchadores apristas."

30   *"Christ at the last supper":* MP, *El derecho de matar* (with Serafín Delmar). Authorship of individual prose poems is specified only at the end of the book. Of fifteen, eight are by Magda: "La sonrisa de Cristo," "El motivo," "El noche," "El poema de la cárcel," "El viento," "1914," "Caminos rojos," and "Círculos violeta." For discussion of "La sonrisa de Cristo," treating the theme of a woman's adultery for love, see Wallace Fuentes, "Becoming Magda Portal," 293.

30   *"the rebellious spirit and revolutionary messianism":* JCM, *Seven Interpretive Essays*, 264.

30   *"rings of anarchy and nihilism"; "exalted tenderness":* Ibid., 264. Mariátegui mentioned "El poema de la cárcel," "La sonrisa de Cristo," and "Círculos violeta" as most truly embodying Magda's spirit, her "charity, compassion, and exalted tenderness." Ibid., 264.

31   *Trampolín; Hangar, ex-Trampolín:* A facsimile reprint of the four issues appeared in *Hueso húmero* (Lima), no. 7 (October–December 1980). MP wrote a preface, "Una revista de cuatro nombres" (A Review with Four Titles). Publication facts are as follows: *Trampolín* [no. 1] (October 1926), with Magda Portal, Serafín Delmar, Alejandro Peralta, Gamaliel Churata, and Julián Petrovick; *Hangar, ex-Trampolín*, no. 2, 2a (semimonthly, October 1926); *Rascacielos, ex-Hangar*, no. 3 (November 1926), dir. Serafín Delmar; *Timonel, ex-Rascacielos*, no. 4 (March 1927), dir. Magda Portal.

31   *short-lived reviews:* For an extensive of list of Peruvian reviews of 1920–30, including *Más allá, Vórtice, Claridad, Kosko, Hélice, Kuntur, Jarana*, and *La Sierra*, see Gonzales Smith, *Poética y ideología en Magda Portal*, 36–37.

32   *"as many as one thousand workers":* Klaiber, *Religion and Revolution in Peru*, 125.

32   *the objection of his mother:* Wiesse, *José Carlos Mariátegui*, 64–66. Wiesse was a frequent contributor to *Amauta* and, with her husband, José Sabogal, a member of Mariátegui's inner circle. See Unruh, "Las rearticulaciones inesperadas," 93–110. This essay is translated as Unruh, "Ad-Libs by the Women of *Amauta*."

34   *"X-rays revealing the body of Peru":* "José Carlos Mariátegui: 16 de abril de 1930," 5, MPP, BENSON.

34   *"its formidable work of education":* JCM, "Defensa del marxismo," 1306.

34   *"The messianic millennium will never come":* JCM, "La lucha final," 500.

34   *"The masses can't do without myth":* JCM, "La lucha final," 501.

34   *"Revolutionary and social myths":* JCM, *Siete ensayos de interpretación*, 193.

35   *a regular contributor:* In addition to poems and an occasional review, Magda contributed polemical prose to *Amauta*: "Andamios de vida" (January 1927) and "Réplica de Magda Portal" (March 1927). Writing in a manifesto-like mode, she defends the vanguardist literary style against hostile attack by Miguel Ángel Urquieta, who answers her in the journal in his "Izquierdismo y seudoizquierdismo artísticos" (March 1927). Although MP's futurist imagery tends to overwhelm argument, her remarks signal a move toward embracing a more socially conscious tendency in vanguard literature. She also rejects a concern with loveliness in poetry, which she associates with Rubén Darío and an earlier generation. "Beauty for its own sake is sterile," she said, "and art must be creative." See Unruh, "Ad-Libs by the Women of *Amauta*," 177–78. See also Wallace Fuentes, *Becoming Magda Portal*, 312–26, on MP's polemic with Urquieta.

35   *"out of my league":* "Mis recuerdos de José Carlos Mariátegui," 1, MPP, BENSON.

36   *"Mariátegui was the teacher":* "Magda Portal in San Francisco," A 12, MPP, BENSON.

36 *His black eyes, gleaming:* Basadre, introduction to *Seven Interpretive Essays*, xxviii–xxix.
36 *Julia Codesido and activist Ángela Ramos:* "Mis recuerdos de José Carlos Mariátegui," 3, MPP, BENSON.
37 *"hardly more than sorcerers' apprentices":* Ibid., 2
37 *"not wanting to miss a single one":* Ibid., 3.
37 *Mariátegui radiated:* "José Carlos Mariátegui: 16 de abril de 1930," MPP, BENSON.
37 *"intellectuals, not just women":* "Magda Portal in San Francisco," A 24, MPP, BENSON.
37 *Klaiber described photos:* Klaiber, *Religion and Revolution in Peru*, 125–26.
38 *"Cerro de Pasco, despite its climate":* "José Carlos Mariátegui en el recuerdo," MPP, BENSON.
38 *Contrary to established procedures:* Beals, *Fire on the Andes*, 315.
39 *"Two women implicated in plot":* "Magda Portal in San Francisco," A 14, MPP, BENSON.
39 *"in which article after article":* JCM, *Mariátegui total*, 258–59.
40 *"I hold poets Serafín Delmar":* Ibid., 1860. The letter is dated June 24, 1927.

CHAPTER 3

41 *"Triumphant Mexico"; "decadent Europe":* MP, *La vida que yo viví: Trazos cortados*, 30, MPP, BENSON.
41 *Peru's high-sierran songs:* MP, "Panorama intelectual de México," 188.
42 *"An overwhelming impression of power":* MP, *La vida que yo viví: Trazos cortados*, 33–34, MPP, BENSON.
42 *"a new concept of a Latin American people":* Ibid., 31.
42 *"the many goals the revolution proposed":* Ibid., 31.
43 *"We became associated . . . with left-wing elements":* Ibid., 30.
43 *"a moral organization":* Catlin, "Mural Census," 242.
44 *to drive "the Bolshevik" Kollantai:* Porter, *Alexandra Kollantai*, 440.
44 *Mella came to Mexico:* See Dumpierre, *J. A. Mella*, 85–89.
45 *poet Gabriela Mistral:* Franco, *Plotting Women*, 103.
45 *"formidable work of mass education"; "a giant step":* MP, "Los libros de la revolución mexicana," 41.
45 *excommunication by the Catholic Church:* See Brenner, *The Wind That Swept Mexico*, 77.
45 *"ripping the heart and soul":* Beals, *Latin America*, 70.
46 *"people of all races":* Haya de la Torre, *Impresiones de la Inglaterra*, 104.
47 *"One understands after just a few weeks why the mere mention":* Ibid., 115.
48 *"the new organization of the Party":* Ibid., 102; see also 114.
48 *American anarchist Emma Goldman concluded:* Goldman, *My Disillusionment with Russia*.
48 *"simply a paintbrush":* Willett, *Art and Politics in the Weimar Period*, 103.
50 *"We aren't just a few . . . who go forward with firm resolve":* Haya de la Torre, *Impresiones de la Inglaterra*, 87.
50 *"The A.P.R.A. represents, therefore":* Cited in Sánchez, *Apuntes para una biografía del APRA*, 50.
51 *"surrounded by porters carrying shiny leather suitcases":* Ravines, *The Yenan Way*, 19.
51 *"was nothing to them compared to safeguarding":* Enríquez, *Haya de la Torre*, 100.
51 *The lecture titles included "Europe and the Two Americas":* Sánchez, *Apuntes para una biografía del APRA*, 72.
52 *"I didn't understand yet what imperialism was":* "José Carlos Mariátegui en el recuerdo," 10, MPP, BENSON.
52 *"Haya's arrival in Mexico":* Ibid., 9–10.
52 *"With J. C. Mariátegui, at the get-togethers":* MP, *La vida que yo viví: Trazos cortados*, 34, MPP, BENSON.
52 *"Night after night, Haya conversed with us":* Ibid., 33.
52 *"Haya . . . went straight to the point":* Ibid., 34.

52 *"barely contaminated by political thought"*: "Magda Portal in San Francisco," A 8, MPP, BENSON.

52 *"were vague, unformulated, barely more than impulses"*: MP, *La vida que yo viví: Trazos cortados*, 33, MPP, BENSON.

53 *"It was nearly inevitable . . . that when Haya arrived"*: "Magda Portal in San Francisco," B 8; see also A 13, MPP, BENSON.

53 *"[The United States] had instigated a war"*: Zinn, *A People's History of the United States*, 399.

53 *"half joking, half in earnest"*: MP, *La vida que yo viví: Trazos cortados*, 34, MPP, BENSON.

54 *Una esperanza y el mar*: These books by Magda and Serafín are announced as being "in press" in their review *Timonel* (Lima) March 1927; their deportation was in June.

54 *"GREAT FRIEND / LIFE'S PRISM"*: Delmar, *Radiogramas del Pacífico*, 31–32.

54 *"Midnight birds / circled my heart's shipwreck"*: "El viajero de todos los mares," in MP, *Una esperanza y el mar*

55 *"essentially lyrical"; "compassionate in the same way"*: JCM, *Seven Interpretive Essays*, 264, 265.

55 *"This poetess of ours"*: Ibid., 266.

55 *The eternal and dark contrast*: Ibid., 265.

55 *"If my poetry's an obstacle"*: "Magda Portal in San Francisco," A 8, MPP, BENSON.

55 "would not publish another book of poetry": MP, *La mujer en el partido del pueblo*, 7.

55 *"a homicidal act"*: "Mis recuerdos de José Carlos Mariátegui," 4, MPP, BENSON.

55 *"I opened my handbag, took out my manuscript"*: "Magda Portal in San Francisco," A 8–9, MPP, BENSON.

56 *By Daniel Reedy's count*: Reedy, *Magda Portal: La pasionaria*, 79.

56 *"saturated with a certain precocious fatalism"*: MP, *Trazos cortados*, 27, memoir, fifty-one-page version, DAEMP.

57 *The APRA leader scorned the idea*: See Haya de la Torre, "El estado antiimperialista"; excerpt trans. in Haya de la Torre, *Aprismo*, 163–70.

57 *exerted substantial influence*: See Hodges and Gandy, *Mexico, 1910–1982*, 131–32.

58 *The Plan de México was written by*: Sánchez, *Apuntes para una biografía del APRA*, 76; see also "Esquema del Plan de México," Martínez de la Torre, *Apuntes para una interpretación marxista de historia social del Perú*, vol. 2, 290–93; see also Eugenio Chang-Rodríguez, *Una vida agonía, Víctor Raúl Haya de la Torre*, 277–82.

60 *"influential members of the Lima proletarian community"*: Stein, *Populism in Peru*, 147; discussion of Haya's ties with Lima's labor movement relies on Stein's account.

60 *"In nearly every meeting of organized labor"*: Ibid., 148. Stein went on to remark that not all labor leaders endorsed Haya's leadership. Prominent anarchists were suspicious of his nonproletarian background; they questioned his motives, fearing he was wresting control of the labor movement from working class leaders with the aim of furthering his own career (149).

60 *In a letter dated April 16, 1928*: Martínez de la Torre, *Apuntes para una interpretación*, vol. 2, 296–98.

61 *You are doing much harm*: Haya, letter to JCM, May 20, 1928, in ibid., 298–99.

61 *Magda, as witnessed by fellow Aprista Esteban Pavletich*: Pavletich told Jesús Chavarría in an interview, November 9, 1966, that "Magda Portal participated in the Mexico City episode and typed Haya de la Torre's reply to Mariátegui." Pavletich also told Chavarría that he himself was present "when Haya dictated the letter to Magda Portal." In Chavarría, *José Carlos Mariátegui*, 212n73.

62 *a demagogue, a would-be caudillo*: See JCM, letter to Eudocio Ravines, December 31, 1988, in JCM, *Mariátegui total*, 1959–60.

63 *"the ferocious absorption of man by the machine"*: MP, *El nuevo poema y su orientación*, 10.

63 *"the least lyrical and most thorough exponent"*: Ibid., 19; see also Monguió, *La poesía postmodernista peruana*, 134.

64 *"individualist sentimentalism so typical"*: MP, *El nuevo poema y su orientación*, 9.

64 *"The poem of today"*: Ibid., 26.

64   *"However deep its understanding"*: Ibid., 23.

65   *"We are foes of Wall Street / and its Monroe Doctrine"*: El hombre de estos años, 17.

65   *"coordinating his art with—not subordinating it to"*: "El poeta aprista"; see also Delmar, "Interpretación social del arte en América" and "Posición del poeta en el movimiento de transformación social."

66   *on receiving this ultimatum*: See Martínez de la Torre, *Apuntes para una interpretación*, vol. 2, 281–85.

66   *"unconditional services" as "soldiers of APRA"*: Haya de la Torre, letter, February 5, 1928, cited as epigraph in Haya de la Torre, *¿A dónde va Indoamérica?*

66   *Aprista donations apparently did not amount*: Hodges, *Intellectual Foundations of the Nicaraguan Revolution*, 94–96, also 135.

67   *former Aprista Jacobo Hurwitz*: Albers, *Shadows, Fire, Snow*, 193.

67   *"a vendetta of slander"*: Constantine, *Tina Modotti*, 139.

67   *"pernicious foreigner"*: Hooks, *Tina Modotti*, 168–71; see also Wolfe, *The Fabulous Life of Diego Rivera*, 230–32.

67   *taking her turn in the revolving honor guard*: MP, *Trazos cortados*, 35, memoir, fifty-one-page version, DAEMP.

67   *"with a huge red star and gold hammer and sickle"*: Hooks, *Tina Modotti*, 167.

67   *"crocodile tears"*: Martínez de la Torre, *Apuntes para una interpretación*, vol. 2, 363.

68   *"counted on the support of three of the four"*: Ibid., 367.

68   *"the only one to oppose"*: Ibid., 367.

68   *"to take away Serafín del Mar's woman, Magda"*: Haya de la Torre, letter to Eudocio Ravines, March 22, 1929, in Pedro Planas, *Los orígenes del APRA*, cited in Reedy, *Magda Portal: La pasionaria*, 159.

68   *"his admiration for Magda went back"*: Reedy, *Magda Portal: La pasionaria*, 159.

69   *"restless and avid for action"*: Pavletich, letter to JCM, July 30, 1929, in JCM, *Mariátegui total*, 2018; also in Martínez de la Torre, *Apuntes de una interpretación*, vol. 2, 365–66.

69   *"The saddest thing . . . is that the Mexican government"*: Modotti, letter, March 6, 1929, *Amauta*, no. 29 (February–March 1930): 94–95.

69   *Pavletich had drafted a number*: Martínez de la Torre, *Apuntes para una interpretación marxista de historia social del Perú*, vol. 2, 363–64.

69   *"We protested the Mexican cell's opposition"*: Sergio Caller, letter to Guillermo Mercardo, October 25, 1929, in ibid., 369–70.

70   *In Paris, the cell split*: Ibid., see 335–46.

70   *"the Apristas in Paris could all fit on a couch"*: Sánchez, *Apuntes para una biografía del APRA*, 112.

70   *"had little meaning, because with or without"*: Eudocio Ravines, letter to JCM, March 19, 1929, in Martínez de la Torre, *Apuntes para una interpretación*, vol. 2, 339.

70   *APRA is a continental organization*: Haya de la Torre, letter to César Mendoza, September 29, 1929, in Basadre, *Historia de la República del Perú*, 6th ed., 163.

70   *Our group, dispersed in various countries"*: "Magda Portal in San Francisco," A 19–20, MPP, BENSON.

70   *"The too notorious truth is that APRA"*: Amauta, no. 28 (January 1930): 97.

70   *"petit bourgeois revolutionary nationalist"*: JCM, letter to Nicanor A. de la Fuente, September 10, 1929, in JCM, *Mariátegui total*, 1592.

71   *deviations from Comintern positions*: This episode is explored by Flores Galindo in *La agonía de Mariátegui*, 17–36; see also Chavarría, *José Carlos Mariátegui*, 158–60.

71   *Historians have noted that Haya de la Torre*: Melis, "El diálogo creador," 1591; see also Flores Galindo, *La agonía de Mariátegui*.

72   *"What is my religion? Love, not the small love"*: "Unos minutos de charla con Magda Portal, la gran revolucionaria."

72   *"the emerald, island-scattered Caribbean"*: MP, *La vida que yo viví: Trazos cortados*, 36, MPP, BENSON.

72 *the stamped visa:* The visa issued by the Colombian consulate in Puerto Rico is dated July 30, 1929; anticipated date of travel, "August 4, 1929." DAEMP.

72 *Havana paper El Diario de Cuba:* MP, "Capitalismo y colonialización," clipping, MPP, BENSON. *Note:* All citations from journalistic accounts of MP's Caribbean tour derive from clippings MP placed in the MMP, BENSON, sometimes without dates or full attribution.

73 *"able to give luster to a continent":* "Magda Portal y la emancipación."

73 *"luminous synthesis":* "Síntesis luminosa del problema mexicano."

74 *"Perhaps another time:* Manuel Rivera Matos, "La conferencia de Magda Portal en el Teatro Municipal," San Juan, Puerto Rico, date and newspaper unattributed, circa July 1929, clipping in MPP, BENSON.

74 *"in any authentic battle for social justice":* Ibid..

74 *"created a sensation that traveled vertiginously":* Alcantara, "Fué un exitazo la conferencia de ilustre luchadora Magda Portal, líder del APRA," *El Mundo* (Santo Domingo) n.d., clipping, MPP, BENSON.

75 *In her talk on Mexico:* MP, *América latina frente.*

75 *"She is all nerve, all action":* Alcantara, "Llegó esta mañana la ilustre escritora."

75 *"lean on sentimentality, advancing like soldiers":* "Vibraciones: Magda Portal."

75 *"the Chronicler" in Barranquilla, Colombia:* "Nos parece que."

76 *"who love the ideal and have blind faith":* "Unos minutos de charla con Magda Portal."

76 *"a very twenty-first-century":* "Llegó ayer a Barranquilla Magda Portal, la escritora," *La Prensa,* Barranquilla, Colombia. Clipping, n.d., MPP, BENSON.

76 *"astonished and disconcerted":* "El espíritu cultivado y ágil de Magda Portal," clipping, n.d., MPP, BENSON.

76 *"amazed at her knowledge of what has hitherto":* "Llegó ayer a Barranquilla Magda Portal, la escritora," *La Prensa* (Barranquilla), n.d., clipping, MPP, BENSON.

76 *When Magda Portal reached our shores:* Angel S. Suazo, "Antes y después de haber oído a Magda Portal," República Dominicana, date and newspaper name not included in clipping, MPP, BENSON.

76 *"Magda Portal: twenty-eight years old":* "Unos minutos de charla con Magda Portal," clipping, MPP, BENSON.

76 *"a mosaic of small countries"; "splintered and enfeebled"; "Either we come together":* "El imperativo de la hora indoamericana," date unavailable, clipping, MPP, BENSON.

77 *"My daughter is waiting for me in Puerto Rico":* "Unos minutos de charla con Magda Portal."

77 *"insisted on speaking to me in English":* MP, *La vida que yo viví: Trazos cortados,* 39, MPP, BENSON.

77 *"Compañera Magda's campaign in Puerto Rico":* Emilio R. Delgado, letter to JCM, October 17, 1929, in JCM, *Mariátegui total,* 2037.

77 *"She seemed unsettled, pale, thin":* Lyra, "Gloria, la hijita de Magda Portal."

78 *"Magda Portal is with us":* Joaquín García Monge, letter to JCM, October 30, 1929, in JCM, *Mariátegui total,* 2039.

78 *Augusto Leguía's regime now exhibited:* See JCM, letter to Joaquín García Monge, November 26, 1929, in JCM, *Mariátegui total.*

78 *"We're working in poverty here":* JCM, letter to Esteban Pavletich, November 7, 1929, in JCM, *Mariátegui total,* 2042–43.

78 *Early in 1930 he wrote Waldo Frank:* Letter from JCM to Waldo Frank, February 25, 1930, in JCM, *Mariátegui total,* 1956.

79 *"I hope you are still in touch with Magda":* JCM, *Mariátegui total,* 2030.

79 *"was already committed to the party Haya":* Levano, "Una mujer de pelea," 63.

79 *"was less timely for Peru than the APRA":* Andradi and Portugal, "Yo soy Magda Portal," 214.

79 *"José Carlos Mariátegui wrote me of his desire":* "Magda Portal in San Francisco," A 18–19, MPP, BENSON. In Buenos Aires, Mariátegui hoped to consult a specialist about an artificial limb and also to meet with Communist officials who had censured his party's independent positions.

80   *"U.S. officials treated the Panamanians as inferiors"*: MP, *La vida que yo viví: Trazos cortados,* 45, MPP, BENSON.

CHAPTER 4

95   *"The Aprista struggle was all-consuming"*: Forgues, "Nací para luchar," 54.

95   *Luis Alberto Sánchez recalled how he learned:* Sánchez, *Testimonio personal,* 245.

96   *"If Mariátegui had arrived"*: "Magda Portal in San Francisco," B 13, MPP, BENSON.

96   *"The country was in crisis"*: Ibid., A 28.

96   *It was not, however, the unrest of the impoverished masses:* This is the conclusion of Steve Stein, *Populism in Peru,* 89.

96   *"the indolent and lazy rabble"*: Ibid., 86.

96   *"a cholo like us"*: Ibid., 102. *Cholo* is a derogatory term referring to a person of mixed ancestry: European, Native American, sometimes African as well.

97   *Decades later Ravines would denounce Communism:* In her 1981 interview ("Magda Portal in San Francisco," MPP, BENSON), Magda spoke scornfully of Ravines, deriding him as an opportunist and false leftist. In the early days of party building in Peru he had seemed to her "less interested in building a social movement in the country than in organizing committees in support of Russian bolshevism." MP, *La vida que yo viví: Trazos cortados,* 49, MPP, BENSON; see also "Magda Portal in San Francisco," A 23, MPP, BENSON.

97   *"ruled out any possible fusion"*: MP, *La vida que yo viví: Trazos cortados,* 48, MPP, BENSON.

97   *Magda Portal, Serafín Delmar, and Julián Petrovick were in Chile:* Sánchez, "Odisea y Calvario de Magda Portal."

98   *"We could barely see to draft the founding document"*: MP, *La vida que yo viví: Trazos cortados,* 51, MPP, BENSON.

98   *Some fifty-five names, including those of Magda:* Sánchez, *Apuntes para una biografía del* APRA, 201; see also 292.

98   *"Magda was a woman who took charge"*: Sánchez, *La literatura peruana,* 1559.

98   *"austere and self-sacrificing" "Magda and Serafín were the mandarins"*: Sánchez, "Cuaderno de Bitácora," 38–39.

99   *"Magda changed houses some twenty times"*: Tealdo, "Historia del APRA," 8.

99   *"The youngest candidate for Peru's presidency"*: "José Carlos Mariátegui en el recuerdo," 15, MPP, BENSON.

99   *Haya's wanting us to prepare for elections:* MP, *La vida que yo viví: Trazos cortados,* 54, MPP, BENSON.

100   *compelled the men to yield:* "Magda Portal en la Inmortalidad," 13.

100   *Aleksandra Kollantai among others:* See Mullaney, "Alexandra Kollontai," 55–96.

100   *"First there was the Executive Committee"*: Andradi and Portugal, "Yo soy Magda Portal," 215.

100   *permanent seat on the party's National Executive Committee:* Aprista women's leaders Carmen Rosa Rivadeneyra, Josefina del Valle, and Rosa Michellini de Casas were also seated on this committee.

100   *She went from province to province"*: Seoane, "Escorzo de Magda Portal."

100   *"Declaration of Women's Rights"*: MP, *El Aprismo y la mujer,* 60.

101   *unanimously approved:* See ibid., 59.

101   *"The cultural level of the Peruvian woman"*: Ibid., 17. See also MP, "Rol de la mujer revolucionaria."

101   *"married women, mothers, teachers, professional women"*: Basadre, *Historia de la República del Perú,* 6th ed., 311.

101   *"the vote of the woman who works is more valuable"*: MP, *El Aprismo y la mujer,* 17.

101   *"The women's vote was 'premature,' they said"*: Andradi and Portugal, "Yo soy Magda Portal," 215.

103   *"Until age fifteen I was a Catholic"*: Ibid., 230.

103 *"the mother of the modern women's movement"*: Klarén, *Peru*, 379.

103 *At salons, or tertulias, initiated by novelist Juana Manuela Gorriti*: See Villavicencio, *Del silencio a la palabra*, 110–15; see also Berg, "Juana Manuela Gorriti," 226–40.

103 *But women also took part in dangerous labor actions*: Villavicencio, *Del silencio a la palabra*, 161–62.

104 *"their delicate brains might be damaged"*: Felisa Moscoso de Carbajal, *Ligeros pensamientos consagrados a la mujer*, Lima, 1901, cited in Villavicencio, *Del silencio a la palabra*, 103–4.

104 *"We had heard much about conditions in Peru"*: Carrie Chapman Catt, letter, February 19, 1923, to Hay, cited in Miller, *Latin American Women*, 80–81; see 259n26.

104 *"In Peru there were few claims to the sisterhood"*: Ibid., 80.

104 *Founded by Zoila Aurora Cáceres*: Guardia, *Mujeres peruanas*, 72.

105 *"upper-class women with no ideology beyond winning the vote"*: MP, *El Aprismo y la mujer*, 5.

105 *a mere 4 percent*: Miller, *Latin American Women*, 120.

105 *"What could be more democratic"*: Tealdo, "Historia del APRA."

105 *in his luggage a silken presidential sash*: Enríquez, 75.

106 *"this great wealth of Peru"*: Ibid., 75.

106 *"To go up against Sánchez Cerrismo"*: MP, *La vida que yo viví: Trazos cortados*, 55, MPP, BENSON.

106 *"was founded on principles considered sacred"*: Statement of August 4, 1931, cited in Basadre, *Historia de la República del Perú*, 6th ed., 159.

106 *"a singular mix of puritanism and bohemianism"*: Sánchez, *Apuntes para una biografía del APRA*, 50.

106 *"'No, this is impossible!'" he said"*: "Magda Portal in San Francisco," A 26, MPP, BENSON.

107 *August 23, 1931, in a major speech*: For an excerpt from Haya's speech, see Haya de la Torre, *Aprismo* 185–94; for treatment of this electoral contest and the Aprista project in general, see also Chang-Rodríguez, *Una vida agónica.*

107 *"attired in blue shirts—symbolically [he was] the sun"*: Pike, *The Politics of the Miraculous in Peru*, 155; see also 154–57.

108 *"a dark-skinned cholo who was even suspected"*: Pike, *The Modern History of Peru*, 251.

108 *"The defenders of the established order"*: Pike, *The Politics of the Miraculous in Peru*, 128.

108 *"nothing to fear"*: F. M. Dearing, "Confidencial 1931," "Entrevista a Haya de la Torre y el Embajador de Norteamérica," *Análisis*, no 1 (January–March), cited in Cotler, *Clases, estado y nación en el Perú*, 241–42; see also Masterson, *Militarism and Politics in Latin America*, 61n16.

108 *"never talking down or giving orders"*: "Magda Portal in San Francisco," A 28, MPP, BENSON.

109 *"For the first time, I think, there was an opening"*: Ibid., A 28.

109 *"sickly, neglected children being auctioned"*: MP, *La vida que yo viví: Trazos cortados*, 65, MPP, BENSON.

109 *"time is measured by the arrival of Magda Portal"*: Ibid., 66.

109 *"Señor APRA, no? APRA—justicia!"*: "Magda Portal in San Francisco," C 19, MPP, BENSON.

110 *"I spoke all over the region"*: Ibid., B 23.

110 *"I sent a telegram: 'Come now, we're ready'"*: Ibid., B 21a.

111 *the legitimacy of Sánchez Cerro's presidency*: Historians seem to concur that Sánchez Cerro won without fraud. See Stein, *Populism in Peru*, 192–95; see also Basadre, *Historia de la República del Perú*, vol. 11, 201–4.

112 *"The government . . . believed this assassination [attempt]"*: Tealdo, "Historia del APRA."

112 *"I heard a loud knock at the door"*: Graciela Pareja Moreno, interview by the author, assisted by Rocío Revolledo Pareja, Lima, August 15, 1993.

113 *He testified that Melgar Márquez*: See Basadre, *Historia de la República del Perú*, 6th ed., 246–47; see also J. Melgar Márquez, "La vida heróica por la libertad en el Perú."

114 *Summarily convicted, the sailors were executed*: MP wrote an elegiac poem in commemoration, "Han muerto ya," in MP, *Costa Sur*, 97, reprinted in MP, *Constancia del ser*, 178.

115 *When Carleton Beals visited Chan Chan*: Beals, *Fire on the Andes*, 189–90.

115   *"The Indians, having exhausted every legal recourse":* Ibid., 99.

115   *"some twenty were brought down to Chan Chan":* Ibid., 99.

115   *"Women too were among the tortured":* MP, *El Aprismo y la mujer,* 31.

116   *"Frequent pilgrimages are made to martyr graves":* Beals, *Fire on the Andes,* 191.

116   *"paved the way for an emergence of a social Christianity":* Klaiber, *Religion and Revolution in Peru,* 62.

116   *"a p r i s m o / 6,000 crosses adorn":* MP, *Costa sur,* 101.

117   *"Magda's correspondence":* MP maintained a very active correspondence; the loss of so much of it, especially her letters to Serafín Delmar, leaves a notable gap in the record.

118   *"They took my mother, my married sister":* MP, *La vida que yo viví: Trazos cortados,* 59, MPP, BENSON.

118   *"liberated from absurd patriotic prejudices":* MP, *El Aprismo y la mujer,* 30.

118   *"WAR IS THE PERPETUATION OF TYRANNY!":* Ibid., 76; see also MP, "A Juana [de] Ibarbourou."

119   *"She also took part in conspiracies":* Seoane, "Escorzo de Magda Portal."

119   *A distinguished and widely respected military officer, General Oscar Benavides:* See Pike, *The Modern History of Peru,* 268–76.

119   *"This hatred is not exactly class hatred":* "La obra del odio," letter (in MS) to editor of *La Noche,* under pseudonym "Marius," dated La Paz, May 22, 1933, MPP, BENSON.

120   *"Magda was very close to Haya":* Sánchez, "Cuaderno de Bitácora," 38–39.

120   *League of Revolutionary Writers:* For more on this organization, see Chang-Rodríguez, *Una vida agónica,* 222.

121   *"my little daughter Gloria, witness":* Hidalgo, Portal, Delmar, Berrios, Lova, Martínez, Alegría, and Petrovick, *Cantos de la Revolución.*

121   *"the most dramatic testimony to the awakening Peruvian feminism":* Pike, *The Politics of the Miraculous in Peru,* 126

121   *"Our struggles, comrades, are not based on our sex":* MP, *La trampa,* 2nd ed., 146.

121   *"the Aprista woman should put forward her ideas":* MP, *El Aprismo y la mujer,* 56.

122   *"The individual woman struggles not only":* Ibid., 48.

122   *"Education is of the whole person";* "Woman's great error": Ibid., 43.

122   *"acting not as man's adjunct":* Ibid., 48.

123   *The Women's Command, for example, had a special committee:* Andradi and Portugal, "Yo soy Magda Portal," 216.

123   *"strictly a matter of personal conscience, unless":* MP, *El aprismo y la mujer,* 20.

123   *"The new woman is self-disciplined":* Ibid., 50.

123   *"Yankee flapper type";* "feminine boy, sportive, agile, bold": Ibid., 51.

124   *"Aprismo is a revolution":* Ibid., 51.

124   *"Partly masculine and partly feminine in spirit":* Ibid., 52.

124   *"the human pair will share the work":* Ibid., 53.

125   *"Compañeras . . . we are the authors":* MP, "Mensaje a las mujeres apristas de Cuba," cited in Alberto Arredondo, "Actividades Apristas: Expulsados del Partido Aprista; Mensaje de Magda Portal a las Mujeres Cubanas," *Futuro* (Havana), no 6 (February 15, 1935): 10, reprinted in Castro, *Haya de la Torre,* 153.

125   *"I arrived somewhere, organized a committee":* "Magda Portal in San Francisco," B 15–16, MPP, BENSON.

126   *"Revolutions aren't made without bloodshed":* Ibid., C 15–16.

126   *"I was just talking, not inciting revolution":* Ibid., B 24.

126   *"absolutely ignorant":* MP, *La vida que yo viví: Trazos cortados,* 71, MPP, BENSON.

127   *"If I'm going to be poisoned like a rat":* "Magda Portal in San Francisco," B 27, MPP, BENSON.

127   *"I am Magda Portal":* Ibid., B 28.

128   *"each a mask of atrocious suffering":* MP, *La vida que yo viví: Trazos cortados,* 76, MPP, BENSON.

128   *"'Political, right?' said one of the inmates":* Ibid., 77.

128   *"I felt better, more stable":* Ibid., 77–78.

129   *"But we soon realized":* Reyes, "Magda Portal a través de mi compañera."

130 *"I believe and continue to believe that Aprismo"*: Cited in Enrique S. Portugal P., "Una mujer indoamericana que debe ser libertada."

130 *"They invented love affairs"*: Andradi and Portugal, "Yo soy Magda Portal," 221.

130 *"difficulties with her imprisoned lover"*: Reedy, "Aspects of the Feminist Movement," 61.

130 *"to go back and forth between prisons"; "She was playing innocently"*: Sánchez, "Odisea y Calvario de Magda Portal."

131 *"My freedom is not satisfying"*: MP, "Saludo de Magda Portal."

131 *"were expiating the enormous crime"*: MP, "De González Prada."

132 *His friends agreed that someone of his particular sensibility*: Marín, "Evocación de Serafín Delmar."

132 *"allay or confirm his anxieties"; "the faith of an illumined man"*: Sánchez, "Serafín Delmar."

132 *Aprista members of this organization included*: Guardia, *Mujeres peruanas,* 90.

133 *"her suitcases splashed with stickers"*: "Magda Portal no quiere hablar de política."

134 *"A slender woman of great nervous intensity"*: "Magda Portal, líder aprista."

134 *"whose seriousness made her seem much older"*: Ibid.

134 *"Magda Portal came to us with her daughter"*: Sánchez, *Testimonio personal,* vol. 2, 193.

134 *Asked about Serafín during an interview*: "Una hora con Magda Portal."

134 *Haya sent encouraging letters to the jailed Apristas*: See Haya de la Torre, *Cartas de Haya de la Torre.*

134 *As reported in the Havana newspaper Patria*: Vegas León, "Las torturas y los crímenes," reprinted in Castro, *Haya de la Torre,* 152–53.

134 *"Where, then, workers of the world"*: "Conciencia de clase," MPP, BENSON.

135 *"the blackest point on the map"*: MP, "El Perú, el punto negro en el mapa de Indomerica, *La Voz del Interior* (Córdoba, Argentina), clipping, n.d. DAEMP.

135 *At a tribute offered her by the Chilean Socialists"*: "Hoy es homenaje a Magda Portal."

137 *"Magda wandered America in exile"*: Sánchez, *La literatura peruana,* 1559–60.

137 *"certain inexplicable modesty"; "erroneous sense"; "detracted from revolutionary effort"*: Sánchez, "Qué libro leyó esta semana?"

137 *"We hear people say, 'So and so gave up everything'"*: Ibid.

137 *"Nobody can give back to you the nights"*: "Magda Portal in San Francisco," C 28, MPP, BENSON.

137 *I think there's a moment in which one is lucid*: Ibid., D 11.

CHAPTER 5

139 *"Everybody visited him"*: "Magda Portal in San Francisco," C 2, MPP, BENSON.

139 *"Haya de la Torre, c/o Lima, Peru"*: Haya de la Torre, *Aprismo,* 12.

140 *"the goodwill of one man"*: MP, ¿Quiénes traicionaron el pueblo? 9.

140 *"We are stagnating"*: MP, Letter to Haya de la Torre, June 20, 1941, MPP, BENSON.

140 *"I have always believed you to be the quintessential Indo-American"*: Ibid.

140 *"Everyone [in Peru] down to the most downtrodden"*: Haya de la Torre, letter to MP, July 7, 1941, MPP, BENSON.

141 *the first of two stunning blows*: "Magda Portal, la poetisa."

141 *"Women will now demonstrate"*: MP, *La mujer en el partido del pueblo,* 4.

142 *"democratic euphoria"*: MP, ¿Quiénes traicionaron el pueblo? 12.

142 *"politics in a higher sense, as a school"*: MP, "Experiencia política de la mujer peruana."

142 *coalition of centrist-to right parties*: This was called the Frente Democrático Nacional (National Democratic Front).

142 *"There is no doubt of the sincerity of this alliance"*: MP, "Nada tiene la mujer."

143 *"one of the most emotion-charged moments"*: Pike, *The Politics of the Miraculous in Peru,* 207.

143 *"His speech astonished us all"*: "Magda Portal in San Francisco," C 5, D 2–4, MPP, BENSON.

144 *"political decomposition"*: MP, ¿Quiénes traicionaron el pueblo? 20.

144 *disdainful treatment by Haya de la Torre*: Valcárcel, "Una luz que no se apaga."

144   *stopping in hundreds of villages and small towns:* Reedy, *Magda Portal: La pasionaria,* 235.

145   *"I'm not getting on any airplane, compañera":* "Magda Portal in San Francisco," C 7, MPP, BENSON.

145   *"fifteen-year Calvary":* MP, *La mujer en el partido del pueblo,* 25.

146   *"hundreds"; Francisca Steward, Carmen Saldías:* Ibid., 17.

146   *Ollé, Fisher, Lizárraga, Bedoya, Perone:* Ibid., 19.

146   *"The odd thing is that I never felt any discrimination":* "Magda Portal in San Francisco," B 19, MPP, BENSON.

146   *"deterred from pursuing their goal of attaining":* MP, *La mujer en el partido del pueblo,* 31.

147   *Haya went to the podium—I stood:* "Magda Portal in San Francisco," C 8, MPP, BENSON.

147   *"arrogance" and "infallibility":* MP, *¿Quiénes traicionaron el pueblo?* 18.

148   *"Living in luxury and maintaining two residences":* Pike, *The Politics of the Miraculous in Peru,* 221n73.

148   *purportedly received payments from the U.S. Embassy:* Ibid., 205, with reference to Villanueva, *El Apra y el ejército,* 30–32.

148   *"his nightly outings in a luxury automobile":* Ibid., 205, with reference to Villanueva, *El Apra en busca del poder,* 45.

148   *would benefit by overthrowing the regime of Manuel Prado Ugarteche:* Pike, *The Politics of the Miraculous in Peru,* 205, with reference to Villanueva, *El Apra y el ejército,* 30–32.

148   *"by maintaining contact with leading Apristas":* U.S. ambassador Cooper to secretary of state, reporting on a meeting between Haya de la Torre and Maurice J. Broderick, cited in Masterson, *Militarism and Politics in Latin America,* 97n38.

148   *"U.S. capital bears no resemblance to that studied by Marx and Engels":* Cited in Enríquez, *Haya de la Torre,* 15.

149   *"[Haya] and his movement have been the strongest bulwark":* Cited in Haya de la Torre, *Aprismo,* 29.

149   *"The National Executive Committee should stay out of it":* Tealdo, "Historia del APRA."

149   *"A party that started out so well!":* Ibid.

150   *"Magda screamed and tore her hair":* Graciela Pareja Moreno, interview by the author, assisted by Rocío Revolledo Pareja, Lima, August 15, 1993.

150   *"Compañera Gloria Delmar, daughter of leader Magda Portal":* "Gloria Del Mar."

150   *"I will never forget the prostrate form of Gloria":* Sánchez, "Cuaderno de Bitácora."

151   *Aprista students carried the casket:* "Ayer se efectuó la inhumación."

151   *Several knowledgeable accounts confirm that Gloria:* Zoila Maxwell (Zoila Bernal León y León), who was close to Magda Portal at this time, had no doubt that Gloria was involved in a love affair with an older man, someone in the APRA. Author conversation with Zoila B. Maxwell, 1994. Graciela Pareja Moreno also believed this to be the case, interview with the author, assisted by Rocío Revolledo Pareja, Lima, August 15, 1993.

151   *Gloria had only recently (in Chile), learned from her mother:* Rocío Revolledo Pareja (Magda's niece) reported this, in contradiction to Graciela Pareja Moreno's assertion that Gloria was raised to understand her parentage. Graciela Pareja Moreno, interview by the author, assisted by Rocío Revolledo Pareja, Lima, August 15, 1993.

152   *"I won't let words approach you / I refuse":* "Balada triste," in MP, *Constancia del ser,* 129.

152   *"There is narcissism or masochism in those who relate":* MP, *Trazos cortados,* 2–3, memoir, fifty-one-page version, DAEMP.

153   *"that failure to include the central thing":* MP, "Trazos cortados," not the shorter version of MP's memoir by the same name but a brief essay on José María Arguedas, 1975, MPP, BENSON.

153   *"My daughter was born at the end of November":* MP, *La vida que yo viví: Trazos cortados,* 9, MPP, BENSON.

153   *"instinctive refusal"; "Seething in my mind were so many desires":* Ibid., 19.

153   *"like a sunflower to the light":* MP, "Resonancias alrededor de una época," 2–3, MPP, BENSON.

153   *"ever-new beginnings without continuity":* Ibid.

154   *A prose sketch published in 1979:* MP, "El viaje inútil."

155   *"sounding the alarm against the new totalitarianisms"*: Haya de La Torre, letter to MP, March 24, 1947, MPP, BENSON.

155   *"the exclusion on Haya's order of compañeras"*: Enríquez, *Haya de la Torre*, 172.

155   *"We thought . . . that after consulting with the party's masses"*: "Defraudada y traicionada."

155   *"During the party congress, in the second half of '48"*: Sánchez, "Cuaderno de Bitácora," 38–39.

155   *"'We have come to the conclusion,' Haya declared"*: "Magda Portal in San Francisco," D 6, C 10, MPP, BENSON.

156   *"Nobody protested. The majority stayed put"*: Andradi and Portugal, "Yo soy Magda Portal," 217.

157   *"On the eve of the uprising I remember talking"*: Ibid., 220.

157   *"Three insurrectionary movements"*: "Magda Portal in San Francisco," C 11–13, MPP, BENSON.

158   *"That stupid thing that Haya did!"*: Zoila B. Maxwell, interview by the author, Berkeley, October 3, 1993.

158   *"Magda at this time was one of the most recognizable women"*: Ibid.

159   *"elegantly attired in a silk dress"*: "Dramática presentación de Magda Portal."

159   *her lawyer, Luis Bramont Arias, read a long statement*: Luis Bramont Arias, transcript of statement to Señor Jefe de la Zona Judicial de Marina, September 15, 1949, MPP, BENSON.

160   *"Well, the Political Bureau, how can I put it"*: "Dramática presentación de Magda Portal."

160   *"Magda later admitted that she had in fact been part"*: Andradi and Portugal, "Yo soy Magda Portal," 219–20.

160   *Magda had tried unsuccessfully to raise funds*: This account derives from Reedy's discussion in *Magda Portal: La pasionaria*, 170; see also Villanueva, *La sublevación aprista del 48.*

160   *"that had betrayed all the people's hopes"*: MP, *¿Quiénes traicionaron el pueblo?* 24.

160   *"slippery slide into the abyss"*: MP, *¿Quienes traicionaron el pueblo?* Ibid., 12.

160   *"to confront with valor even one major social problem"*: MP, ibid., 13.

160   *"politics of the double face"*: MP, ibid., 15.

160   *"The leaders promised—'over our dead bodies'"; "but over the corpses"*: MP, ibid., 18.

160   *"was to agree to build a cenotaph"*: Ibid., 20.

161   *"of the sort that afforded women no civil standing"*: Ibid., 23.

161   *"in the People and in Youth"*: Ibid., 30.

161   *"mendacious traffickers in hope"*: Ibid., 30.

161   *"I couldn't just leave without saying a word"*: "Magda Portal in San Francisco," C 19, MPP, BENSON.

161   *APRA leaders Ramiro Prialé, Carlos Manuel Cox*: Masterson, *Militarism and Politics in Latin America*, 135.

162   *"a political death wish"; "disillusioned with a leadership that had brought"*: Pike, *The Politics of the Miraculous in Peru*, 237.

162   *the APRA chief had betrayed the insurrectionary plotters*: See Villanueva, *La sublevación aprista del 48.*

162   *"because of the ambivalence and treason"*: Cited in Andradi and Portugal, "Yo soy Magda Portal," 218.

162   *"had begun identifying with the upper classes"*: Ibid., 217.

162   *"in his youth a pioneer in revolutionary struggles"*: "Magda Portal in San Francisco," C 17, MPP, BENSON.

163   *Peru's women were finally accorded the full vote*: A constitutional reform giving Peru's women various rights, including the unrestricted vote, passed September 7, 1955.

163   *declared the Aprista Party of Peru defunct*: See Reedy's account of this episode in *Magda Portal: La pasionaria*, 266–67.

163   *"I may be an Aprista"*: Graciela Pareja Moreno, interview by the author, assisted by Rocío Revolledo Pareja, Lima, August 15, 1993.

163   *even such staunch friends as Salvador Allende*: See Villavicencio, "Aprender a recordarte."

163   *"When I left, they said hideous things about me"*: "Magda Portal in San Francisco," C 20, MPP, BENSON.

164 *"twenty heroic years"; "synonymous with* APRA," *"depersonalized"; "a spirit of sacrifice pre-vailed"; "caught up in a dialectic of nostalgia"; "The epoch of the supreme leader is over"*: Tealdo, "Historia del APRA."

164 *"the unpublished intellectual work of more than twenty years"*: "Noticia," in MP, *Constancia del ser.*

164 *"From her I absorbed many things"*: MP, *Trazos cortados,* 21, memoir, fifty-one-page version, DAEMP.

165 *welcomed her Aprista friends into their home*: Zoila Maxwell, an Aprista in the 1940s, met and became friends with Magda in 1939 or 1940; she remembered Magda's mother as "a very beautiful woman with striking blue eyes and a very kind face; you fell in love with her immediately." She recalled that Magda's friends Antenor Orrego and Alcides Spelucín "liked to come to her house and be with her mother. They came for several Christmases." Zoila B. Maxwell, interview by the author, Berkeley, October 3, 1993.

165 *"Never, never abandon your sister Magda"*: Graciela Pareja Moreno, interview by the author, assisted by Rocío Revolledo Pareja, Lima, August 15, 1993.

165 *"taken a job with Cerro de Pasco"*: Zoila Maxwell, interview by the author, Berkeley, October 3, 1993. Zoila also confided that Magda would have accepted an offer of marriage from the distinguished lawyer Dr. Bernardino León y León, a match that Zoila promoted; Dr. León y León told her he would have welcomed the marriage if he were in better health. Zoila said that Magda would have accepted his offer, which was not forthcoming, and not much later he died of a heart attack. Note that Dr. León y León was permitted by the nuns to visit Magda during her solitary confinement in Santo Tomás.

165 *Why then the six thousand dead of Trujillo*: Tealdo, "Historia del APRA."

166 *"We need a death, we need a death"; "What you have done is a betrayal"*: Andradi and Portugal, "Yo soy Magda Portal," 220.

166 *"Passionate and vehement, she embraced the ideals"*: MP, *La trampa,* 2nd ed., 145.

166 *"Or so her romantic imagination allowed her to suppose"*: Ibid., 145.

167 *"she believed in love"*: Ibid., 119.

167 *"three failed relationships"; "a kind of physical repugnance for the act of love"*: Ibid., 117.

167 *"Mariel, may women always curse you!"*: Ibid., 125.

167 *"as if women had a right to be equal to men"*: Ibid., 144.

167 *"so as to recruit women, so it could not be said"*: Ibid., 144.

167 *"In the center of the leader's bedroom"*: Ibid., 157.

167 *Not only his enemies but many a devoted Aprista*: Pike, *The Politics of the Miraculous in Peru,* 101.

168 *"A party can't sustain itself without an all-encompassing symbology"*: *La trampa,* 2nd ed., 154–55.

168 *"Great crowds always overwhelm her"*: Ibid., 145–46.

168 *"'For centuries the people have borne the yoke'"*: Ibid., 147–48.

168 *"'My husband gets drunk and beats me, compañerita'"*: Ibid., 149.

169 *"to friends of the leader, or opportunists"*: Ibid., 151.

169 *"the book they wanted to kill me for writing"*: Andradi and Portugal, "Yo soy Magda Portal," 219.

169 *reproached her for having left the party*: Forgues, "Nací para luchar," 61.

169 *"the chosen* CIA *candidate"*: Beals, *Latin America,* 106.

CHAPTER 6

171 *"We cannot grasp the relative insignificance"*: "JCM, *Mariátegui total,* 501.

173 *The bookstore was then liquidated*: MP, "Liquidación de la agencia en el Perú de la Editorial Fondo de Cultura Económica," report, n.d., MPP, BENSON.

173 *"to eat for a number of months"*: Rocío Revolledo Pareja, conversation with the author, Berkeley, February 22, 1997.

174 *"I wrote on everything"*: "Magda Portal in San Francisco," C 29, MPP, BENSON.

174 *"at no time in this century, prior to the 1930s"*: Masterson, *Militarism and Politics in Latin America,* 219.

174 *An agricultural census taken in 1961 revealed:* Werlich, *Peru,* 17.

174 *"who sympathized with the revolutionary objectives"*: Masterson, *Militarism and Politics in Latin America,* 166.

174 *Peruvian military aided by the U.S. Central Intelligence Agency:* Ibid., 216–17.

175 *Javier Heraud:* As her niece recalled, Magda sympathized with Javier Heraud. Rocío Revolledo Pareja, e-mail to author, August 28, 2001.

176 *"its messiah-like leader, its secretive and rigidly disciplined"*: Masterson, *Militarism and Politics in Latin America,* 275.

177 *"was neither with communism nor against it"*: MP, "Ni con el comunismo ni contra el comunismo."

177 *In a manuscript version of a talk she delivered on the occasion of her inception:* "Compañeros, quiero, en primer lugar," n.d., DAEMP.

178 *In an opinion piece dated in manuscript February 25, 1980:* "El Perú y el mundo: Afganistan," editorial, February 25, 1980, on letterhead of the Lima newspaper *Ojo,* MPP, BENSON.

179 *"That day when woman will take her place"*: "Con magnífica velada de arte."

179 *"the symbolic figure who opened the way"*: "Magda Portal, la poetisa de los pobres."

179 *"Of course!"*: "Lampo."

179 *"without cataclysmic bloodshed"*: "Con magnífica velada de arte."

179 *when asked by Sara Beatriz Guardia to discuss her erotic experiences:* Sara Beatriz Guardia, interview by the author, Barranco, Peru, August 25, 1993.

179 *Abortions? Not one, but several:* Andradi and Portugal, "Yo soy Magda Portal," 230–31.

180 *she traveled to Mexico City:* Cecilia Bustamante recounts that Magda visited her in Austin before they traveled together by train to Mexico City. Bustamante, *Magda Portal y sus poderes.*

180 *the 1981 interview so often cited in these pages:* "Magda Portal in San Francisco," MPP, BENSON.

180 *"The principal task of the writer in our time is to denounce"*: "Poesía," Cuestionario planteado a la poetisa Magda Portal por la revista trimestral de poesía "Poesía," a cargo de Miguel Angel Rodríguez Rea, co-director, y Eduardo Farro Castillo, editorialista, MPP, BENSON.

181 *"The injustices he lived and witnessed"*; *"I am sick with disappointment, rebellion, dissatisfaction"*: MP, "Trazos cortados," essay on José María Arguedas, 1975, MPP, BENSON.

181 *"There is only one real social idea"*: "Compañeros, quiero, en primer lugar," DAEMP.

181 *"the protagonist of a broken dream"*: Sánchez, "Cuaderno de Bitácora," 38–39.

181 *"a few stellar spirits whose names defined epochs"*: "Compañeros, quiero, en primer lugar," DAEMP.

182 *Flora Tristan, Precursora, which appeared in 1983:* For a discussion of MP's treatment of Tristan compared with that of Argentinean Silvina Bullrich, see Stacey Schlau, "In Search of a Foremother: Silvina Bullrich and Magda Portal on Flora Tristán," *Spanish American Women's Use of the Word, Colonial Through Contemporary Narrative,* 81–104; see also Busse, "Flora Tristan and Peruvian Feminists," 124–28. "Flora Tristan, Precursor," a version of MP's speech, trans. Kathleen Weaver, is in MPP, BENSON.

182 *"the bedside-table book of Peruvian feminists:* "Magda Portal descansa en paz en las profundidades del mar," 9.

182 *Don Pío:* In fact, Don Pío welcomed his unknown niece as a long-term guest, gave her an allowance, and offered a lesser inheritance—before disinheriting her entirely when *Peregrinations of a Pariah* appeared in France; copies of the book were burned by the bishop of Arequipa in the public square.

183 *"that female vanity that is the legacy"*: MP, "Retrato de una mujer."

183 *women, who petitioned the government:* Sara Beatriz Guardia, interview by the author, Barranco, Peru, August 25, 1993.

183 *"I'm going forward, forward, I don't go back"*: "Magda Portal, la poetisa de los pobres."

184 *"Perhaps my final words will go unheard"*: "Quizá nadie oirá," manuscript, DAEMP.

184   *In an article commemorating the anniversary of the siege:* MP, "Leningrado 1945," DAEMP.
185   *"to pay their final respects":* "Magda Portal descansa en paz."
186   *"pooled in a circle where, just moments":* Ibid.
186   *"Your voice shall be mine":* "Clamor," in MP, *Costa sur,* 13.

SELECTED POEMS

The principal text for translation is *Constancia del ser.* Additional sources are "Oración al mar," *Flechas,* December 1924; "El viajero de todos los mares," in *Una esperanza y el mar,* 1927; nos. 5 and 7, in "18 cantos emocionados de 'Vidrios de amor,'" *Repertorio Americano* (Costa Rica), December 21, 1929; "Tarde de lluvia en Praga," *Quehacer* (Lima), November 1983; and "Sin tiempo," manuscript, the Estate of Magda Portal, Lima. Some Spanish texts are modified slightly for consistency, and several titles (first lines) are offered for numbered poems. For comments on the translation process, see Weaver, "Magda Portal."

SELECTED REFERENCES

For an extensive bibliography of works by and about Magda Portal, the reader is referred to Daniel R. Reedy, "Bibliografía cronológica de Magda Portal" and "Bibliografía sobre Magda Portal," in *Magda Portal: La pasionaria peruana*, 349–86 (Lima: Ediciones Flora Tristán, Centro de la Mujer Peruana Flora Tristán, 2000).

WORKS BY MAGDA PORTAL

"A Juana [de] Ibarbourou." *Claridad* (Buenos Aires) 14, no. 294 (1935).

América latina frente al imperialismo y Defensa de la revolución mexicana. Lima: Editorial Cahuide, 1931.

"Andamios de vida," *Amauta*, no. 5 (January 1927): 12.

El Aprismo y la mujer. Lima: Editorial Cooperativa Aprista "Atahualpa," 1933.

"Capitalismo y colonialización: La conquista de mercados!" *El Diario de Cuba*, May 28 1929.

Constancia del ser. Lima: Talleres Gráficos P. L. Villanueva, 1965.

Costa sur. Santiago de Chile: Imprenta Nueva, 1944.

"De González Prada, que sembró fructiferamente en el corazón de los jóvenes peruanos, a Haya de la Torre, el esforzado paladín de América." *Señales* (Buenos Aires), September 18, 1935.

El derecho de matar. With Serafín Delmar. La Paz, Bolivia: Imprenta Continental, 1926.

"18 cantos emocionados de 'Vidrios de amor.'" Series of untitled poems dated 1924. *Repertorio Americano* (Costa Rica), December 21, 1929.

Una esperanza y el mar: varios poemas a la misma distancia. Lima: Imprenta Minerva, 1927.

"Experiencia política de la mujer peruana." *Vanguardia* (Buenos Aires), August 20, 1939.

Flora Tristán. Santiago de Chile: Imprenta Nueva, 1944.

Flora Tristán: La precursora. Lima: Ediciones "Páginas Libres." El texto integro de la conferencia dictada por Magda Portal en la Escuela de Derecho de la Universidad de Chile, el 28 de Octobre de 1944, con motivo de la inauguración del Primer Congreso de Mujeres de Chile, n.d.

Flora Tristán: Precursora. With Otilia Navarrete, Renée Castro-Pozo, Sonia Canales, Carmen C. P. de Urteaga, and Elena Quiñe de Delgado. Lima: Editorial La Equidad, 1983.

Hacia la mujer nueva. In *El Aprismo y la mujer.* Lima: Editorial Cooperativa Aprista "Atahualpa," 1933.

"Leningrado 1945." In *La guerra y la paz 1939/45.* Published to commemorate the fortieth anniversary of the victory over fascism, celebrated May 1985. Lima: Soviet-Peruvian Cultural Association.

"Los hermanos Peralta." *El Comercio* (Lima), June 21, 1977.

"Los libros de la revolución mexicana." Review of *Lecturas populares,* by Esperanza Velásquez Bringas. *Amauta* (Lima) no. 11 (January 1928): 41.

"Mi descubrimiento de Flora Tristán." In *Flora Tristán: Una reserva de utopia,* by Magda Portal, Denys Cuche, Daniel Armogathe, Jacques Grandjonc, Stéphane Michaud, and Maritza Villavicencio, with an introduction by Alfonso Ibáñez. Proceedings of the first international colloquium on Flora Tristan, Dijon, May 3–4, 1984. Lima: Tarea, Centro de la mujer peruana, Flora Tristán, 1985.

La mujer en el partido del pueblo. Lima: Imprenta "El Cóndor," 1948. Pamphlet. Magda Portal's address to the First National Convention of Aprista Women, November 14–24, 1946.

"Ni con el comunismo ni contra el comunismo." *APRA* 1 (June 19, 1931).

El nuevo poema y su orientación hacia una estética económica. México: Ediciones A.P.R.A, 1928.

"Panorama intelectual de México: Las canciones populares." *Repertorio Americano* (San José, Costa Rica) 16, no. 12 (1928).

"El poeta de los espejos iluminados: Serafín Del Mar." *Variedades* (Lima) 21, no. 896 (1925): 970–71.

"Prólogo-Manifiesto." Unsigned editorial by Magda Portal and Federico Bolaños. In *Flechas* (Lima), ed. Federico Bolaños and Magda Portal, no. 1 (October 23, 1924).

¿Quiénes traicionaron el pueblo? Lima: Imprenta Salas, 1950.

"Replíca de Magda Portal," *Amauta,* no. 7 (March 1927): 28.

"Una revista de cuatro nombres." Preface to *Hueso húmero* (Lima), no. 7 (October–December 1980): 101–104.

"Rol de la mujer revolucionaria: El voto femenino." *Repertorio Americano,* June 6, 1931.

"Saludo de Magda Portal a los amigos solidarios de la Argentina y Chile." *Claridad* (Buenos Aires) 15, no. 301 (1936).

La trampa. 1st ed. Lima: Editorial Raíz, 1957.

———. 2nd ed. Lima: Editorial Poma, 1982. Excerpts "Aprismo and the Woman," and "Women in the Party" translated in *Women in Latin American History,* ed. June E. Hahner. Los Angeles: University of California–Los Angeles Latin American Center, 1976.

"El viaje inútil." *Ojo* (Lima), January 21, 1979.

"La vieja casa y sus fantasmas." *Revista Autoeducación,* July 1985.

INTERVIEWS

Andradi, Esther, and Ana María Portugal. "Yo soy Magda Portal." In *Ser mujer en el Perú.* Lima: Tokapu Editores, 1979. This interview is extensively translated by Marcy Schwartz in *Women's Writing in Latin America: An Anthology,* ed. Sara Castro-Klarén, Silvia Molloy, and Beatriz Sarlo. Boulder, Colo.: Westview Press, 1991.

Forgues, Roland. "Nací para luchar." In *Palabra Viva,* vol. 4, *Los poetas se desnudan.* Lima: El Editorial Quijote, 1991.

"Lampo." *Quehacer* (Lima), no. 25 (November 1983).

Levano, César. "Una mujer de pelea: Magda Portal cuenta su vida dolorosa y plena." *Caretas* (Lima), August 17, 1987.

"Magda Portal in San Francisco." Interview by Kathleen Weaver, Janet Rigg, and Allan Francovich. San Francisco, July 1–2, 1981. Typescript, in Spanish.

"Nada tiene la mujer de inferior al hombre." *Claridad de los Trabajadores y para los Trabajadores* (Lima), May 25, 1945.

"Retrato de una mujer." *La Tortuga* (Lima), no. 23 (1985).

Tealdo, Alfonso. "Historia del APRA: Entrevista con Magda Portal." DDT (un biseminario contra toda clase de parásitos políticos; Lima) 1, no. 2 (1950).

Weaver, Kathleen. "An Interview with Magda Portal: The Early Years." Translated by Kathleen Weaver. In *Contemporary Women Writing in Latin America*, vol. 1, *Contemporary Women Writing in the Other Americas*, ed. Georgiana M. M. Colvile. Lewiston, N.Y.: Edwin Mellen Press, 1996.

OTHER WORKS

Albers, Patricia. *Shadows, Fire, Snow: The Life of Tina Modottii.* Berkeley and Los Angeles: University of California Press, 1999.

Alcantara. "Llegó esta mañana la ilustre escritora peruana Magda Portal, la más destacada mujer de la revolución social que está sacudiendo la América." *El Mundo* (Santo Domingo), July 9, 1929.

Alencastre G., Manuel. "La vigencia de la ANEA: 1938–1997." *El Comercio* (Lima), October 10, 1997.

Arenal, Electa, and Stacey Schlau. *Untold Sisters: Hispanic Nuns in Their Own Works.* Translated by Amanda Powell. Albuquerque: University of New Mexico Press, 1989.

"Ayer se efectuó la inhumación de los restos de la c. Gloria Delmar Portal." *La Tribuna* (Lima), January 6, 1947.

Baines, John M., *Revolution in Peru: Mariátegui and the Myth.* With an introduction by Juan Mejía Baca. University: University of Alabama Press, 1972.

Basadre, Jorge. *Historia de la República del Perú.* 5th ed., aumentada y corregida. Vols. 1–11. Lima: Ediciones "Historia," 1961–68.

———. *Historia de la República del Perú.* 6th ed., aumentada y corregida. Vol 11. Lima, Editorial Universitaria, 1968.

———. Introduction to *Seven Interpretive Essays on Peruvian Reality,* by José Carlos Mariátegui. Translated by Marjory Urquidi. Austin: University of Texas Press, 1971.

Beals, Carleton. *Fire on the Andes.* Illustrated by José Sabogal. Philadelphia: J. B. Lippincott, 1934.

———. *Latin America: World in Revolution.* New York: Abelard-Schuman, 1963.

Berg, Mary G. "Clorinda Matto de Turner (1852–1909), Peru." In *Spanish American Women Writers: A Bio-bibliographical Source Book,* ed. Diane E. Marting. New York: Greenwood Press, 1990.

———. "Juana Manuela Gorriti (1818–1892), Argentina." In *Spanish American Women Writers: A Bio-bibliographical Source Book,* ed. Diane E. Marting. New York: Greenwood Press, 1990.

Brenner, Anita. *The Wind That Swept Mexico.* Photographs by George B. Leighton. New York: Harper and Bros., 1943.

Busse, Erika. "Flora Tristan and Peruvian Feminists in the Twentieth Century." *Journal of Women's History* 15, no. 3 (2003): 124–28.

Bustamante, Cecilia. *Magda Portal y sus poderes.* Austin, Tex.: Extramares Editions, 2003.

Castañeda Vielakamen, Esther. *El vanguardismo literario en el Perú: Estudio y selección de la revista "Flechas" (1924).* Lima: Amaru Editores, 1989.

Castañeda Vielakamen, Esther, and Elizabeth Toguchi Kayo. "Magda Portal y su irrupción en la vanguardia. *Warmi Nayra: Revista del círculo de mujeres Magda Portal* 1 (November 1991): 28–37.

Castro, Luis Alva. *Haya de la Torre: Peregrino de la unidad continental.* Vol. 2. Lima: Fondo Editorial "V. R. Haya de la Torre," 1990.

Castro-Klarén, Sara, ed., *Narrativa femenina en América Latina: Prácticas y perspectivas teóricas/Latin American Women's Narrative: Practices and Theoretical Perspectives.* Madrid: Iberoamericana; Frankfurt: Vervuert, 2003.

Castro-Klarén, Sara, Silvia Molloy, and Beatriz Sarlo, eds. *Women's Writing in Latin America.* Boulder, Colo.: Westview Press, 1991.

Catlin, Stanton L. "Mural Census." In *Diego Rivera: A Retrospective,* ed. Cynthia Newman Helms. Retrospective curated by Linda Downs and Ellen Sharp. New York: Founders Society, Detroit Institute of Arts and W. W. Norton, 1986.

"Cenizas de Magda Portal arrojan hoy al mar." *Expreso* (Lima), July 13, 1989.

Chang-Rodríguez, Eugenio. *Una vida agónica: Víctor Raúl Haya de la Torre,* Lima: Fondo Editorial del Congreso del Perú, 2007.

Chavarría, Jesús. *José Carlos Mariátegui and the Rise of Modern Peru, 1890–1930.* Albuquerque: University of New Mexico Press, 1979.

Claridad (Buenos Aires) 14, no. 294 (1935). Issue devoted to Magda Portal.

Claridad (Buenos Aires) 15, no. 301 (1936). Issue devoted to Serafín Delmar.

Colvile, Georgiana M. M., ed. *Contemporary Women Writing in Latin America.* Vol. 1 of *Contemporary Women Writing in the Other Americas.* Lewiston, N.Y.: Edwin Mellen Press, 1996.

"Con magnífica velada de arte ha sido clausurado exposición femenina de Viña . . . Charla de la poestisa peruana Magda Portal." *El Mercurio* (Santiago de Chile), March 3, 1940.

Constantine, Mildred. *Tina Modotti: A Fragile Life.* New York: Rizzoli International, 1983.

Cotler, Julio. *Clases, estado y nación en el Perú.* Perú Problema 17. Lima: Instituto de Estudios Peruanos, 1978.

Cox, Carlos Manuel. "Luchadores apristas: Magda Portal y Serafín Delmar." *Claridad* (Buenos Aires) 15, no. 301 (1936).

Cruz, Juana Inés de la. *A Sor Juana Anthology.* Translated by Alan S. Trueblood. Foreword by Octavio Paz. Cambridge: Harvard University Press, 1988.

"Defraudada y traicionada—según declaró—Magda Portal levantó su voz para acusar al aprismo." *La Crónica* (Lima), February 11, 1950.

Delmar, Serafín [Reynaldo Bolaños]. "Autobiografía." In *Los campesinos y otros condenados.* Santiago de Chile: Ediciones Orbe, 1942.

———. *El hombre de estos años.* México: Ediciones A.P.R.A., 1929.

———. "Interpretación social del arte en América." [México, D.F., 1928]. *Claridad* (Buenos Aires) 15, no. 301 (1936).

———. "El poeta aprista." *Claridad* (Buenos Aires) 15, no. 301 (1936).

———. "Posición del poeta en el movimiento de transformación social." [Lima penitentiary, 1936]. *Claridad* (Buenos Aires) 15, no. 301 (1936).

———. *Radiogramas del Pacífico.* Lima: Imprenta Minerva, 1927.

Dijkstra, Sandra. *Flora Tristan: Feminism in the Age of George Sand.* London: Pluto Press, 1992.

"Dramática presentación de Magda Portal ante el consejo de guerra." *Última Hora* (Lima) 1, no. 25 (1950).

Dumpierre, Erasmo. *J. A. Mella: Biografía.* Havana: Editorial de Ciencias Sociales, 1975.

Enríquez, Luis Eduardo. *Haya de la Torre: La estafa polítca más grande de América.* Lima: Ediciones del Pacífica, 1951.

Eshleman, Clayton. Introduction to *César Vallejo: The Complete Posthumous Poetry.* Translated by Clayton Eshleman and José Rubia Barcia. Berkeley and Los Angeles: University of California Press, 1978.

Espejo Asturrizaga, Juan. *César Vallejo: Itinerario del hombre, 1892–1923.* Lima: Seglusa Editores, 1989.

"El espíritu cultivado y ágil de Magda Portal desconcierta y asombra." *La Prensa* (Barranquilla), August 1929.

Flechas (Lima). Dir. Federico Bolaños and Magda Portal, no. 1 (October 23, 1924); no. 3 (November 29, 1924).

Flores Galindo, Alberto. *La agonía de Mariátegui: La polémica con la Komintern.* Lima: DESCO, Centro de Estudios y Promoción del Desarrollo, 1980.

Franco, Jean. *Plotting Women: Gender and Representation in Mexico,* New York: Columbia University Press, 1989.

"Gloria Del Mar." *La Tribuna* (Lima), January 4, 1947.

Goldman, Emma. *My Disillusionment in Russia.* London: C. W. Daniel, 1925. The Emma Goldman Papers. Berkeley Digital Library SunSITE. http://sunsite.berkeley.edu/ Goldman/Writings/Russia.

Gonzales Smith, Myriam. *Poética e ideolgía en Magda Portal: Otras dimensiones de la vanguardia en Latinoamérica.* Lima: Instituto de Estudios Peruanos, 2007.

Grünfeld, Mihai G., ed. *Antología de la poesía latinoamericana de vanguardia (1916–1935).* Introduction by Mihai G. Grünfeld. Madrid: Hiperión, 1995.

Guardia, Sara Beatriz. *Mujeres peruana: El otro lado de la historia.* 2nd ed. Lima: Tempus Editores, 1986.

———, ed. *Mujeres que escriben en América Latina: Simposio Internacional Escritura Femenina e Historia en América Latina.* Lima: Centro de Estudios la Mujer en la Historia de América Latina, 2007.

Hahner, June E., ed. *Women in Latin American History.* Los Angeles: University of California–Los Angeles Latin American Center, 1976.

Haya de la Torre, Víctor Raúl. *¿A dónde va Indoamérica?* 3rd ed. Santiago de Chile: Editorial Ercilla, 1936.

———. *Antiimperialismo y el APRA.* Santiago de Chile: Ediciones Ercilla, 1936.

———. *Aprismo: The Ideas and Doctrines of Víctor Raúl Haya de la Torre.* Edited and translated by Robert J. Alexander. Kent, Ohio: Kent State University Press, 1973.

———. *Cartas de Haya de la Torre a los prisioneros apristas.* Edited by Carlos Manuel Cox. Lima: Editorial Nuevo Día, 1946.

———. "El estado antiimperialista." In *Antiimperialismo y el APRA.* Santiago de Chile: Ediciones Ercilla, 1936.

———. *Impresiones de la Inglaterra imperialista y la Rusia soviética.* Buenos Aires: Editorial Claridad, 1932.

Haya de la Torre, Víctor Raúl, and Luis Alberto Sánchez. *Correspondencia, 1924–1976.* Vol. 1, *1924–1951*; vol. 2, *1952–1976.* Lima: Mosca Azul Editores, 1982.

Hays, H. R. "The Passion of César Vallejo." In *César Vallejo: Selected Poems,* trans. H. R. Hays, ed. Louis Hammer. Old Chatham, N.Y.: Sachem Press, 1981.

Hernández Novás, Raúl. "Vida de un poeta." In *Poesía Completa: César Vallejo.* Edición crítica y estudio introductorio. Havana: Editorial Arte y Literatura, Casa de las Americas, 1988.

Herrera, Oscar. "Magda Portal." *Claridad* (Buenos Aires) 14, no. 294 (1935).

Hidalgo, Alberto, Magda Portal, Serafín Delmar, Gerardo Berrios, Juan José Lova, Aurelio Martínez, Ciro Alegría, and Julián Petrovick. *Cantos de la Revolución.* Colección Literatura, Serie "San Lorenzo." Lima: Editorial Cooperativa Aprista Atahualpa, 1933.

Hodges, Donald C. *Intellectual Foundations of the Nicaraguan Revolution.* Austin: University of Texas Press, 1986.

Hodges, Donald C., and Ross Gandy. *Mexico, 1910–1982: Reform or Revolution?* 2nd ed. London: Zed Press, 1983.

Hooks, Margaret. *Tina Modotti: Photographer and Revolutionary.* London; San Francisco: Pandora, 1993.

"Una hora con Magda Portal." *La Nación* (Santiago de Chile), December 10, 1939.

"Hoy es homenaje a Magda Portal." *La Opinión* (Santiago de Chile), April 14, 1940.

Hurlburt, Laurance P. "Diego Rivera (1886–1957): A Chronology of His Art, Life, and Times." In *Diego Rivera: A Retrospective,* ed. Cynthia Newman Helms. Retrospective curated by Linda Downs and Ellen Sharp. New York: Founders Society, Detroit Institute of Arts and W. W. Norton, 1986.

"El imperativo de la hora indoamericana." *El Mundo* (Santo Domingo), July 1929.

Irving, Evelyn Uhrhan. "Juana de Ibarbourou (1892–1979)." In *Spanish American Women Writers: A Bio-bibliographical Source Book,* ed. Diane E. Marting. New York: Greenwood Press, 1990.

Johnson, Julie Greer. "Sor Juana Inés de la Cruz (1648?–1695)." In *Spanish American Women Writers, A Bio-bibliographical Source Book,* ed. Diane Marting. New York: Greenwood Press, 1990.

———. *Women in Colonial Spanish American Literature.* Westport, Conn.: Greenwood Press, 1963.

"Juegos Florales de 1923, Acta-Fallo del Jurado." *El Tiempo* (Lima), August 23, 1923.

Klaiber, Jeffrey L. *Religion and Revolution in Peru, 1824–1976.* Notre Dame: University of Notre Dame Press, 1977.

Klarén, Peter F. *Peru: Society and Nationhood in the Andes.* New York: Oxford University Press, 2000.

Kollantai, Aleksandra. "New Woman." In *The New Morality and the Working Class.* Transcribed for marxists.org, 2001, from *The Autobiography of a Sexually Emancipated Communist Woman,* trans. Salvator Attansio (New York: Herder and Herder, 1971). http://www.marxists.org/archive/kollonta/works/new.htm.

Lavrin, Asunción, and Rosalva Loreto, eds. *Diálogos espirituales: Manuscritos femeninos hispanoamericanos, siglos XVI–XIX.* Puebla, Mexico: Instituto de Ciencias Sociales y Humanidades de la Benemérita Universidad Autónoma de Puebla, Universidad de las Américas, Puebla, 2006.

Levano, César. "Una mujer de pelea: Magda Portal cuenta su vida dolorosa y plena." *Caretas* (Lima), August 17, 1987.

Lyra, Carmen. "Gloria, la hijita de Magda Portal." *Repertorio Americano* (Costa Rica), April 1932.

"Magda Portal descansa en paz en las profundidades del mar." *Diario La República* (Lima), July 14, 1989.

"Magda Portal en la Inmortalidad." *Extra* (Lima), July 12, 1989.

"Magda Portal, la poetisa de los pobres, ha muerto." *Diario La República* (Lima), July 13, 1989.

"Magda Portal, líder aprista, sufrió prisiones, es antiimperialista y no cree en el Tío Sam." *Ercilla* (Santiago de Chile), November 29, 1939.

"Magda Portal no quiere hablar de política." *Vea* (Santiago de Chile), November 20, 1939.

"Magda Portal y la emancipación de América Latina." *La Opinión* (Santa Domingo), July 16, 1929.

Mariátegui, José Carlos. "Defensa del marxismo." In *Mariátegui total,* ed. Sandro Mariátegui Chiappe. Vol. 1. Lima: Empresa Amauta, 1994.

———. "La lucha final." In *Mariátegui total,* ed. Sandro Mariátegui Chiappe. Vol. 1. Lima: Empresa Amauta, 1994. Originally published in *Mundial* (Lima) 5, no. 240 (1925).

———. *Mariátegui total.* Edited by Sandro Mariátegui Chiappe. Vol. 1. Lima: Empresa Amauta, 1994.

———. *Seven Interpretive Essays on Peruvian Reality.* Translated by Marjory Urquidi. Austin: University of Texas Press, 1971.

———. *Siete ensayos de interpretación de la realidad peruana.* Lima: Biblioteca "Amauta," 1972.

Marín, Juan. "Evocación de Serafín Delmar." *Claridad* (Buenos Aires) 15, no. 301 (1936).

Martínez de la Torre, Ricardo. *Apuntes para una interpretación marxista de historia social del Perú.* Vols. 2 and 4. Lima: Empresa Editora Peruana, 1948.

———. "La reforma universitaria en la Argentina." *Amauta* (Lima), nos. 30, 31, 32 (1929–1930).

Marting, Diane E., ed. *Spanish American Women Writers: A Bio-bibliographical Source Book.* New York: Greenwood Press, 1990.

Masterson, Daniel M. *Militarism and Politics in Latin America: Peru from Sánchez Cerro to Sendero Luminoso.* New York: Greenwood Press, 1991.

Matto de Turner, Clorinda. *Torn from the Nest.* Translated by John Polt. Edited by Antonio Cornejo Polar. New York: Oxford University Press, 1998.

Melgar Márquez, José. "La vida heróica por la libertad en el Perú." *Claridad* (Buenos Aires) 15, no. 301 (1936).

Melis, Antonio. "El diálogo creador de José Carlos Mariátegui." In *Mariátegui total,* by José Carlos Mariátegui, ed. Sandro Mariátegui Chiappe. Vol. 1. Lima: Empresa Amauta, 1994.

Mella, Julio Antonio. *¿Qué es el A.R.P.A.?* Pamphlet. Reprinted in *Amauta* (Lima), no. 31 (June–July 1930); no. 32 (August–September 1930).

Meza, Ladislao F. "Magda Portal, laureada." *Mundial* (Lima), August 1923.

Miller, Francesca. *Latin American Women and the Search for Social Justice.* Hanover: University Press of New England, 1991.

Monguió, Luis. *La poesía postmodernista peruana.* Berkeley and Los Angeles: University of California Press, 1954.

Mullaney, Marie Marmo. "Alexandra Kollontai: The Female Revolutionary as Visionary." In *Revolutionary Women: Gender and the Socialist Revolutionary Role.* New York: Praeger, 1983.

"Nos parece que." *La Prensa* (Barranquilla, Colombia), September 4, 1929.

Paz, Octavio. *Sor Juana; or, The Traps of Faith.* Translated by Margaret Sayers Peden. Cambridge: Harvard University Press, 1988.

Pike, Fredrick B. *The Modern History of Peru.* London: Weidenfeld and Nicolson, 1967.

———. *The Politics of the Miraculous in Peru: Haya de la Torre and the Spiritualist Tradition.* Lincoln: University of Nebraska Press, 1986.

Porter, Cathy. *Alexandra Kollantai: A Biography.* London: Virago, 1980.

Portugal P., Enrique S. "Una mujer indoamericana que debe ser libertada." *Claridad* (Buenos Aires) 14, no. 294 (1935).

Ravines, Eudocio. *The Yenan Way.* New York: Charles Scribner's Sons, 1951.

Reedy, Daniel R. "Aspects of the Feminist Movement in Peruvian Letters and Politics." *Secolas Annals* 6 (March 1975).

———. *Magda Portal: La pasionaria peruana; Biografía intellectual.* Lima: Ediciones Flora Tristán, Centro de la Mujer Peruana Flora Tristán, 2000.

———. "Magda Portal: Peru's Voice of Social Protest." *Revista de Estudios Hispánicos* 4, no. 1 (1970).

Reyes, Carlos. "Magda Portal a través de mi compañera." *Claridad* (Buenos Aires) 15, no. 299 (1936).

Sabat de Rivers, Georgina. *Estudios de literatura hispanoamericana: Sor Juana Inés de la Cruz y otros poetas barrocos de la colonia.* Barcelona: Lecturas Hispánicas y Universales, 1992.

Sánchez, Luis Alberto. *Apuntes para una biografía del APRA.* Vol. 1, *Los primeros pasos (1923–1931).* Lima: Mosca Azul Editores, 1978.

———. "Cuaderno de Bitácora." *Caretas* (Lima), July 17, 1989.

———. *La literatura peruana.* Vol. 4. Lima: Ediciones de Ediventas, 1966.

———. "Odisea y Calvario de Magda Portal." *Claridad* (Buenos Aires) 14, no. 294 (1935).

———. "¿Qué libro leyó esta semana?" *Ercilla* (Santiago de Chile), January 14, 1945.

———. "Serafín Delmar." *Claridad* (Buenos Aires) 15, no. 301 (1936).

———. *Testimonio personal.* 2nd ed. Vol. 1, *El aquelarre (1900–1931);* vol. 2, *El purgatorio (1931–1945).* Lima: Mosca Azul Editores, 1987.

———. *Víctor Raúl Haya de la Torre o el político.* Lima: E. Delgado Valenzuelo, 1979. Primera edición, Santiago de Chile: Editorial Ercilla, 1934.

Salgado, María A. "Alfonsina Storni (1892–1938)." In *Spanish American Women Writers, A Bio-bibliographical Source Book,* ed. Diane E. Marting. New York: Greenwood Press, 1990.

Schlau, Stacey. *Spanish American Women's Use of the Word: Colonial Through Contemporary Narratives.* Tucson: University of Arizona Press, 2001.

Seoane, Manuel. "Escorzo de Magda Portal." *Claridad* (Buenos Aires) 14, no. 294, (1935).

"Síntesis luminosa del problema mexicano fué la conferencia que dictó el domingo Magda Portal." *Listín Diario* (Santo Domingo), July 22, 1929.

Smith, David. "Vallejo's Book of the Abyss." Preface to César Vallejo, *Trilce,* trans. David Smith. New York: Grossman, 1973.

Stein, Steve. *Populism in Peru: The Emergence of the Masses and the Politics of Social Control.* Madison: University of Wisconsin Press, 1980.

Tristan, Flora. *Flora Tristan, Utopian Feminist: Her Travel Diaries and Personal Crusade.* Translated and edited by Doris Beik and Paul Beik. Bloomington: Indiana University Press, 1993.

———. *Flora Tristan's London Journal, 1840.* Translated by Dennis Palmer and Giselle Pincetl. Translation of *Promenades dans Londres.* Boston: Charles River Books, 1980.

———. *The London Journal of Flora Tristan.* Translated by Jean Hawkes. London: Virago, 1982.

———. *Peregrinations of a Pariah*. Translated and edited by Jean Hawkes. London: Virago, 1986.

———. *Le Tour de France: Journal, 1843–1844*. Paris: Maspéro, 1980.

———. *The Workers' Union*. Translated by Beverly Livingston. Urbana: University of Illinois Press, 1983.

"Unos minutos de charla con Magda Portal, la gran revolucionaria." *Listín Diario* (Santo Domingo), July 10, 1929.

Unruh, Vicky. "Ad-Libs by the Women of *Amauta*: Magda Portal and María Wiesse." In *Performing Women and Modern Literary Culture in Latin America*. Austin: University of Texas Press, 2006.

———. *Latin American Vanguards: The Art of Contentious Encounters*. Berkeley and Los Angeles: University of California Press, 1994.

———. "Las rearticulaciones inesperadas de las intelectuales de *Amauta* Magda Portal y María Wiesse." In *Narrativa femenina en América Latina: Prácticas y perspectivas teóricas/Latin American Women's Narrative, Practices, and Theoretical Perspectives,* ed. Sara Castro-Klarén. Madrid: Iberoamericana; Frankfurt: Vervuert, 2003.

Urquieta, Miguel Ángel. "Izquierdismo y seudoizquierdismo artísticos." *Amauta*, no. 7 (March 1927).

Valcárcel, Gustavo. "Una luz que no se apaga." *El Nacional* (Lima), July 16, 1989.

Vallejo, César. *The Black Heralds*. Translated by Richard Schaaf and Kathleen Ross. Pittsburgh: Latin American Literary Review Press Series Discoveries, 1990.

———. *The Complete Poems: A Bilingual Edition*. Edited and translated by Clayton Eshleman. Foreword by Mario Vargas Llosa. Berkeley and Los Angeles: University of California Press, 2007.

Vegas León, Guillermo. "Las torturas y los crímenes de la isla de el Frontón." *Patria* (Havana) 2, no. 22 (1938). Reprinted in Luis Alva Castro, *Haya de la Torre: Peregrino de la unidad continental,* vol. 2 (Lima: Fondo Editorial "V. R. Haya de la Torre," 1990).

"Un viaje accidentado y penoso soportó Magda Portal viniendo a La Paz." *El Diario* (La Paz, Bolivia), January 20, 1939.

"Vibraciones: Magda Portal." *La Nación* (Barranquilla, Colombia), August 13, 1929.

Villanueva, Víctor. *El APRA en busca del poder, 1930–1940*. Lima: Editorial Horizonte, 1975.

———. *El APRA y el ejército*. Lima: Editorial Horizonte, 1977.

———. *La sublevación aprista del 48: Tragedia de un pueblo y un partido*. 4th ed. Lima: Editorial Milla Batres, 1973.

Villavicencio, Martiza. "Aprender a recordarte." *Viva!* (Lima), September 1989.

———. *Del silencio a la palabra: Mujeres peruanas en los siglos XIX–XX*. Lima: Ediciones Flora Tristán, 1992.

Virgillo, Carmello. "Gabriela Mistral (1889–1957)." In *Spanish American Women Writers: A Bio-bibliographical Source Book,* ed. Diane E. Marting. New York: Greenwood Press, 1990.

Wallace Fuentes, Myrna Ivonne. "Becoming Magda Portal: Poetry, Gender, and Revolutionary Politics in Lima, Peru, 1920–1930." Ph.D. diss., Duke University, 2006.

Weaver, Kathleen, "Magda Portal: Translation in Progress." *Translation Review* 32, no. 22 (1990): 41–43.

Werlich, David P. *Peru: A Short History*. Carbondale: Southern Illinois University Press, 1978.

Wiesse, María. *José Carlos Mariátegui: Etapas de su vida.* Lima: Ediciones Hora del Hombre, 1945.

Willett, John. *Art and Politics in the Weimar Period: The New Sobriety, 1917–1933.* New York: Pantheon Books, 1978.

Williams, William Carlos. "The American Background." In *Selected Essays of William Carlos Williams.* New York: Random House, 1954.

Wolfe, Bertram D. *Diego Rivera: His Life and Times.* New York: Knopf, 1939.

———. *The Fabulous Life of Diego Rivera.* New York: Stein and Day, 1963.

Zinn, Howard. *A People's History of the United States.* Rev. ed. New York: Harper Collins, 1995.

INDEX

Page numbers in *italics* indicate photographs.

Printed in Great Britain
by Amazon